ACKNOWLEDGMENTS

The National Council for Behavioral Health and Mental Health First Aid USA wish to acknowledge the tremendous efforts of Mental Health First Aid Australia and the members of the international expert panels whose consensus was used to develop the Mental Health First Aid Action Plan and guidelines.

We are also grateful for the generous commitment of time by the members of the National Council's Medical Director Institute and the employees of the National Council of Behavioral Health whose expertise was used to develop this manual. A special thank you to:

AMY GOLDSTEIN, PhD

BONNEY GULINO SCHAUB, MS, RN

JACK S. PETRAS, LMHC

ANTHONY SALERNO, PhD

CHERYL S. SHARP, MSW

CHANGE MATRIX, LLC

We wish to also thank the National Trainers, Mental Health First Aid Instructors, and First Aiders for the thoughtful feedback they provided to help improve this manual. We thank them for their continued efforts to guide people toward appropriate treatments and supports, and for reducing the stigma around mental health and substance use disorders.

The artwork in this manual has been contributed by artists with lived experience. With their consent, we proudly honor their bravery, recognize their talents, and thank them for their support. To learn more about each artist, or view their additional artwork, please visit www.keepingartinmind.com.

UNITED STATES-BASED INFORMATION

Mental Health First Aid USA has added some content and information to make the material relevant for adults in the United States. All data included in the manual is based on young adults and adults in the United States unless noted that it was an international study.

The following section and chapters have been added by Mental Health First Aid USA:

- **SECTION 1:** Introduction to Mental Health First Aid
    - ○ Call to Action
    - ○ About the Program
    - ○ How the Manual is Organized
    - ○ Key Themes in the Manual
        - » Trauma
        - » Stigma
        - » Culture
        - » Recovery and Well-being
    - ○ The Role of the First Aider

- **CHAPTER 1:** Mental Health in the United States

- **CHAPTER 2:** Mental Health First Aid
    - ○ ALGEE for Adults with Developmental Disabilities
        - » Mental Health First Aid: Cultural Considerations
        - » Important Considerations

- **CHAPTER 3:** Self-Care for the Mental Health First Aider

- **CHAPTER 6:** Trauma and Trauma-related and Stressor-related Disorders

- **CHAPTER 7:** Bipolar Disorder

- **CHAPTER 10:** Substance Use Disorder
    - ○ What are Substance Use Disorders and Addiction
    - ○ Prevalence of Substance Use Disorders
    - ○ Commonly Misused Substances

All new content is also noted in the table of contents in the manual, at the beginning of the chapters where it appears, and in specific chapters throughout the manual.

TABLE OF CONTENTS

* Content denoted with an asterisk refers to material developed by Mental Health First Aid USA to make the course more relevant for the United States. This new content was developed with input from experts in mental health..

TABLE OF FIGURES

INTRODUCTION TO MENTAL HEALTH FIRST AID

In this first section, you'll learn about mental health and mental health challenges and about Mental Health First Aid. You'll also learn about the practice of self-care.

TIMOTHY AMUSSEN, *Agios Tree*

"Agios Tree" depicts how adaptable and constant nature can be and what I strive to achieve.

CALL TO ACTION

When you use the skills you learn in Mental Health First Aid (MHFA), you are the first line of support for a person in need. You are there to help them feel less distressed, and you can be a vital source in helping them seek further assistance. Your body language, what you say, and how well you listen can have a powerful impact. The quality and type of support you offer through listening can enhance coping and self-esteem. With an accurate view of mental health challenges and using a strengths-based holistic perspective, you can help people help themselves. You can also be an advocate, empower your community, and improve self-care.

As a First Aider, you can be the one to make a difference in the life of someone with a mental health or substance use challenge. Your First Aid actions can be a first step in someone's recovery journey.

Today millions of people across the United States, known as First Aiders, have been trained in a Mental Health First Aid program. This means that millions of people know how to recognize and respond to someone experiencing a mental health or substance use crisis. As the number of Americans facing mental health challenges continues to grow, this is more important than ever before.

A core aspect of giving Mental Health First Aid is being fully present and listening. As human beings, we have a fundamental need to be understood. Not necessarily agreed with, but understood. Being fully present and truly listening can help minimize feelings of distress and may be the most effective step as you help someone seek support or treatment that fosters their well-being.

Communication and effective listening are the core skills of Mental Health First Aid. Listening involves all of you, not just your ears. The way you are perceived can be based on body language and tone of voice, so it is important to recognize what your nonverbal language is saying. To effectively offer Mental Health First Aid, it is important to suspend your judgment or biases.

It is important to note that First Aiders do not diagnose or treat mental health or substance use challenges. Instead, First Aiders serve as a vital link between a person experiencing a new or worsening mental health or substance use challenge and appropriate professional supports, self-help, and other support strategies.

ABOUT THE PROGRAM

PROGRAM OVERVIEW

Mental Health First Aid was designed to extend the concept of first aid training to mental health and substance use challenges.

Mental Health First Aid teaches participants to recognize the signs and symptoms that suggest a potential mental health or substance use challenge, how to listen nonjudgmentally and give reassurance to a person who may be experiencing a mental health or substance use challenge, and how to refer a person to appropriate support and services.

HISTORY OF MENTAL HEALTH FIRST AID

Mental Health First Aid was created in Australia in 2000 by Betty Kitchener, an educator and mental health consumer, and Professor Tony Jorm, a mental health researcher.

In 2008, the National Council, the Maryland Department of Health and Mental Hygiene, and the Missouri Department of Mental Health brought Mental Health First Aid to the United States, with the goal of making Mental Health First Aid training as common as CPR.

EFFICACY OF MENTAL HEALTH FIRST AID

A 2018 study of the Adult and Youth Mental Health USA curricula concluded that the program:

- Reduced stigma around mental illness.
- Increased participant knowledge about mental health.
- Raised participant confidence to use the MHFA 5-step action plan (ALGEE®).

> **Mental illness** is a substantial health issue, and public misunderstanding, prejudice, and discrimination can rob people of important life opportunities and achieving meaningful supports. That MHFA training has such clear positive long-term effects on trainees, particularly on those who have had no previous mental health training, provides support for the continued expansion of this education program across public and private systems to increase community understanding and support for individuals struggling with mental illness."
>
> —Banh, et al., 2018

A range of studies, including randomized controlled trials, have shown that Mental Health First Aid training improves knowledge, reduces stigmatizing attitudes, and increases first aid actions toward people with mental health challenges. The continuing attention to research and evaluation is an important factor in the Mental Health First Aid program's growth worldwide.

Summaries of evaluation studies are available on the Mental Health First Aid website at https://www.mentalhealthfirstaid.org/about/research/.

DISCLAIMER

The content of this manual is informational in nature and is not intended to be, and should not be, used as a substitute for medical care, counseling, peer support, or treatment of any kind.

GOALS OF MENTAL HEALTH FIRST AID

The vision is for Mental Health First Aid to become as common as CPR and for Mental Health First Aid training to be available to everyone in the United States.

The symptoms of a mental health or substance use disorder can be difficult to detect. Even if friends and family notice a change, they may not know how to intervene or direct the person to proper treatment. All too often, those in need of mental health services do not get them until it is too late. First Aiders learn how to offer initial help in both noncritical mental health or substance use situations and in a crisis using the Mental Health First Aid 5-step action plan known as ALGEE. This manual offers concrete tools and answers to key questions like "As a First Aider, what can I do?" "Am I required to offer assistance?" and "Where can someone find help for a mental health issue or challenge?"

This manual introduces First Aiders to specific disorders; their risk factors; and the warning signs of depression, anxiety, bipolar disorder, psychotic disorders, eating disorders, substance use disorders, suicidal thoughts, and nonsuicidal self-injury. The Mental Health First Aid program builds an understanding of the importance of early intervention and provides strategies for giving support and help.

By the end of the course, each participant will have the knowledge and confidence to assist a person in need.

HOW THIS MANUAL IS ORGANIZED

The Mental Health First Aid USA Manual provides overviews of the following mental health and substance use challenges: depression, anxiety, bipolar disorder, eating disorders, psychosis, substance use disorders, suicide, nonsuicidal self-injury, and mental health crises.

The following is the general format of each chapter:

- What is (the condition or behavior)?

- Prevalence of (the condition or behavior).

- Signs and symptoms of (the condition or behavior).

- What causes (the condition or behavior)?

- Impact of trauma on (the condition or behavior).

- Stigma around (the condition or behavior).

- The importance of early intervention for (the condition or behavior).

- The MHFA action plan for (the condition or behavior).

- The chapters on specific mental disorders appear in Section 2.

The final chapter of the manual provides strategies for crises that may work for many mental disorders and harmful behaviors, including panic attacks, traumatic events, psychotic episodes, drug overdose, aggressive behavior, suicidal thoughts and behavior, and nonsuicidal self-injury.

Use the table of contents and the table of figures to navigate your way through the text. References and a glossary of terms can be found at the end of this manual. Terms that are defined in the glossary are italicized throughout the text.

KEY THEMES IN THIS MANUAL

While the framework of Mental Health First Aid is the same regardless of the mental disorder, there are differences in the way you provide support and the type of help you give.

Many factors shape a person's experience with a mental health or substance use disorder. Trauma, stigma, and culture can impact a person's journey through recovery and well-being. Chapters in Section 2 discuss how trauma and stigma fit in with the mental health or substance use challenges addressed.

TRAUMA

The Substance Abuse Mental Health Services Administration (SAMHSA) defines individual trauma as an event, series of events, or set of circumstances that is experienced by an individual as physically or emotionally harmful or life threatening and that has lasting adverse effects on the individual's functioning and mental, physical, social, emotional, or spiritual well-being.

A person can experience one event that has a lifetime impact on their overall well-being and their capacity to cope. A series of such events can have a cumulative impact.

Examples of traumatic experiences might include childhood abuse or neglect and growing up in a dysfunctional family where there might be addiction, domestic violence, or a parent who is absent from the home because of divorce, incarceration, or death. Trauma is often a contributing factor for all the disorders presented in the manual. We take a wider look at trauma in Chapter 6: Trauma and Trauma-related and Stressor-related Disorders.

Figure 1

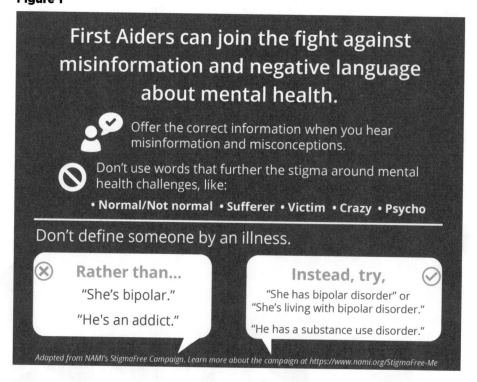

First Aiders can join the fight against misinformation and negative language about mental health.

Offer the correct information when you hear misinformation and misconceptions.

Don't use words that further the stigma around mental health challenges, like:

• **Normal/Not normal** • **Sufferer** • **Victim** • **Crazy** • **Psycho**

Don't define someone by an illness.

Rather than...	Instead, try,
"She's bipolar."	"She has bipolar disorder" or "She's living with bipolar disorder."
"He's an addict."	"He has a substance use disorder."

Adapted from NAMI's StigmaFree Campaign. Learn more about the campaign at https://www.nami.org/StigmaFree-Me

STIGMA

Fear and misunderstanding are often referred to as stigma. Stigma involves negative attitudes (prejudice) and negative behaviors (discrimination).

In the United States, there is still a great deal of stigma associated with mental health and substance use disorders. People are often ashamed to discuss their symptoms and may be reluctant to seek treatment and support because of concerns about what others will think. For example, with depression, they may deny that they are depressed if asked about it and may not seek treatment and support because of concerns about what others will think (Vega, Rodriguez, & Ang, 2010).

Stigma surrounding mental illness can lead to people being excluded from jobs, housing, social activities, and relationships. Additionally, people with mental health challenges can begin to believe the negative things that others say about them.

Studies show that better understanding of the experiences of people with mental disorders can reduce or eliminate stigma and discrimination (Corrigan & Watson, 2002). Avoiding stigmatizing and discriminating language and terminology is addressed in this manual and in the course.

CULTURE

Culture is a combination of a person's values, norms, expectations, and identity that can affect their perceptions, the actions they take, and how they interact with others. It impacts how communities and families are organized. The diversity in the United States has grown for many decades, and our population is going to continue to change and shift (United States Census Bureau, 2017).

Cultural differences can result in differing beliefs about health, in the way health is discussed and decisions are made, and the way individuals think about and treat health or cope with symptoms (Abdullah & Brown, 2011). Cultural differences affect whether people do well in treatment.

Researchers looking at the effects of historical trauma on health have stated that members of some ethnic minority communities may see mental health professionals as part of the problem rather than part of the solution (Gopalkrishnan N., 2018). First Aiders establish trust by listening and being genuine, enabling them to sensitively explain the benefits of care from a mental health professional.

RECOVERY AND WELL-BEING

Conversations about mental illness have finally begun to shift away from focusing only on the "illness" or "deficit" model of describing mental illness. It has become more common to hear people talk about well-being and recovery.

Recovery is a personal journey with the goals of hope, empowerment, and autonomy. The definition of well-being is unique to the individual and may include physical, mental, professional, and social health.

As the existing stigmas in public attitudes about depression and mental illness are addressed, more people will speak publicly about mental health and substance use disorders and recovery, encouraging others to seek help and pursue their own recovery.

THE ROLE OF THE FIRST AIDER

As a First Aider, you can be the one to make a difference in the life of someone with a mental health or substance use challenge. Your First Aid actions can be a first step in someone's recovery journey.

Once you are trained in Mental Health First Aid, there are a number of ways to help build the community. You can be an advocate, empower your community, and improve self-care.

SUMMARY

By reading this manual and participating in a Mental Health First Aid training, you will be able to participate in discussions designed to increase your knowledge of the signs and symptoms of mental health and substance use challenges and reduce negative thoughts around mental health conditions. You will be more comfortable and will be able to apply the MHFA 5-step plan, ALGEE.

In the Mental Health First Aid course you will not be trained in how to diagnose mental disorders or substance use disorders. The information provided in this course is for Mental Health First Aid only. It is not intended to be and should not be relied upon as a substitute for professional mental health advice.

TERMS WITHIN THIS MANUAL

The terms generally used throughout this manual are a person with a mental health challenge or mental disorder. "Mental disorder" and "mental illness" are used to mean the same thing.

Some people have symptoms of mental disorders (such as confused thinking or extreme highs and lows in mood), but the symptoms are not severe enough to warrant the diagnosis of a mental disorder. In these cases, we use the term mental health challenge. In the manual, we do not use the term "brain disease," because not all brain diseases are categorized as mental illness, and not all mental illnesses are categorized as brain diseases.

Some additional terms that describe mental health challenges are emotional and behavioral disorder, extreme emotional distress, psychiatric illness, mental illness, mental health condition, mental breakdown, nervous breakdown, nervous exhaustion, and burnout.

The term behavioral health refers to the fields of both mental health and substance use.

In this manual, young adult refers to those ages 18 to 24. First Aiders should understand that because they are still developing, young adults can think and behave more like youth than adults until their early 20s. As they mature, their judgment generally begins to improve, and they are capable of generating several solutions to problems; this can help them in stressful situations and interpersonal conflicts.

We use the term family to mean anyone a person identifies as family.

One term that is important to understand in thinking about mental health is what is known as gender identity. At birth, babies are assigned male or female based on physical characteristics. This refers to the sex or assigned gender of the child. Meanwhile, gender identity refers to an internal sense that people have of who they are based on an interaction of biological traits, developmental influences, and environmental conditions. Exploration of one's gender identity can occur at any point in the lifespan, from childhood through older adulthood (Rafferty, 2018).

For some people, the match between their assigned gender and gender identity is not clear. When this happens, discomfort or distress can result — at any point in the person's life (Coleman et al., 2012). Transgender is the umbrella term that incorporates differences in gender identity that involve having one's assigned biological sex not match one's felt identity (American Psychological Association [APA], 2015).

Mental Health First Aid USA covers only the most common and most severe types of mental health challenges and disorders. However, you may apply what you read in Mental Health First Aid USA to mental health challenges that are not covered.

ELLA SCHEUERELL, *My Inner Scream*

After experiencing anxiety and depression for more than a decade, I still have to remind myself in moments of panic or sadness: This moment will pass. It is easy to get lost in the overwhelming ebbs and flows of mental health disorders; however, I work hard to find balance every day and not judge myself in the process. Artistic expression, specifically ceramics, is one tool I use to process the ups and downs of my mental health. I often illustrate symptoms, coping mechanisms, challenges, and even strengths I have because of my mental health on the surfaces of my pottery.

CHAPTER 1: MENTAL HEALTH IN THE UNITED STATES

MENTAL HEALTH

What Are Mental Health And Mental Well-Being?

The term mental health describes the health of a person's mind and their thoughts, feelings, and actions.

The World Health Organization defines mental health as "a state of well-being in which the individual realizes their own abilities, can cope with the normal stresses of life, can work productively and fruitfully, and is able to make a contribution to their community."

Some people with a diagnosable mental health challenge like depression or schizophrenia can realize their own abilities, cope with the normal stresses of life, work productively and fruitfully, and contribute to their community. Their levels of emotional, psychological, or social well-being may range from high to low.

On the other hand, some people who have no serious or diagnosable mental health challenges may not be able to realize their own abilities, cope with the normal stresses of life, work productively and fruitfully, and contribute to their community (Galderisi et al., 2015).

Figure 2 illustrates the idea that mental health is not always severely affected by a mental illness, and that a person who does not have a mental illness does not always have optimal mental health.

Figure 2

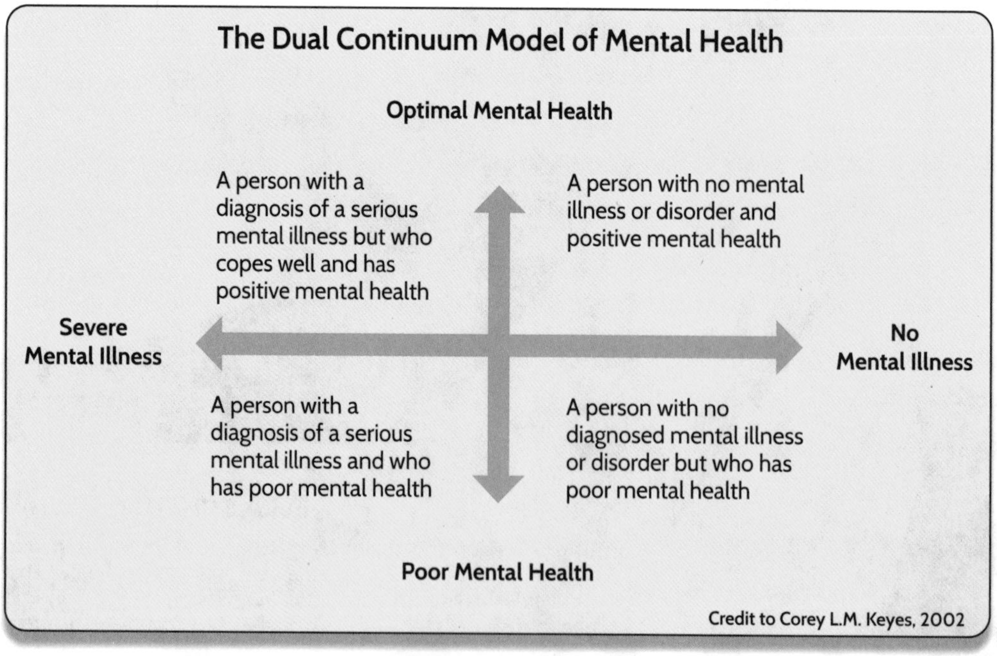

The Dual Continuum Model of Mental Health

Optimal Mental Health

A person with a diagnosis of a serious mental illness but who copes well and has positive mental health

A person with no mental illness or disorder and positive mental health

Severe Mental Illness

No Mental Illness

A person with a diagnosis of a serious mental illness and who has poor mental health

A person with no diagnosed mental illness or disorder but who has poor mental health

Poor Mental Health

Credit to Corey L.M. Keyes, 2002

WHAT IS MENTAL ILLNESS?

Mental illnesses are diagnosable health conditions involving changes in emotion, thinking, or behavior (or a combination of these). Mental illnesses are associated with distress and/or problems functioning in social, work, or family activities. The various types of diagnosable mental illnesses are called mental disorders.

The Diagnostic and Statistical Manual of Mental Disorders® (DSM-5) is a handbook used by professionals to diagnose individuals with mental disorders. Because it is one of the most widely used systems for classifying mental disorders, many of the descriptions about the signs and symptoms of mental disorders in this manual are from the DSM-5.

Centers for Disease Control and Prevention (CDC) states that mental disorders are conditions that affect a person's thinking, feeling, mood, or behavior and affect their ability to function or relate to others. When a mental health problem in adults is severe, it is usually called serious mental illness (SMI).

Some of the main categories of mental disorders are mood disorders*, anxiety disorders, personality disorders, psychotic disorders, eating disorders, trauma-related disorders, and substance use disorders. Some mental disorders are more common than others. For example, depression and anxiety disorders are common, while schizophrenia and anorexia are not (SAMHSA, 2014). Personality disorders and narcissistic and paranoid personality traits are not discussed in this manual. Information on personality traits and personality disorders is found in the Helpful Resources section.

*Find definitions of terms like **mood disorder** in the Glossary of Terms at the end of the manual.*

The table defines each type of mental disorder and gives examples for each category (American Psychiatric Association, DSM-5 Task Force, 2013).

CATEGORY	DESCRIPTION	EXAMPLES
Mood Disorders	Mental disorders marked by the elevation or lowering of a person's mood	Depression, bipolar disorder (also called manic depression), seasonal affective disorder (also called major depressive disorder with seasonal pattern)
Anxiety Disorders	Disorders characterized by intense worry about future events that disrupts a person's ability to perform at work, school, or in relationships	Generalized anxiety disorder, social anxiety disorder
Personality Disorders	Ways of thinking, feeling, and behaving that are markedly different from acceptable cultural norms and cause difficulty in relationships	Borderline personality disorder, narcissistic personality disorder, antisocial personality disorder, paranoid personality disorder
Psychotic Disorders	Severe mental disorders featuring abnormal thinking and perception that cause a person to lose touch with reality	Schizophrenia, schizoaffective disorder
Eating Disorders	Serious illnesses tied to irregular eating habits, severe stress, or concerns about body image, characterized by too much or too little food intake	Anorexia nervosa, bulimia nervosa, orthorexia nervosa
Trauma-related Disorders	Disorders that result following a traumatic or stressful event	Post-traumatic stress disorder, acute stress disorder
Substance Use Disorders	Disorders that occur when the recurrent use of substances causes impairment, including health problems, disability, and/or failure to meet personal obligations	Alcohol use disorder, opioid use disorder

About People With Intellectual Disabilities And Mental Health

You may work with someone with a developmental disability that involves intellectual disability. If you see serious changes in the way that the person typically acts or handles their emotions, do not assume that these changes are caused by their intellectual disability.

About People With Developmental Disabilities And Consent To Care/Guardianship

If you are involved in a conversation about whether a person with a developmental disability will get care, try to find out if the person can make their own health care treatment decisions. (The term for this is decisional capacity.)

When adults with developmental disabilities have incomplete decisional capacity, a legal guardian (often a family member) gives consent for care.

HOW COMMON ARE MENTAL HEALTH CHALLENGES IN ADULTS?

Close to one in five adults in the United States has a mental illness or substance use disorder.

The National Survey on Drug Use and Health, a national survey administered by SAMHSA, shows that an estimated 46.6 million people, or 18.9 percent of adults ages 18 years or older, experience a mental illness or substance use disorder each year.

Figure 3

1 in 5

In the United States, every year, one in five (18.9 percent) American adults experiences a mental disorder.

SAMHSA, 2018

PERCENTAGE OF U.S. ADULTS WITH MENTAL DISORDERS IN ANY ONE YEAR

Type of mental disorder	Anxiety Disorders	Major Depressive Disorder	Substance Use Disorder	Bipolar Disorder	Eating Disorders	Schizophrenia
% of adults	21.3%[1]	7.1%[2]	7.6%[2]	1.8%[1]	0.05-0.44%[3]	0.3-0.6%[4]

Results from 2017 National Survey on Drug Use and Health and other surveys. These statistics come from various studies because no study encompasses all these types of mental disorders.

The table shows the percentage of adults with some of the most common mental disorders.

Not including substance use disorders, researchers estimate that in a 1-year period, 24.8 percent of adults have a mental disorder (Bagalman & Napili, 2014).

Mental disorders often occur simultaneously. For example, it is not unusual for a person with an anxiety disorder to also develop depression, or a person who is depressed to also have a substance use disorder. Co-occurrence, dual diagnosis, and comorbidity are terms used to describe the presence of more than one mental disorder. Of adults in the United States with any mental disorder in any 1-year period, 14.4 percent have one disorder, 5.8 percent have two disorders, and 6 percent have three or more (Kessler et al., 2005a).

Impact Of Mental Disorders

Most mental health challenges and disorders come with distress and real pain. They can affect the ability to work and form relationships, and they can lead to the use of alcohol and other drugs. They are disruptive for the family as well. All of this can happen even when the disorder is treated.

Mental health challenges and disorders are the leading cause of disability in the United States and Canada (National Institute of Mental Health [NIMH], 2017). They account for 25 percent of years of life lost due to disability or early death (U.S. Burden of Disease Collaborators, 2013). Disability refers to the amount of disruption a health problem causes to a person's ability to study, work, look after themselves, and carry on relationships with family and friends.

Mental and behavioral disorders are the second most debilitating illnesses, with cardiovascular illnesses the most debilitating. When scientists include mental and behavioral disorders and neurological disorders in the tally, this group is more debilitating than cardiovascular illnesses. Neurological disorders are diseases of the nervous system, such as epilepsy, Alzheimer's disease, and Parkinson's disease.

[1] Kessler, R. C., Petukhova, M., Sampson, N. A., Zaslavsky, A. M., & Wittchen, H.-U. (2012). Twelve month and lifetime prevalence and lifetime morbid risk of anxiety and mood disorders in the United States. International Journal of Methods in Psychiatric Research, 21(3), 169-184.

[2] Substance Abuse and Mental Health Services Administration. (2018). Key substance use and mental health indicators in the United States: Results from the 2017 National Survey on Drug Use and Health (HHS Publication No. SMA 18-5068, NSDUH Series H-53). Rockville, MD: Center for Behavioral Health Statistics and Quality, Substance Abuse and Mental Health Services Administration.

[3] Udo, T., & Grilo, C. M. (2018). Prevalence and correlates of DSM-5-defined eating disorders in a nationally representative sample of U.S. adults. Biological Psychiatry, 84(5), 345-354.

[4] Kessler, R. C., Birnbaum, H., Demler, O., Falloon, I. R., Gagnon, E., Guyer, M., Howes, M. J., Kendler, K. S., Shi, L., Walters, E., ... Wu, E. Q. (2005). The prevalence and correlates of nonaffective psychosis in the National Comorbidity Survey Replication (NCS-R). Biological Psychiatry, 58(8), 668-76.

Mental Health First Aid And People With Developmental Disabilities

The First Aider may encounter people with developmental disabilities.

CDC states that developmental disabilities are a variety of disorders acquired before age 18, including:

- Intellectual disability (formerly called mental retardation).
    - Intellectual disability involves "significant limitations in both intellectual functioning (reasoning, learning, problem solving) and adaptive behavior, which covers a range of everyday social and practical skills," according to the American Association on Intellectual and Developmental Disabilities.
    - Most people who have an intellectual disability have a mild disability.
- Autism spectrum disorders (ASDs) (formerly called autism).
    - ASDs may or may not involve intellectual disability.
- Physical disorders such as vision impairment, epilepsy, and cerebral palsy.

Prevalence of developmental disabilities

One in six children in the United States has one or more developmental disabilities (CDC, 2012).

Prevalence of intellectual disabilities

Intellectual disabilities are not common. About 1 percent of the population has an intellectual disability (McKenzie et al., 2016).

About ASD

In 2013, the American Psychiatric Association merged four distinct autism diagnoses into one umbrella diagnosis of ASD. These diagnoses are autistic disorder, childhood disintegrative disorder, pervasive developmental disorder-not otherwise specified (PDD-NOS), and Asperger syndrome.

People with ASD may have an intellectual disability, or they may be well above average in intelligence.

People with ASD have difficulties with social communication and connection, along with limited interests or repetitive behaviors. They may or may not have problems understanding language or expressing themselves, but they may also have unusual speech patterns or repeat words or phrases.

People with ASD may have unusual movements or responses to sounds, sights, and touch, or may express discomfort with change.

Seizures, intense anxiety, and difficulty paying attention are common among people with ASD.

Signs And Symptoms Of Mental Health Challenges In A Person With Developmental Disabilities

Any major change in the person's thoughts, feelings, or behavior that affects daily functioning and that is persistent or worsens over time could indicate a mental health challenge.

HOW MENTAL HEALTH CHALLENGES CAN AFFECT THE WAY A PERSON WITH DEVELOPMENTAL DISABILITIES THINKS, FEELS, BEHAVES, AND APPEARS

Thoughts

- Seeing things that are not present
- Self-doubt related to common tasks
- Lack of confidence
- Increased distrust for people

Emotions

- Anger
- Easily agitated
- Sadness
- Frustration
- Guilt
- Doubt
- Worry

Behaviors

- Physical complaints, such as headaches, pain, weight loss, or weight gain
- Resisting going to bed, doing things instead of going to bed, waking a lot
- Decrease in skills
- Changes to speech (being more talkative or louder than usual, asking repeated questions or speaking quickly)
- Changing quickly between activities
- Increased difficulties completing tasks
- New self-injury or increased self-injury
- Shouting, swearing, screaming, or lashing out at others
- Being unwilling to take part in their normal activities or participating but not appearing to enjoy them
- Being unwilling to eat meals, throwing meals away, or spitting out the food
- Seeking excessive reassurance that they are doing well or that they are a good person
- Obsessive behaviors such as arranging, organizing, hand washing
- Withdrawing from others
- Seeking more attention
- Acting much more confident than usual

Adapted from: www.idhealtheducation.edu.au

Appearance and Well-being

- Decreased or increased body movement
- Appearing fearful or uncharacteristically suspicious even of those who are familiar to the person
- Unnecessarily confrontational
- Nervous

Importance Of Early Intervention For People With Mental Health Challenges

Studies show that with proper care and treatment, people with mental health and substance use challenges get better, and many recover completely. Recovery refers to the process in which people are able to live, work, learn, and participate fully in their communities. There are more treatments, services, and community support systems than ever before, and they work.

The first step is early diagnosis and appropriate services (Centers for Disease Control and Prevention [CDC], 2016). Early intervention refers to recognizing the warning signs of a mental health or substance use problem and acting before it becomes worse.

It is during this early intervention phase that Mental Health First Aid can play an important role. Research suggests that people are more likely to seek help if someone close to them suggests it (Jorm, 2011).

Early diagnosis and appropriate treatment can help people achieve relief from distress; prevent symptoms from becoming more serious; and reduce the likelihood of issues with work, family, school, relationships, and substance use. It can keep medical costs down and reduce the overall burden on family members.

Phases Of Mental Health Challenges And Of Treatments (The Spectrum Of Interventions)

There are many different states of mental health, including well-being and the time when a person becomes unwell. Mental Health First Aid is one of many ways to help someone, and Figure 3 shows when Mental Health First Aid is appropriate.

The term mental health promotion encompasses all care, from prevention programs, to early intervention, to treatment, and on to continuing care.

Prevention

For the person who is well or shows some mild symptoms, prevention programs are appropriate.

Prevention programs include policies or practices to reduce stress in the workplace, as well as stress management courses, parenting skills training, and education about substance use and addiction and about physical exercise to improve mood. Some children, youth, and young adults receive resilience training programs in school.

How Does The First Aider Know When To Seek Help?

Consult the tables in each chapter listing signs and symptoms to help you know when to be concerned and to use Mental Health First Aid. In general, First Aiders should pay attention when they notice major changes in a person's thoughts, feelings, or behaviors, where these changes are interfering with work performance, relationships, or participation in usual activities.

Figure 4

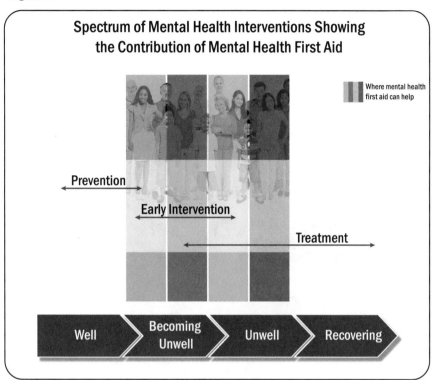

Spectrum of Mental Health Interventions Showing the Contribution of Mental Health First Aid

Early Intervention

Early intervention refers to recognizing the warning signs of a mental health or substance use problem and acting before it gets worse. Early intervention can prevent symptoms from becoming more serious. It can reduce the likelihood of the person losing their job, dropping out of school, experiencing relationship breakups, and having problems with the law or with alcohol and other drugs.

Many people have a long delay between developing a mental disorder and receiving appropriate treatment and support. The longer the delay in getting help, the more difficult recovery can be.

For the person who is moving from mild mental health challenges to a mental illness, early intervention approaches such as Mental Health First Aid can be helpful.

Figure 5

Types of Help

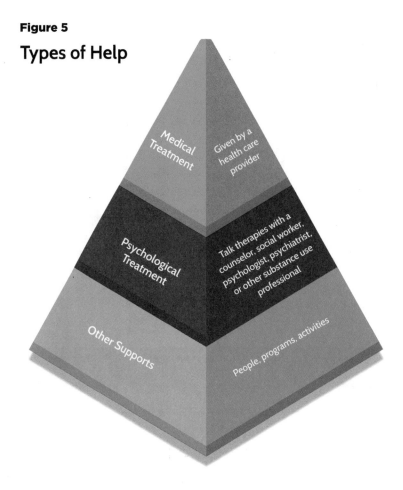

Medical Treatment

Given by a health care provider

Psychological Treatment

Talk therapies with a counselor, social worker, psychologist, psychiatrist, or other substance use professional

Other Supports

People, programs, activities

Treatment And Supports

For a person with a mental illness, treatments and supports are available to assist in the recovery process.

Treatment and supports can be medical treatments, psychological treatments, and activities or other supports that research has shown to help promote mental health.

The right combination of treatment and supports make people feel better or better able to manage their day-to-day life.

Figure 5 illustrates that everyone can use supports like self-care strategies to improve their mental health, while those experiencing increased stress or a mental health challenge or crisis can benefit from psychological treatments, and for some, a doctor might recommend adding medical treatments. All three types of help can be used together, or a person may benefit from only one.

Medical treatments

Medical treatments include prescribed medications and other treatments given by health care professionals such as a psychiatrist or other medical doctor. For mental disorders, medications might include antidepressants, antipsychotics, or mood stabilizers, while for addiction, medications include those that deter the person from misuse or overuse of the addictive substance.

Medication is usually combined with appropriate psychological treatments, such as counseling and other supports.

Psychological treatments

Psychological treatments involve changing the way the person thinks or behaves to:

- Reduce symptoms.

- Increase life skills.

- Reduce problem behaviors, like using too much alcohol.

These treatments are called counseling or "talk therapies" because they usually involve talking face-to-face and developing a supportive relationship with a mental health professional, such as a counselor, social worker, psychologist, psychiatrist, or substance use professional. Therapy can happen one-on-one, in a group, or with family members. Online counseling (eHealth or apps) is available.

Other supports

Other supports include people, programs, or activities that can help the person reduce or manage symptoms of mental health challenges. Only some will be available, and only some will match the person's interests. The following are examples.

- **People** can include anyone in the person's life who can be supportive to their recovery. This could include friends, siblings, neighbors, employers, and religious leaders.

- **Programs** could include mentoring programs, peer support groups, or peer mentors. Peer supporters — others who have experienced mental health challenges — can provide valuable help in recovery.

- **Activities** might include sports, art, music, theater, yoga, running, hiking, meditation, volunteering, or employment. For some mental health challenges, and when recommended by a medical professional, helpful activities might include a peer support group, a rehabilitation program, complementary treatments, life coaching, or lifestyle changes.

Professionals Who Can Help

Many types of mental health professionals in various settings can help.

Job titles and specialties can vary by state. For example, in some states, nurse practitioners are allowed to prescribe medication.

A brief description of some of the more common behavioral health professionals follows. Those who can assess and provide therapy are listed first, followed by those who can prescribe and monitor medications.

Behavioral Health Specialists

Therapists can help someone better understand and cope with thoughts, feelings, and behaviors. They can also offer guidance and help improve a person's ability to achieve life goals. These mental health professionals may also help assess and diagnose mental health conditions.

Substance use professionals evaluate, assist in treatment, and promote the recovery of people with substance use disorders. They also work to prevent substance use disorders.

Certified peer specialists/certified peer support specialists receive training that enables them to use their own lived experiences to promote hope, personal responsibility, empowerment, education, and self-determination (Mental Health America, 2018).

Psychologists are trained to diagnose and treat psychiatric disorders, but they are not medical doctors (MDs). Some states allow psychologists to prescribe some medications. A psychologist usually has a doctoral level degree and may hold either a PhD or a PsyD. During the course of psychology training, a psychologist may specialize in treating a particular area of mental illness or substance use disorder (for example, intravenous drug use or obsessive-compulsive disorder).

The American Psychological Association maintains an online database of members where First Aiders can search by the ages served and area of expertise.

Neuropsychologists are psychologists who specialize in the functioning of the brain and how it relates to behavior and cognitive ability. Most have completed post-doctoral training in neuropsychology. They may have either a PhD or a PsyD.

Neuropsychologists perform neuropsychological assessments, which measure a person's strengths and weaknesses over a broad range of cognitive tasks, and they provide a report that highlights cognitive strengths and weakness and forms the basis for developing a treatment plan.

Neuropsychologists who have passed national proficiency exams are certified by the American Board of Professional Psychology-Neuropsychology.

First Aiders can search the database of the American Association of Clinical Neuropsychology for a neuropsychologist.

Social workers A licensed clinical social worker (LCSW) has a master's degree in social work and is licensed by state agencies. LCSWs are required to have significant supervised training and expertise in clinical psychotherapy. The training must be approved by state licensing boards, which maintain a public list of all LCSWs. Social workers are not medical doctors; when they use the title of "Dr." it is because they have a PhD.

First Aiders can search the database of their state licensing board for an LCSW.

Medical Doctors

General practitioners (also known as family doctors or primary care physicians)

For many people developing a mental illness, their general practitioner will be the professional they first turn to for help. This person can provide immediate support and treatment and will often make a referral to a specialist. This is a more traditional approach to care of a person with a mental health challenge or disorder.

A general practitioner can recognize symptoms of a developing mental illness and can:

- Look for a possible physical cause.
- Explain the illness and how the person can best be helped.
- Prescribe medication if needed.
- Refer the person to a psychologist or other mental health professional who can help the person learn ways of coping with and overcoming the illness.
- Refer the person to a psychiatrist, particularly if the symptoms are severe or long lasting.
- Link the person to peer support or other support in their community.

Psychiatrists focus on treating people with severe or long-lasting disorders. They are experts in medication and can help people who may have side effects or interactions with other medications.

Most psychiatrists work in private practice, at mental health centers, or in hospitals.

Neurologists are medical doctors who specialize in the diagnosis and treatment of disorders of the brain, spine, and nervous system.

Medical doctors who are trained in addiction medicine work to prevent, evaluate, diagnose, treat, and promote the recovery of those with the disease of addiction and substance-related health conditions, and of those who show unhealthy use of substances.

Advanced Practitioners

Nurse practitioners are registered nurses who have master's-level clinical training in a health care specialty area, such as mental health, women's and newborn health, or elder and adult health. In many states, under physician supervision they prescribe some medications and recommend treatments.

Physician assistants (PAs): In many states, physician assistants can prescribe some medications. Like nurse practitioners, physician assistants usually work in a health care specialty under physician supervision.

Integrated Care

Medical practices offering both medical care and mental and behavioral health care are known as integrated care.

Integrated care can work well because people with mental and substance abuse disorders may have hypertension, diabetes, obesity, and cardiovascular disease (National Council for Behavioral Health, 2018). These illnesses are aggravated by inadequate physical activity, poor nutrition, smoking, and substance use.

First Aiders should be familiar with available services within primary care or behavioral health settings.

Professionals Who Assist Young Adults Still In School

School psychologists are trained in psychology and education and receive a Specialist in School Psychology (SSP) degree. For young adults still in school, they can identify learning and behavior challenges; evaluate students for special education services; and support social, emotional, and behavioral health. The National Association of School Psychologists has more information.

A report on the neuropsychological assessment serves as evidence for requesting school accommodations such as an Individualized Education Plan (IEP) and as a baseline for measuring whether what the school offers is working.

Neuropsychologists work one-on-one with young adults struggling in school to help them devise learning strategies to build on their strengths and compensate for their weaknesses.

If someone can't pay for mental health services, they may be able to turn to their local community-based behavioral health care clinic. Some communities may have Certified Community Behavioral Health Clinics (CCBHCs). CCBHCs offer comprehensive mental health and substance use disorder services.

Finding Care That The Person Can Afford

Health insurance and managed care organizations have varying levels of coverage for mental health services, so it is important to find out what will be covered by particular institutions or doctors. You might assist in calling the person's health insurance company for a list of professionals who specialize in working with mental health and substance use disorders.

For people without health insurance, help may be available. They might be able to get services from a community mental health center or behavioral health care clinic, federally qualified health care center, or other local health resource. Some may be able to get care from a faith-based organization, school, or university.

RECOVERY FROM MENTAL AND SUBSTANCE USE DISORDERS

Many people are unaware that mental and substance use disorders can be treated and that recovery is possible. Recovery from mental illness is a process of change through which people improve their health and well-being, live self-directed lives, and strive to reach their full potential. Recovery is also a term used to describe the period of time when people with mental illness come to accept the challenge of their illness and work to overcome it (SAMHSA, 2017).

Research has found that there are four major dimensions that support recovery:

- **Health –** Overcoming or managing one's disease(s) or symptoms and making informed, healthy choices that support physical and emotional well-being.

- **Home –** Having a stable and safe place to live.

- **Purpose –** Conducting meaningful daily activities and having the independence, income, and resources to participate in society.

- **Community –** Having relationships and social networks that provide support, friendship, love, and hope.

The First Aider's Role

You should understand that hope, the belief that these challenges and conditions can be overcome, is the foundation of recovery. The role you play in fostering hope may be the most valuable contribution you can make in supporting someone in a mental health crisis.

As you offer support, recall that setbacks aren't failures, but rather are part of the recovery process. Help the person (and their family, as appropriate) to recall this as well. Because setbacks are a natural part of life, resilience becomes a key component of recovery.

You may play a role in encouraging the person to take action that will benefit their recovery, such as helping them get to a meeting of others experiencing similar issues, or encouraging them to keep their job. Recovery is more likely when a person has opportunities for education, employment, and support from others experiencing similar issues (Jorm, 2011). Support groups have been found to be helpful for both people with mental disorders and their families (Worrall et al., 2018).

Family members often become the champions of their loved one's recovery. But families of people with mental disorders may have increased family stress, guilt, shame, anger, fear, anxiety, loss, grief, and isolation. Families need access to support.

WELL-BEING

Well-being follows a period of recovery.

Achieving well-being allows a person to perform well at work, in their studies, and in family and other social relationships. The person learns to cope with illness, crisis, or trauma and associated challenges while adjusting their lifestyle.

For well-being, a person aims to balance the emotional, financial, social, spiritual, occupational, physical, intellectual, and environmental dimensions of their lives in a way that works for them (Swarbrick & Yudof, 2006). A brief look at these eight dimensions of well-being follows:

- When a person is emotionally well, they cope effectively, have positive self-regard, and create satisfying relationships.
- Financial wellness comes with experiencing satisfaction with current and future financial situations.
- Developing a sense of connection, belonging, and a well-developed support system can help a person feel socially well.
- Spiritual well-being occurs when people attend to their sense of purpose and meaning in life. Spiritual well-being can involve a focus on the here and now rather than on the past or the future.
- Occupational well-being comes from personal satisfaction and enrichment with one's work and with volunteering, studying, caregiving, contributing to the community, or other activities that provide a meaning and purpose to life.
- Physical activity as appropriate, healthy foods, and restful sleep all contribute to physical well-being.
- Intellectual well-being can be attained when people recognize ways to expand their knowledge and skills through intellectually stimulating activities.
- Safe environments lead to environmental well-being.

A Note On Resilience

Resilience is a person's ability to "bounce back" or overcome adversity. The American Psychological Association put out a statement in 2018 defining resilience and affirming that every person can develop resilience:

> Being resilient does not mean that a person does not experience difficulties or distress. Emotional pain and sadness are common in people who have suffered major adversity or trauma in their lives. In fact, the road to resilience is likely to involve considerable emotional distress. Resilience is not a trait that people either have or do not have. It involves behaviors, thoughts and actions that can be learned and developed in anyone.

Resiliency is strengthened through the presence of protective factors, which are characteristics that decrease one's vulnerability to health risks. Protective factors for mental disorders include optimism and the ability to frame adverse events in a positive light; social and familial support; and a sense of purpose or meaning in life (Masten & Wright, 2010). Specific protective factors for certain mental health challenges are outlined in Section 2.

MENTAL HEALTH FIRST AID

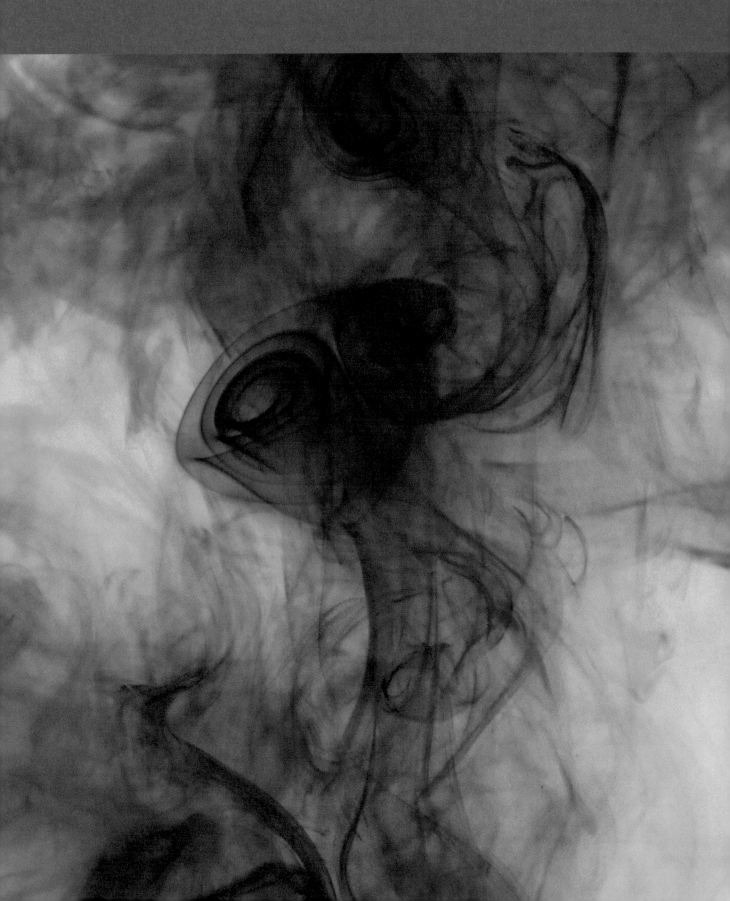

CHAPTER 2:
MENTAL HEALTH FIRST AID

WHAT IS MENTAL HEALTH FIRST AID?

First aid is the help given to a person who is ill or injured before professional medical treatment can be obtained.

Mental Health First Aid is help for a person experiencing a mental health challenge, mental disorder, or a mental health crisis. The first aid is given until appropriate professional help is received or until the crisis resolves.

Mental Health First Aid aims to:

- Preserve life when a person may be a danger to self or others.

- Prevent the problem from becoming more serious.

- Promote recovery and resiliency.

- Provide comfort.

- Help to identify appropriate resources and guide the person toward them.

To administer Mental Health First Aid, the First Aider must know:

- How to recognize signs and symptoms of mental health challenges.

- How to offer and provide initial help.

- How to guide people and their family toward appropriate treatments and other supportive help.

Mental Health First Aid does not teach people to diagnose or provide therapy.

In a crisis, Mental Health First Aiders can help ensure that the emergency medical technicians (EMTs) provide the same level of care and compassion toward the mental illness as they would a physical illness.

WHY MENTAL HEALTH FIRST AID?

Some of the many reasons Mental Health First Aid is beneficial are:

People may not be well informed about how to recognize mental health challenges and how to get help. They may not know how to seek help or what sort of help is best. First Aiders help with this.

> Knowledge of Mental Health First Aid can help you help others. You can also share the Mental Health First Aid training with others who can benefit from it.

There Are More Treatments, Services, And Community Support Systems Than Ever Before, And They Work.

The first step is getting people the help they need. First Aiders play a crucial role in offering immediate first aid and assisting the person and their family get connected to appropriate help.

Mental Health First Aid Has Been Found To Be Effective.

Peer-reviewed studies show that trained Mental Health First Aiders:

- Grow their knowledge of signs, symptoms, and risk factors of mental illnesses and addiction.

- Can identify multiple types of professional and self-help resources for people with a mental illness or addiction.

- Increase their confidence in and likelihood to help an individual with a mental health challenge.

- Increase their intention to provide Mental Health First Aid to an individual with a mental health challenge.

- Increase the amount of help provided to an individual with a mental health challenge.

Studies also show that Mental Health First Aid reduces negative attitudes toward individuals with mental illnesses. This can allow people to benefit from relationships that otherwise would not be possible.

The National Council's Medical Director Institute's report, Mass Violence in America, states that Mental Health First Aiders can help people understand that the large majority of people with mental health challenges are not violent toward others, and do not deserve to be treated as if they are a threat.

In the Mass Violence in America, the authors state that mental health professionals and others should pay attention to individuals with narcissistic and/or paranoid personality traits who are fixated on thoughts and feelings of injustice and who have few social relationships; people who have had recent stresses; and people with new onset psychosis. They add that quality and comprehensive mental health care is a necessary component of a fight against mass violence, and recommend more research on the role in mass violence of social alienation, poor schools, poverty, discrimination, and the lack of job opportunities. The Helpful Resources section has additional information.

Personality disorders and difficult personality traits such as narcissism and/or nondelusional paranoia are understood in the context of what mental health professionals call "The Big Five Personality Traits" (Grohol, 2019). Personality traits generally become more established from ages 7 through 10.

The Big Five Personality Traits

Extraversion – The level of sociability and enthusiasm

Agreeableness – The level of friendliness and kindness

Conscientiousness – The level of organization and work ethic

Emotional stability (also called neuroticism) – The level of calmness and tranquility

Intellect/imagination (also called openness) – The level of creativity and curiosity

Researchers have found that nondelusional paranoia is related to childhood trauma and social stress (Lee, 2017). Those with narcissistic personality traits may not see how they contribute to problems or how their actions affect other people (Ronningstam, 2014).

Mental Disorders Are Common.

In the United States, almost half of adults (46.4 percent) will experience a mental illness during their lifetime. Every year, around one in five (18.9 percent) is affected.

Stigma Can Lead People To Hide Their Issues And Delay Seeking Help, But Mental Health First Aid Can Reduce Stigma.

Stigma involves negative attitudes (prejudice) and negative behavior (discrimination). People are often ashamed to discuss mental health and substance use issues with family, friends, teachers, and/or work colleagues and may be reluctant to seek treatment and support because of concerns about what others will think.

Stigma can lead to exclusion of people with mental disorders from jobs, housing, social activities, and relationships. People with mental disorders can internalize the stigma and begin to believe the negative things others say about them.

Understanding that effective treatments are available may reduce stigma and encourage a person to seek help.

Myths And Misunderstandings About Mental Illness May Lead People To Ignore Symptoms.

Some common myths are that people can use willpower to pull themselves out of a mental health or substance use disorder, that only weak people have mental disorders, and that it is better to avoid psychiatric treatment. Another myth is that people with mental disorders are dangerous.

A lack of knowledge about mental illness may result in someone denying symptoms when they appear (Svensson, Hansson, & Stjernswärd, 2015).

Sometimes A Person In Severe Distress Cannot Take Effective Action To Help Themselves.

People with mental disorders may not have the insight that they need help or may be unaware that effective help is available. In this situation, people close to them can make sure they get appropriate help.

Family And Friends Might Help The Person To Develop An Advance Directive, Wellness Plan, Relapse Prevention Plan, And/Or Personal Directive.

What is an advance care directive?

An advance care directive is a document describing how a person wants to be treated when they are unable to make their own decisions due to their present state of illness. This is an agreement made between the person, their family, and sometimes their primary health care provider. It is not usually a legal document, but this varies between states and territories.

What is an enduring power of attorney?

An enduring power of attorney is a legal agreement allowing a person to appoint someone of their choice to manage their legal and financial affairs. This is developed when a person is of sound mind. As the agreement is "enduring," it will continue to apply if the person becomes unable to make their own decisions (legally described as being of "unsound mind").

What is an enduring power of guardianship?

An enduring power of guardianship is a legal agreement allowing a person to appoint someone of their choice to manage, where necessary, medical and welfare decisions on their behalf. It comes into effect only when the person becomes unable to make their own decisions.

The laws regarding advance care directives, enduring power of attorney, and enduring power of guardianship can vary among different states and territories, and legal advice should be sought.

People Are Resilient And Can Recover From Mental Health Challenges.

Studies show that people with mental health challenges get better and many recover completely. In fact, many people are extremely resilient and are able to use their life experiences to help them grow (Bonanno et al., 2011). For people with trauma, this is described as post-traumatic growth (PTG) (University of North Carolina at Charlotte, 2014).

People May Not Be Able To Get To Appointments.

Many factors can make a person unable to get to appointments, such as lack of transportation or money or a lack of understanding of insurance and of our health care system. When you know about available resources, you can better help individuals and families.

Professional And Other Support Services Are Not Always Available When A Mental Health Issue Arises.

When a professional such as a psychiatrist is not available in a crisis, a First Aider can help.

THE MENTAL HEALTH FIRST AID ACTION PLAN

The Mental Health First Aid 5-step action plan to help people with mental health challenges is ALGEE. Figure 6 shows the steps of ALGEE.

Figure 6

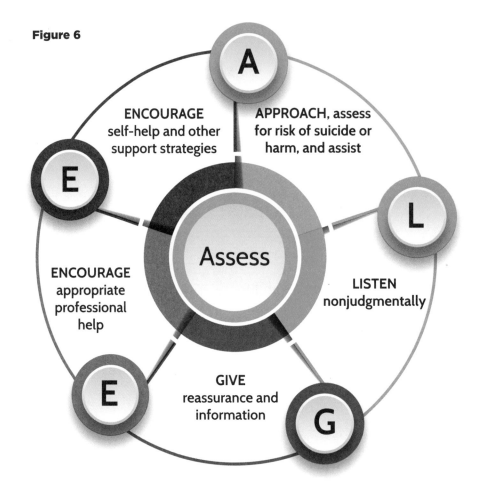

To understand ALGEE, think about when you first learned First Aid. In a First Aid course, participants learn all the steps for first aid in order, even though they will not always need to take all steps. Similarly, Mental Health First Aiders learn ALGEE's five steps, but will not always use all five and will not always use them in order.

The First Aider has to use good judgment and be flexible and responsive to the person they are helping. For example, when you listen nonjudgmentally as you assist someone, you are doing two of the steps at once.

In this chapter, we present ALGEE for adults first, and then ALGEE for adults with developmental disabilities.

In Section 2, you will learn about ALGEE for each mental disorder, while in Chapter 13: First Aid for Mental Health Crises you will learn how to assess and assist in mental health crisis situations.

As a First Aider, you will assist the person until appropriate professional help arrives or the crisis resolves.

ALGEE FOR ADULTS

ACTION A: Approach, Assess For Risk Of Suicide Or Harm, And Assist

A First Aider should approach the person, look out for any crises and assist the person in dealing with them. The key points for the First Aider are to:

- Approach the person about their concerns.

- Find a suitable time and space where both people feel comfortable.

- If the person does not initiate a conversation with the First Aider about how they are feeling, the First Aider should say something to them.

- Respect the person's privacy and confidentiality.

Possible crises might include:

- The person may harm themselves by attempting suicide, using alcohol or substances to become intoxicated, attempting to achieve extreme weight loss, or engaging in nonsuicidal self-injury such as cutting or scratching the skin. (In nonsuicidal self-injury situations, the self-injury is intentional but is not a suicide attempt.)

- The person experiences extreme distress, such as a panic attack or a reaction to a traumatic event. Every individual has their own unique way of reacting to traumatic events.

- The person's behavior is very disturbing to others (they become guarded or frightened or lose touch with reality).

If the person appears to be at risk of harming self or others, the First Aider must get help immediately.

- Call 911 immediately.
  - ◦ Tell the dispatcher that the person is suicidal or at risk of harming self or others, so they can send officers with specific training in crisis de-escalation and mental illness.
  - ◦ Do not leave the person alone.
- If the crisis is occurring in the workplace, follow the established crisis protocol.
  - ◦ If you do not know the protocol or if support is not available, call 911 immediately.
    - » Tell the dispatcher that the person is suicidal, to allow for the dispatcher to send officers with specific training in crisis de-escalation and mental illness.

Important signs that a person MAY BE suicidal:

- Threatening to hurt or kill themselves.

- Seeking access to lethal means: pills, weapons, etc.

- Talking or writing about death, dying, or suicide.

- Expressing hopelessness, no reason for living, having no sense of purpose in life, or not wanting to be alive.

- Sudden changes in behavior.
  - Ends friendships, drastic drop in grades, starting or engaging in more arguments with family members.
  - Withdrawing from friends or family or activities they normally participate in.
  - Having a sudden, dramatic change in mood or irritability.
  - Dramatic changes in sleep: sleeping all the time or being unable to sleep.
  - Giving away prized possessions.

If you have concerns that a person may be having suicidal thoughts, call 911. Suicidal thoughts or behaviors are an emergency and must be considered as such.

If you have no concerns that the person is in crisis, you can move on to another action. If at any point your concern for the person's safety increases, put any worries about damaging your relationship with the person aside and focus solely on the person's safety.

You can provide the following resources to the person:

- National Suicide Prevention Lifeline at 1-800-273-TALK (1-800-273-8255).
- Crisis Text Line (text "MHFA" to 741741).

Be aware that the person may not wish to open up to you until they feel that you care enough, are trustworthy, and willing to listen. It is also possible that they may hide or downplay their problem, particularly if they feel guilty about upsetting or disappointing you.

Some people may fear opening up about their problems in case their vulnerability is perceived as weakness. Let the person know that you are available to talk when they are ready; do not put pressure on them to talk right away.

If you are having a private discussion with the person and other people arrive, take a private moment to ask whether they want to continue the discussion in front of others, ask others to leave, or schedule another time to continue your discussion.

In a non-crisis situation, what should I do if the person doesn't want help?

Start with finding out the specific reasons why this is the case. For example, a person may be concerned that they cannot afford treatment, may worry that they will not find a doctor they like, or may be worried about being sent to a hospital. These reasons may be based on mistaken beliefs, and you may be able to help them overcome their worry about seeking help.

If they still do not want help, let them know that if they change their mind in the future, they can speak to you. To remain supportive, you can:

- Encourage the person to talk with someone they trust.
- Encourage the person to connect with friends and family.
- Remain patient and nonjudgmental.
- Remain friendly and open.
- Ask if there would be a circumstance or situation where the person would be willing to consider getting help.
- Recall that you should never threaten the person with hospitalization.

ACTION L: Listen Nonjudgmentally

Listening to the person is very important. When listening, it is important to set aside any judgments about them or their situation and to avoid expressing those judgments. Most people experiencing distressing emotions and thoughts want to be heard before being offered helpful options and resources.

Be aware that the person may not wish to open up to you until they feel that you care enough and are trustworthy and willing to listen. It is also possible that they may hide or downplay their problem, particularly if they feel guilty about upsetting or disappointing you.

Some people may fear opening up about their problems in case their vulnerability is perceived as weakness. Let the person know that you are available to talk when they are ready.

When listening nonjudgmentally, your goals are to:

- Allow yourself to really hear and understand what is being said.
- Make it easier for the person to feel they can talk freely about their problems without being judged.
- Respect the person's culture.

To do so, you will:

- Use "I" statements and nonjudgmentally state what you have noticed
    - For example, "I noticed that you look like you might be feeling sad about something."
- Ask questions, but not push. "Is there something going on that is causing you to be sad?" or "Did something happen?"
- Be in the present with them without comparing to your own experience.
    - For example, "A conflict with a co-worker can be tough."
- Be accepting even though you may not agree.
    - For example, if the person says that going to work is too much to handle, empathize with their frustration. It is not the time to convince them to take specific action.
- Make eye contact, nod, smile, and repeat back what you hear to make sure it's correct.
- Be positive with your feedback.

You can be an effective, nonjudgmental listener by paying special attention to two main areas:

- Your attitudes and how they are conveyed.
- Effective communication skills, both verbal and nonverbal.

Attitudes

The key attitudes involved in nonjudgmental listening are acceptance, genuineness, and empathy.

An attitude of acceptance means respecting the person's feelings, culture, personal values, and experiences as valid, even if they are different from your own or you disagree with them. You should not judge, criticize, or trivialize what the person says because of your own beliefs or attitudes. Sometimes this may mean withholding all judgments that you have made about the person and their other circumstances. For example, do not conclude that the person's problems are the result of weakness or laziness — the person's mental disorder is not something they can control, and they are trying to cope.

Genuineness means not holding one set of attitudes while expressing another. Your body language and verbal cues should show your acceptance of the person. For example, you can nod your head, look at the person, and not look at your phone while you have the conversation. Adopting the person's accent, language, slang, or mannerisms does not show genuineness if these are not natural for you.

Empathy means being able to imagine yourself in the other person's place, showing the person that they are truly heard and understood by you. Dr. Brené Brown, a sociologist researcher, describes empathy this way, "Empathy has no script. There is no right way or wrong way to do it. It's simply listening, holding space, withholding judgment, emotionally connecting, and communicating that incredibly healing message of 'You're not alone.'"

A First Aider can show empathy by saying, "It sounds like things are really difficult for you right now. You feel sad all of the time. I am here for you if you want to talk about it." This validates what the person is saying. It shows that the First Aider cares and wants to help.

On the other hand, saying, "I understand exactly what you are going through" may not be helpful because we can never know exactly what the other person is experiencing. This type of statement might shut down the conversation.

Remember that empathy is different from sympathy, which means feeling sorry for or pitying the person. Sympathy can create an uneven power dynamic and can lead the person to feel isolated and disconnected. Empathy is a skill that First Aiders should practice so they can help people feel included, heard, and supported.

Verbal skills

Using the following simple verbal skills will show that you are listening:

- Ask questions that show you genuinely care and want to understand.
- Check your understanding by restating what the person has said and summarizing facts and feelings.
- Listen not only to what the person says, but also how they say it; tone of voice and nonverbal cues will give extra clues about how they are feeling.
- Respect the person's culture by asking about and exhibiting verbal behaviors that convey this respect.
- Use prompts, such as "I see" and "Ah" when necessary to keep the conversation going.
- Be patient if the person is struggling to communicate.
- Do not be critical or express frustration at the person or their symptoms.
- Avoid giving unhelpful advice such as "pull yourself up by your bootstraps," "get a grip," or "cheer up." If this were possible, the person would have done it.
- Do not interrupt the person when they are speaking, especially to share your opinions or experiences.
- Avoid confrontation such as arguing or fighting with the person — unless you need to take more assertive actions to prevent harmful or dangerous acts.

Remember that pauses and silences are okay. The person may need time to think about what has been said or may be struggling to find the words they need. Interrupting the silence may make it difficult for them to get back on track and may damage the rapport you have been building.

With all mental health challenges, recall that there are variations in people's perceptions of depression, whether they seek help, and response to treatment.

You might find that person uses terms that you don't typically use or hear to describe symptoms of mental health challenges and disorders. They may have learned to describe their feelings the way their parents did. For example, in ethnically and culturally diverse low-income communities, a study found that women did not all use the same terms to describe depression. The same physical symptoms and severity of depression were reported across the different ethnic groups; it was the terms that differed. Some terms were blues, sadness, and homesickness (Gonzalez et al., 2011).

ACTION G: Give Reassurance And Information

Once a person with a mental health challenge feels that they have been heard, it can be easier to offer support and information. Reassurance includes emotional support, such as empathizing with how the person feels and voicing hope.

People with a mental health challenge can experience a range of emotions. They might be in denial about their situation, scared to admit what is happening, and uncertain about what to do next. You can offer to provide some information about mental health challenges and explain that mental health challenges are common.

You can provide hope that treatment can help address any current difficulties and can also help prevent more serious problems in the future. Remind the person that what they are experiencing is a disorder.

Be patient, persistent, and encouraging. Understand that the person may be overwhelmed by worry, and it may make it difficult for them to be receptive to support. Let the person know that you will continue to help them. Be on time for any meetings that you arrange with the person. Use your nonjudgmental listening skills each time you are together.

ACTION E: Encourage Appropriate Professional Help

People with mental health challenges will generally get better more quickly and be less likely to have another episode of illness if they get appropriate professional help. Yet people often do not know about the options available to them.

You might offer to help the person learn more about mental health professionals and services and suggest appropriate help.

For a young adult still in school who is reluctant to talk to their family, the First Aider can encourage them to connect with a mental health professional at their school or university. The mental health professional can assess the situation, identify mental health resources, and in some school districts, can find out information about cost and insurance.

ACTION E: Encourage Self-Help And Other Support Strategies

Encourage the person to use self-help strategies and help them identify other supports including supportive people in their social network, programs in their community, and activities they enjoy. Self-help includes physical and mental and emotional self-care strategies.

Physical self-care, or the healthy living habits one develops and practices, is an important aspect of managing the symptoms of mental health challenges. Eating habits, exercise patterns, sleep, recreational activities, and more can have a significant impact on how a person feels and functions. Encourage the person to talk to their doctor about recommended nutrition, exercise, or sleep.

Physical self-care could be challenging for someone living in poverty, with unstable housing, and without access to adequate nutrition. If this is an added burden, First Aiders could help the person connect with additional social services in the community.

Mental and emotional self-care or effective coping skills are important part of managing daily stress and the added challenges of a mental disorder. You can help the person to learn how to use coping skills in the face of stress and challenges. Doing so increases a person's resilience.

Coping skills are:

- Expressing feelings.
- Communicating.
- Connecting with supportive people.
- Exercise.
- Deep breathing.
- Setting realistic goals.
- Setting boundaries.

You might guide the person to improve coping skills through healthy activities such as:

- Talking to a trusted person about feelings or problems.
- Journaling.
- Connecting with community clubs or groups.
- Using online support groups.
- Developing a hobby.
- Creating art or music.
- Writing.
- Meditation.

You can also help the person identify people, programs, or activities that can help them reduce or manage symptoms of mental health challenges.

In cases when someone is hospitalized, you might ask whether the person would like their family and friends to know that they should give the same sort of support as they would to a person with a physical illness. Get-well cards or flowers and calls or visits may be welcome. Family or friends may help out if they cannot manage (Thoits, 2011). Studies show that people with mental disorders who are hospitalized are less likely to receive flowers, get-well cards, and other gifts, and this can lead to feelings of rejection.

If you have contact with the person's family member and have permission to talk about the person, you can encourage the family member to seek the support of their social network, because having a loved one experience a mental health challenge is difficult.

ALGEE FOR ADULTS WITH DEVELOPMENTAL DISABILITIES

Figure 7

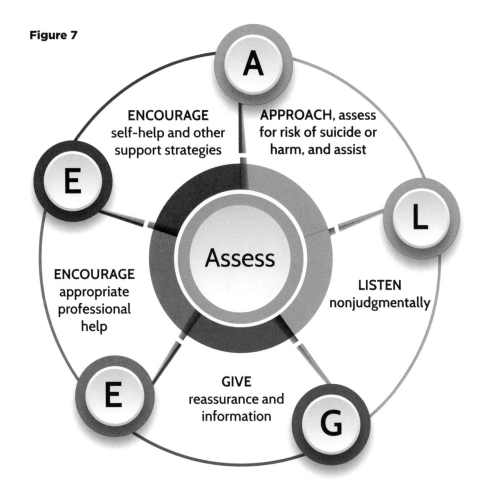

ACTION A: Approach, Assess For Risk Of Suicide Or Harm, And Assist

A First Aider should approach the person, look out for any crises, determine if there is a communication gap, and assist the person in dealing with any crises.

The key points for the First Aider are to:

- Approach the person about your concerns.

- Ask whether you can do anything to help them communicate; you might ask whether they have a book or document explaining their communication needs, or a call a national hotline for help.

- Find a suitable time and space where both people feel comfortable.

- If the person does not initiate a conversation with you about how they are feeling, say something to them.

- A person with intellectual disabilities may not understand the term "suicide," so you may need to say "kill yourself" or "make yourself die" instead. This guidance applies only to those with intellectual disabilities. Recall that not everyone with a developmental disability has an intellectual disability.

- Recall that some people with an intellectual disability may hug or kiss new people. Help the person understand what physical contact you are comfortable with.

- Respect the person's privacy and confidentiality.

- When you contact professional help, try to locate the person's established support system, caregiver, or family to inform them.

- If a person with developmental disabilities reveals abuse, neglect, or exploitation at home, contacting a family member may further endanger them.

  » If this is disclosed during your conversation, you should contact their local department of social services or family services or a law enforcement agency.

- If you offer to assist the person and the person does not want your help, respect this, unless there is a risk of harm to the person or others.

Possible crises might include:

- **The person may harm themselves by attempting suicide,** using alcohol or substances to become intoxicated, engaging in nonsuicidal self-injury such as cutting or scratching the skin, or attempting to achieve extreme weight loss.

  If you have concerns that a person may be having suicidal thoughts, call 911 and do not leave the person alone. Suicidal thoughts or behaviors are an emergency and must be considered as such.

- **The person experiences extreme distress,** such as a panic attack or a reaction to a traumatic event. For a person with an intellectual disability, events such as repeated rejection, living in situations where they lack control, teasing and name calling, and extended hospitalizations can be traumatic.

- **The person's behavior is very disturbing to others** (they become aggressive or sexually inappropriate or lose touch with reality).

  - Sexually inappropriate behavior may involve a participant who is unwilling or participants who are unequal in age, size, or ability.

  - If the police must be involved because of sexually inappropriate behavior, advocate for the person or seek another advocate to assist them.

If the person appears to be at risk of harming self or others, the First Aider must get help immediately.

- Call 911 immediately.

  - Tell the dispatcher that the person is suicidal, to allow for them to send officers with specific training in crisis de-escalation and mental illness.

  - Tell the dispatcher that the person has a developmental disability.

  - Check if the person is wearing a medical alert bracelet or pendant.

  - Try to locate the person's family, legal guardian, caregiver, or someone from their support system.

  - Meet the EMTs on their arrival, before they approach the person, and remind them that the person has a developmental disability.

  - Reassure the person that they are not in trouble, if this is the case.

- If you are working with the person in a setting where there is a crisis protocol, follow the crisis protocol and escort the person to a member of the crisis response team's office.
    - If that person is not available or this is happening outside of the setting where there is a crisis protocol, call 911 immediately. Tell the dispatcher that the person is suicidal and has a developmental disability.

If EMTs refuse to do anything for the person, but you feel the person needs their assistance, do not give up; try to explain to the EMTs what you believe the person needs.

If you believe the person is suicidal, share your concerns with the person's family member or legal guardian and ask if they are also concerned the person may be at risk of suicide.

For additional guidance see Chapter 12: Suicide.

If there is no crisis, but the person is distressed:

- Recall that minor changes can cause distress for a person with a developmental disability. You might try turning off the TV, asking people to be quiet, or moving to another location.
- Ask the person if they have felt this way before, and if so, what has been helpful in the past.

If there is no crisis, but the person is exhibiting sexually inappropriate behavior:

- Redirect the person to another activity or to a private area.
- Ask the person's caregiver or professional helper if strategies are in place for this behavior.

If you have no concerns that the person is in crisis, and the person is not in distress, you can move on to another action.

Important Signs That A Person May Be Suicidal:

- Threatening to hurt or kill themselves.
- Seeking access to lethal means: pills, weapons, etc.
- Talking or writing about death, dying, or suicide.
- Expressing hopelessness, no reason for living, having no sense of purpose in life, or not wanting to be alive.
- Sudden changes in behavior:
    - Ending friendships; a drastic drop in grades; starting or engaging in more arguments.
    - Withdrawing from friends or family or activities they normally participate in.
    - Having a sudden, dramatic change in mood or irritability.
    - Dramatic changes in sleep: sleeping all the time or being unable to sleep.
    - Giving away prized possessions.

ACTION L: Listen Nonjudgmentally

First of all, ask the person if there is anyone they would like to be part of the conversation, such as a family member, caregiver, professional helper, or friend. However, if you believe that the person is not able to speak openly when someone else is present, check whether the person wants to meet alone instead.

Ask the person with developmental disabilities (or their caregiver or professional helper) about their ability to understand and their particular communication needs. It will be important to know whether the person with developmental disabilities will tell you when they do not understand.

Do not pretend to understand the person if you do not. If you are having difficulty understanding them, ask if they would like someone else to be part of the conversation to help you understand.

When someone else is present, speak directly to the person and not to anyone else. If you want to ask the other person a question, check with the person if this is okay before doing so.

The following tips are helpful:

- Do not ask leading questions such as, "You're feeling sad, aren't you?" This may influence them to respond with what they think you want to hear or what they think is the right answer.

- Give the person time to think about what has been said or to express themselves. Consider offering frequent breaks.

- Do not try to finish the person's sentences.

- Do not provide the person with too many options because this may be confusing.

- Use short and simple statements or questions. You might say, "Taking deep breaths and counting to ten can help calm feelings of frustration."

- For important messages, try repeating them. This will increase the likelihood the person will understand and remember.

    ◦ For example, for someone who uses a cell phone and who is telling you that they are feeling sad, you may want the person to show that they can call a helpline. You might phrase your instructions, "If you are feeling sad and you are alone, pick up your cell phone and text 'MHFA' to 741741." Next, repeat the sentence the same way several times.

Additional tips that may be useful include the following:

- If you need to ask when something occurred or how long something has been happening, and the person struggles with dates and times, ask in a way that makes it meaningful for them. For example, you might say, "Have you felt this way since before your birthday, or after?" or "Was that at dinner time or breakfast time?"

- Do not use sarcasm (for example, saying "I bet you love that activity!" when you know the person does not love the activity).

- Do not use abbreviations and acronyms unless the person uses them too. For example, if the person doesn't know what a "CIT" is, don't say, "I am going to call the CIT." Instead, say "I am going to call the Crisis Intervention Team."

- Do not use idioms or colorful expressions such as "under the weather," "wise old owl," or "He's a teddy bear."

- If you ask the person a question that offers a choice of answers, be aware that they might choose the last option. Check their understanding by asking the question again later in a different way.

- Allow the person to talk about their experiences. However, be aware that they may describe their emotional symptoms using physical descriptions. For example, they may say that their heart hurts or that they are sad in their stomach.

- Sometimes repetitive behaviors such as repeating movements or sounds, or touching or moving objects, can help a person manage their emotions. If you think the person is using these behaviors (known as stimming behaviors or self-stimulatory behaviors) in this way, do not try to stop them.

ACTION G: Give Reassurance And Information

Before offering any specific information, check what supports are available to the person. In any case, you should start out by offering general reassuring statements such as, "Thank you for sharing your experience with me. I appreciate your trust. A lot of people have reported similar signs and symptoms, and they have found help from a professional who knows the treatments that can help." You can provide the person or their caregiver or guardian with the national resources listed in Chapter 2: Mental Health First Aid to use until local resources are identified.

The person should know that it is okay to stop you if they are not understanding. As you talk to the person, you might say, "I need to make sure I explain it properly, please let me know if I am not clear."

ACTION E: Encourage Appropriate Professional Help

If mental health professionals with expertise in intellectual disability are available in the local area, share this information as relevant. However, be mindful that the person may not want to use a mental health service that specializes in supporting people with an intellectual disability. If this is the case, you should recommend that the person or their caregiver speak to their primary care doctor first, who will be able to make an appropriate referral.

Keep in mind that there may not be a local mental health professional with training and experience in working with people with an intellectual disability. Give the person and their caregiver information to help them to make a decision about professional help. Explain to them what is involved in the various options as well as the benefits of each option. Try using a clear statement such as, "The choice is yours and I am here to support you."

ACTION E: Encourage Self-Help And Other Support Strategies

Ask the person if they have used self-help strategies in the past that they found helpful. If they have and they need support to use them, provide that support or find others who can.

If you want to suggest self-help strategies, carefully consider whether the person will be able to use the strategies. If the person wants to learn to use self-help strategies, suggest specialized education programs (where available) to assist them to learn these skills.

If the person needs additional support from helpers, but family and friends are under stress, call a national hotline or try other means to find this support for them. You can find information on national hotlines in the Helpful Resources section.

A Note About Appointments

If you have the opportunity to support a person who has an appointment that is not immediate, you can use the following tips:

- Explain what to expect, and make sure they know the time, place, and who they will see.

- If the person thinks they are in trouble because they are going to see a professional, reassure them that they are not.

If you are supporting a person as they go to an appointment, you should:

- Let the health professional know if the person has any specific fears or needs that may affect the appointment (with appropriate consent from the person or their legal guardian).

- Encourage the person to take any book or document explaining their communication needs, if they have this.

- Explain to the health professional the person's communication style and preferences (with appropriate consent from the person or their legal guardian).

- If the professional is having difficulty understanding the person, you should assist, with the person's permission.

MENTAL HEALTH FIRST AID: CULTURAL CONSIDERATIONS

If you are assisting someone from a cultural background different from your own, you may need to ask about and adjust some of your nonverbal behaviors. For example, the person may be comfortable with a level of eye contact different from what you are used to. You might ask if they are comfortable if you stand next to them.

Keep in mind that some people want their family to be part of their mental health decisions, and some people do not. Sometimes that decision is based on the person's culture. Do not assume that because someone is from a certain culture that you know whether they would want to talk with someone in their family first before getting help. You can ask the question directly.

Some people may want help from a chaplain, spiritual leader, or healer. You can ask about their preferences.

It may be helpful to explore and try to understand the person's experiences, values, or belief systems. Avoid generalizations. When unsure what the person sees as appropriate and realistic, always ask. You might seek advice from someone from the same cultural background before approaching the person, if you do not feel there is the urgency of a crisis.

Recall that adopting a new culture can be a contributor to stress. Figure 7 highlights this as one factor of many that can affect a person's well-being.

Someone you wish to help may tell you that they are uncomfortable speaking with you because you do not have the same experiences as they do. When this happens, you should let them know you are going to text the crisis text line (which involves texting "MHFA" to 741741) to find someone who they may feel more comfortable talking to.

Figure 8

What can lead to stress, anxiety, and more?

Trouble Sleeping

Frightening Thoughts

Jumpiness

Flashbacks

Forced to leave your own culture

Trauma

Adopting a new culture

Being poor

Discrimination

Ask the person to tell you if you do or say anything that makes them uncomfortable, and apologize if they tell you that you have. After you apologize, move on, rather than focusing on the mistake or on what you have learned.

If it is natural for you to state your preferred pronouns when you introduce yourself to a new person, you may wish to do so. If a person tells you what pronoun they prefer, use that pronoun.

IMPORTANT CONSIDERATIONS

First Aiders should be aware that:

- Mental Health First Aid does not replace any potential responsibilities, legal responsibilities, or organizational procedures a First Aider has as a mandatory reporter, first responder, or government employee.

- Staying safe is the most important thing for all First Aiders to remember. A First Aider is never required to engage in a situation they are uncomfortable with or where they feel unsafe. If a situation becomes uncomfortable or unsafe, immediately disengage and connect the person with another trained person or professional help.

SELF-CARE FOR THE MENTAL HEALTH FIRST AIDER

CHAPTER 3: SELF-CARE FOR THE MENTAL HEALTH FIRST AIDER

TAKING CARE OF YOURSELF AS A FIRST AIDER

To be able to care for people as a Mental Health First Aider, you must first take care of yourself. It's like the advice we're given on airplanes: put on your own oxygen mask before trying to help someone else with theirs. Taking care of yourself is a valid goal on its own, and it helps you support those around you.

What Is Self-Care?

Self-care refers to activities and practices that you can engage in on a regular basis to reduce stress and maintain and enhance your short- and long-term health and well-being. Self-care is necessary for your effectiveness and success in helping others as a First Aider.

The ups and downs in working with people can have a huge impact on you. But First Aiders who pay attention to their own physical and emotional health are better able to handle a crisis or handle the challenges of supporting someone with mental health or substance use challenges. They adapt to changes, build strong relationships, and recover from setbacks.

Self-care should not be something that you force yourself to do, or something you don't enjoy doing. Self-care should refuel you. Self-care isn't a selfish act either; recall the oxygen mask.

Self-care helps First Aiders identify and manage challenges such as the potential for burnout, stress, and interpersonal difficulties.

- Burnout is a state of emotional, physical, and mental exhaustion caused by excessive and prolonged stress. It occurs when you feel overwhelmed, emotionally drained, and unable to meet constant demands.

- Be aware of your own personal vulnerabilities as a Mental Health First Aider, such as the potential for re-traumatization. Re-traumatization is reliving stress reactions experienced as a result of a traumatic event when faced with a new, similar incident (SAMHSA, 2017).

- Avoid vicarious or secondary traumatic stress if you are working with people who share their own traumatic experiences. Vicarious or secondary traumatic stress is the emotional duress that results when someone hears about the trauma of another (National Child Traumatic Stress Network, 2008).

- Prevent compassion fatigue, which can be experienced by those helping people in distress. It is an extreme state of tension and preoccupation with the suffering of those being helped — so extreme that it can create a secondary traumatic stress for the helper (Figley & Ludick, 2017).

- Achieve more balance in your life by maintaining and enhancing the attention you pay to the different domains of your life in a way that makes sense to you.

Goals Of Self-Care

Self-care is not simply about limiting or addressing professional stressors. It is also about enhancing your overall well-being. Goals of self-care include:

- Taking care of physical and psychological health.
- Managing and reducing stress.
- Recognizing emotional and spiritual needs.
- Fostering and sustaining relationships.
- Achieving balance in different areas of one's life.

People differ in the areas of our life they emphasize and the balance sought among them.

Help For The Helper

After providing Mental Health First Aid to someone in distress, you may feel worn out, frustrated, or even angry. You may need to deal with the feelings and reactions you have set aside during the encounter. It can be helpful to find someone to talk to about what has happened. First Aiders might want to reach out to talk with family or friends. First Aiders may find it helpful to reach out to a mental health professional or to connect with national helplines noted in the Helpful Resources section.

With Self-Care, Where Do I Start?

Stick to the basics. Over time you will find your own rhythm and routine. You will be able to implement more and identify more specific forms of self-care that work for you.

Self-care needs to be something you actively plan, rather than something that just happens. It is an active choice and you must treat it as such. Add certain activities to your calendar, announce your plans to others in order to increase your commitment, and actively look for opportunities to practice self-care.

Although self-care means different things to different people, there's a basic checklist that can be followed by all of us:

- Create a "no" list, with things you know you don't like or that you no longer want to do. Examples might include not checking emails at night, not attending gatherings you don't like, or not answering your phone during lunch or dinner.
- Strive for a nutritious, healthy diet.
- Get enough sleep. Adults usually need 7–8 hours of sleep each night.
- Exercise as appropriate for your own health. Exercise is as good for our emotional health as it is for our physical health. It increases serotonin levels, leading to improved mood and energy. What's important is that you choose a form of exercise that you like.
- Get the recommended routine medical care. It is not unusual for people to put off checkups or visits to the doctor, but it's a bad idea.
- Use relaxation exercises or practice meditation. You can do these exercises at any time of the day.
- Spend enough time with your loved ones.
- Do at least one relaxing activity every day, such as a walk or 30 minutes spent unwinding.
- Do at least one pleasurable activity every day, like cooking, meeting with friends, or going to the movies.
- Look for opportunities to laugh!

Figure 9

Remember you cannot assist others as a First Aider without taking care of yourself. Consider the following questions to guide your self-care plan.

Self-Care

1. Have I decided what I will do for self-care?
2. Who can I speak with now?
3. Who can I call if I feel upset or distressed later?

REMEMBER

The goals of Mental Health First Aid are to:

- Encourage adults to practice nonjudgmental listening
- Empower adults with the skills to promote help-seeking skills and behaviors
- Reduce stigma around mental health and substance use challenges

NOT to diagnose and/or treat themselves or others

FIRST AID FOR MENTAL HEALTH ISSUES

Before being able to give Mental Health First Aid to someone, First Aiders need basic knowledge about mental health challenges, mental disorders, and behaviors, so that they are able to recognize that an illness may be developing. This section provides information on the signs and symptoms of depression, anxiety, bipolar disorder, psychosis, trauma, eating disorders, substance use, and nonsuicidal self-injury. Although each mental disorder is addressed separately, it is important to note that some people have multiple mental disorders.

Remember, First Aiders do not diagnose but rather look for signs and symptoms that a person is having trouble. First Aiders do not have to know what is going on or the cause. It is enough to simply have a supportive conversation and get the person connected to appropriate help.

The resources discussed in this section have been studied during the past decade. Their helpfulness has been demonstrated through these studies.

CHAPTER 4: DEPRESSION

WHAT IS DEPRESSION?

Depression (major depressive disorder) is a common and serious medical illness that negatively affects how people feel, the way they think, and the way they act.

Symptoms of depression vary. And the way it affects people's lives varies depending on how severe their symptoms are.

Depression and depressive disorders are dangerous if left untreated. The good news is that depression is treatable. People who receive proper, timely intervention can be helped. Between 80 and 90 percent of people with depression have a positive outcome from treatment, and almost all patients gain some relief from their symptoms (American Foundation for Suicide Prevention, 2018).

Depression causes feelings of sadness and/or a loss of interest in activities once enjoyed. It can lead to a variety of physical problems and additional emotional problems (for example, irritability). It can interfere with functioning, even if others cannot see the person's pain (American Psychiatric Association, 2013).

People with depression may use alcohol or other drugs as a way of trying to feel better.

Having depression increases the risk of suicide. CDC found that among those who completed suicide in 2015, 75.2 percent had depression/dysthymia (Stone et al., 2017). (Chronic major depression and dysthymia was the term used for persistent depressive disorder at the time of the study.)

Depression is a major risk factor for nonsuicidal self-injury, also known as self-harm. Nonsuicidal self-injury includes cutting and other means of hurting oneself.

Depression is a mood disorder. Mood disorder is a category of mental disorders that includes all types of depression and bipolar disorders. The type of depression that is the focus of this chapter is major depressive disorder, also called clinical depression. It is the most severe and most disabling form of depression.

Half of people with this diagnosis have their first depressive episode by the age of 32 (NIMH, 2017).

When and how people access mental health care, including for depression, differs among groups. For example, Spanish-speaking Latinx in the United States are least likely to access mental health care services and receive treatment for depression (Wong, 2015).

Co-Occurring Mental Disorders

Depression often occurs with ADHD, disruptive behavior disorders, anxiety disorders, and substance use disorders (McIntosh et al., 2009).

Prevalence Of Depression Among U.s. Adults

Depressive disorders affect over 8 percent of adults ages 20 and up (Brody, Pratt, & Hughes, 2018).

Certain populations in the United States are more likely to experience depression than others (SAMHSA, 2017). People who identify as lesbian, gay, bisexual, transgender (LGBT) are more likely to experience depression than those who identify as heterosexual (Bostwick, et al., 2014; Mays, et al., 2017).

SIGNS AND SYMPTOMS OF DEPRESSIVE DISORDER

As a First Aider, you are not trained to diagnose mental disorders or to treat them. Rather, you are trained to pay attention to serious changes in the way people typically learn, behave, or handle their emotions, changes which cause distress and problems getting through the day.

A Note About Depressive Symptoms

Not every person who is depressed has all the symptoms. People differ in the number and severity of symptoms.

Even if the symptoms don't add up to an official diagnosis of a depressive disorder, the impact on life can still be significant.

HOW DEPRESSION AFFECTS THE WAY A PERSON THINKS, FEELS, BEHAVES, AND APPEARS

Thoughts

- Self-criticism
- Self-blame
- Worry about many aspects of their life
- Negative outlook on life
- Inability to concentrate
- Indecisiveness and confusion
- Tendency to believe others see them in a negative light
- Hopeless and helpless thinking with a negative view of:
  - **Self:** "I'm a failure." "It's all my fault." "Nothing good ever happens to me." "I'm worthless." "No one loves me."
  - **The world:** "Life is not worth living." "There is nothing good out there."
  - **The future:** "Things will always be bad."
- Thoughts of death and suicide

Emotions

- Sadness/lack of pleasure
- Anxiety
- Guilt
- Anger
- Sudden mood swings
- Little or no emotion
- Helplessness
- Hopelessness
- Irritability

continues next page

HOW DEPRESSION AFFECTS THE WAY A PERSON THINKS, FEELS, BEHAVES, AND APPEARS

 Behaviors

- Crying spells
- Withdrawn from others
- Slowed down
- Speech may be slow
- Neglect of responsibilities with work, family, or self-care
- Loss of interest in personal appearance and hygiene (perhaps wearing dirty clothes and not bathing or washing)
- Loss of motivation
- Nonsuicidal self-injury
- Having sleeping difficulties or sometimes sleeping too much
- Overeating or loss of appetite
- Using alcohol and other drugs
- Sometimes agitated and unable to relax or settle in one place
- Voice may not change in tone or may be quieter than normal
- Look sad most of the time
- Stand with their shoulders slumped and their head down
- Easily moved to tears
- Upset, angry, or easily distracted
- Show little or no emotion
- Loss of interest in food or sometimes eating too much, resulting in weight loss or gain (American Psychiatric Association, 2013)

 Appearance and Well-being

- Always tired
- Lack of energy
- Weight loss or weight gain
- Headaches
- Irregular menstrual cycle
- Loss of sexual desire
- Unexplained aches and pains

Types Of Depressive Disorders

Major depressive disorder

Major depressive disorder includes the symptoms of depression described in the table. The person may have symptoms once in their life, or the symptoms may stop and start again. The severity of symptoms may be different for each individual.

Persistent depressive disorder

Persistent depressive disorder is a form of depression that has milder symptoms than major depressive disorder that tend to last for several years. As stated, persistent depressive disorder was previously known as chronic major depression and dysthymia.

Pregnancy and depression

Women with depression during pregnancy and after childbirth experience real pain. This type of depression harms the mother-infant relationship and the child's cognitive and emotional development (Avalos et al., 2019).

Women with this type of depression often do not think it requires medical attention.

Sometimes, sadness during or after pregnancy is only "the baby blues," but the baby blues doesn't last more than two weeks (University of North Carolina Department of Medicine, 2018).

Figure 10

Untreated perinatal depression is dangerous.

The Problem

3 - 6

Percentage of women who will have a major depressive episode during or immediately after pregnancy.

American Psychiatric Association, 2013

Perinatal depression can come before or after birth.

Because feeling sad after giving birth is common, women with perinatal depression (depression around pregnancy and childbirth) sometimes go untreated.

Treatment

Treatment helps the mother and improves her relationship with her infant and the child's cognitive development.

Perinatal depression before birth is antenatal depression.

Perinatal depression after birth is postnatal or postpartum depression.

Depression with seasonal pattern

Formerly known as seasonal affective disorder (SAD), depression with seasonal pattern involves a depressive episode at a specific time of year, generally fall and winter (NIMH, Mar 2016).

Bipolar disorder

Bipolar disorder, previously known as manic-depressive disorder, involves bouts of major depression and periods of mania — euphoria, poor judgment, and extreme risk-taking activity. Chapter 7: Bipolar Disorder is dedicated to this disorder.

Special Note On Loss Of A Loved One And Bereavement

Bereavement, or feelings of sadness and grief that occur with the death of a loved one, is a normal experience. A person may express this experience as being "depressed." There is no specific depression diagnosis for bereavement-related grief (Boelen, Reijntjes, & Smid, 2016).

Bereavement grief has some of the same symptoms as major depression, like intense sadness and withdrawal from daily activities. The grieving process is natural and unique to everyone.

Grief and depression are different in important ways and respond to different treatments. And a person may have challenges with both grief and depression.

First Aiders should be careful as they assess the situation before deciding whether to approach and assist. The First Aider can encourage professional help such as seeing a primary care provider, therapist, or psychiatrist.

WHAT CAUSES DEPRESSION?

Depression has no single cause and often involves the interaction of various biological, psychological, and social factors. People may become depressed for no apparent reason or when something very distressing has happened and they feel powerless to control the situation, such as:

- Breakup of a relationship.
- Living in conflict.
- Long-term poverty.
- Loss of a job or difficulty finding a new one.
- Having an accident that results in long-term disability.
- Bullying or victimization.
- Being a victim of crime.
- Developing a long-term physical illness.
- Other mental health conditions.
- Being a long-term caregiver to another person.
- Death of a partner, family member, or friend.

Other ways that depression can be triggered include:

- The effects of medical conditions like Parkinson's disease, Huntington's disease, traumatic brain injury, stroke, hypothyroidism, and lupus (American Psychiatric Association, 2013).
- The hormonal and physical changes and responsibilities of having and caring for a baby.
- The side effects of certain medications or drugs.
- Intoxication or withdrawal from alcohol or other drugs.
- Premenstrual changes in hormone levels (PMS).
- Lack of exposure to bright light in the winter months (see discussion of seasonal affective disorder).

No matter the cause, people with depression should be seen by a professional.

The symptoms of depression are thought to be due to changes in natural brain chemicals called neurotransmitters. Neurotransmitters send messages from one nerve cell to another in the brain. When a person becomes depressed, the brain can have fewer of certain of these chemical messengers. One of these chemicals is serotonin, which helps to regulate a person's mood. Many antidepressant medications work by changing the activity of serotonin in the brain.

Risk Factors For Depressive Disorder

A risk factor for a disorder is something that increases the chances of a person being affected by that particular disorder. Examples of risk factors for developing depression include:

- **History of trauma.** Physical, sexual, or emotional abuse, especially in childhood, raises the risk for depression. The risk increases as the number of these childhood experiences increases.

  In adulthood, combat-related stress, catastrophic loss, serious health challenges, rape, and other traumatic events increase the risk for depression.

- **Previous episodes of depression.**

- **Family members who have had episodes of depression.**

- **Gender.** Women are 70 percent more likely than men to experience depression in their lifetime (NIMH, Feb 2018).

- **Sensitivity.** People with a highly sensitive outlook toward others and a greater tendency to react negatively to criticism from others have increased risk.

- **Social circumstances.** Poverty, being homebound, and some other social circumstances increase a person's risk for depression (Brown et al., 2015).

- **Medical conditions or medications.** Certain medical conditions or medications may increase a person's risk for depression. People should discuss these risks with their doctor before beginning or changing a medication.

Protective Factors For Depressive Disorder

Protective factors include religious or spiritual practices, social support, physical exercise and healthy diet, positive emotions and hope for the future, and active coping skills. Coping skills include journaling, connecting with community clubs or groups, talking to a trusted person about feelings or problems, using online support groups or chat rooms, writing, creating art or music, or developing a hobby. Managing stress and reaction to challenges in a healthy manner can help a person increase their resilience.

Trauma And Depression

A person who experiences trauma has a higher risk of developing a mental disorder such as depression. In fact, that risk increases dramatically with each additional negative childhood experience (Merrick et al., 2017).

Traumatic events experienced as a child are referred to as adverse childhood experiences (ACEs). ACEs include:

- Verbal abuse.

- Physical abuse.

- Sexual abuse.

- Emotional neglect.

- Physical neglect.

- Divorce/parent separation.

- Domestic violence.

- Alcohol/drug exposure.

- Exposure to mental illness and suicide.

- Having a household member in prison.

Traumatic stress refers to reactions that persist and affect a person's daily life after the traumatic event or ACE has ended. Reactions can include intense and ongoing emotional upset, depressive symptoms or anxiety, behavioral changes, difficulties with self-regulation, problems relating to others or forming attachments, loss of previously acquired skills, attention difficulties, nightmares, difficulty sleeping and eating, and physical symptoms such as aches and pains. People may use alcohol or other drugs, behave in risky ways, or engage in unhealthy sexual activity (Kerr et al., 2010).

If the person did not get treatment for traumatic stress, prolonged mental challenges can result, as well as health-risk behaviors such as smoking, eating disorders, substance use, and high-risk activities. The person may have difficulty in establishing fulfilling relationships and maintaining employment.

If a person diagnosed with depression has a history of trauma, other symptoms of post-traumatic stress disorder (PTSD) may also be present, such as persistent, frightening thoughts and memories or flashbacks of a traumatic event or events. Other symptoms may include jumpiness, sleep problems, problems in public settings, avoidance of certain places or situations, depression, headaches, or stomach pains.

Sometimes, people with mental health challenges feel stigmatized, but feel less so when they understand that trauma may have contributed to their challenges and that treatment is available. As a First Aider, you can help the person understand that trauma affects mental health without making them feel that they should talk about their trauma.

If trauma is addressed, and appropriate treatment and supports are provided sooner rather than later, a person's recovery is much more likely. Some ways that it can be addressed include consistent healthy behaviors, a stable and safe living environment, and self-care.

Stigma Around Depression

Because of internal and external stigmas, many people do not seek help even though more and more mental health services are available across the United States.

IMPORTANCE OF EARLY INTERVENTION FOR DEPRESSION

When people get appropriate professional help and effective treatment as early as possible, this is known as "early intervention." Being untreated after one episode of depression makes it more likely the person will have other episodes, so early intervention is key (Ghio et al., 2014).

Mental Health First Aid enables early intervention for people with depressive disorders.

THE MHFA ACTION PLAN FOR DEPRESSION

See Chapter 2: Mental Health First Aid to read about how to use the 5-step MHFA action plan, ALGEE. In this section, we discuss each step briefly and add information about treatments for depression.

ALGEE is a useful way to remember the steps of the action plan you can use to help a person with signs and symptoms of mental disorders. Not every step must be done, and they don't have to be done in order.

Special Considerations For Depression In People With Developmental Disabilities

If you know the person's family, caregiver, or legal guardian, you may wish to first engage with them to talk about your concerns and see if they have noticed similar concerns. However, recall that you must ask the person whether it is okay to speak with the family member. If the person does not have the capacity to make their own health care treatment decisions, you will find out who is permitted to give consent for these decisions for the person.

If you are able to speak with the family, caregiver, or legal guardian, you might listen nonjudgmentally, provide reassurance and information, and then help them connect to professional help or other resources to get help for the person. The way that you engage with the person's family will depend on your role and relationship.

When navigating consent to care, it is important to consider the individual's capacity to make their own health care treatment decisions, known as decisional capacity. When adults with developmental disabilities have incomplete decisional capacity, consent is obtained from a surrogate (such as a family caregiver who serves as a legal guardian) and assent, uncoerced willingness to undergo treatment, from the individual.

If you are the parent or relative, you might be talking directly to your adult relative using the relevant ALGEE action steps. If the person appears to be at risk of self-harm and says that they intend to die, call 911 and do not leave the person alone.

Figure 11

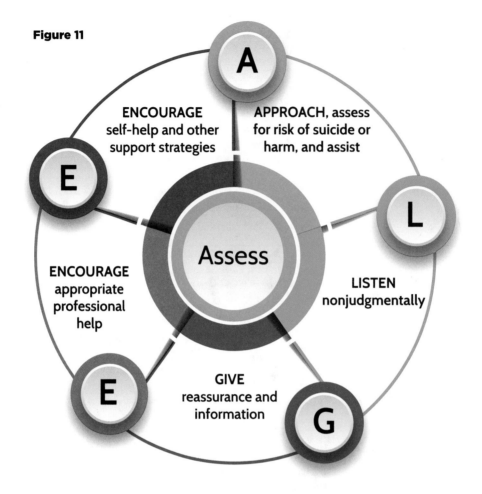

ACTION A: Assess for Risk of Suicide or Harm

If you think that a person may be depressed and in need of help, approach them about your concerns.

As you talk with the person, be on the lookout for any indications that they may be in crisis.

The main crises associated with depression are:

- The person has suicidal thoughts and behaviors.
- The person is engaging in nonsuicidal self-injury.

If you have concerns that the person may be having suicidal thoughts, call 911 and do not leave the person alone.

If the person you are helping is engaging in nonsuicidal self-injury and is also suicidal, call 911. Suicidal thoughts or behaviors are an emergency and must be considered as such.

If you have concerns that the person may be engaging in nonsuicidal self-injury but is not suicidal, see Chapter 11: Nonsuicidal Self-injury.

Encourage the person to talk about their feelings, symptoms, and what is going on in their mind.

If you have no concerns that the person is in crisis, you may ask them how they are feeling and how long they have been feeling that way, then move on to Action L.

ACTION L: Listen Nonjudgmentally

If you believe the person is not in a crisis, you can engage them in conversation.

You will spend time and listen before you try to discuss possible courses of action.

Refer to Chapter 2: Mental Health First Aid to read more about how to listen nonjudgmentally, including how to convey an attitude of acceptance, genuineness, and empathy, and what verbal and nonverbal skills are effective.

ACTION G: Give Support and Information

Once a person with a mental health challenge feels that they have been heard, it can be easier to offer support and information. Reassurance includes emotional support, such as empathizing with how the person feels and voicing hope.

People with a mental health challenge can experience a range of emotions. They might be in denial about their situation, scared to admit what is happening, and uncertain about what to do next. The First Aider can offer to provide some information about mental health challenges and explain that mental health challenges are common.

First Aiders can provide hope that treatment can help address any current difficulties and can also help prevent more serious problems in the future. Remind the person that what they are experiencing is a disorder.

What not to do

Several tips for what not to do are:

- Don't tell someone to "snap out of it" or to "get over it."
- Do not adopt an over involved or overprotective attitude toward someone who is depressed.
- Do not use a patronizing tone of voice or a facial expression that shows an extreme look of concern.
- Do not ignore, disagree with, or dismiss the person's feelings by attempting to say something positive like, "You don't seem that bad to me."

ACTION E: Encourage Appropriate Professional Help

You might help the person find a local mental health professional. Sometimes it is difficult to get an appointment with a mental health program. You may need to provide support in navigating the system.

If the person would like you to accompany them to an appointment with a mental health professional or doctor, that is acceptable. Your role as the First Aider is to provide encouragement throughout the process. You can best provide encouragement by waiting in a common area and being positive and optimistic. It is important to respect privacy and boundaries; do not ask prying questions after the appointment.

Remember not to take over the steps necessary for setting up the appointment. A person with depression needs to make their own decisions as much as possible and express their feelings and experiences in their own words.

It may take some time to get a diagnosis and find a health care provider with whom the person is able to establish a good relationship. You should encourage the person not to give up seeking appropriate professional help.

Information about professionals who can help can be found in Chapter 1: Mental Health in the United States.

Treatments available for depressive disorder

Research has shown that depression in adults is treatable. A range of treatments are available for both. For some, it may be necessary to treat the depression with medication.

When the professional identifies an episode of depression that is so severe that the person is unable to care for themselves or where the person is a danger to themselves or others, they may be admitted to a hospital for 24-hour care. Most people with depression, however, can be treated effectively at home or outside a hospital.

Psychological therapies

Therapy with a mental health professional has shown to be effective in treating depression. Here are some examples of these treatments:

- **Cognitive behavioral therapy (CBT)**, which is based on the idea that how a person thinks affects the way the person feels. When people get depressed, they think negatively about most things. They may have thoughts about how hopeless the situation is and how helpless they feel, with a negative view of themselves, the world, and the future. CBT helps the person recognize unhelpful thoughts and change them to more realistic ones (Craske, 2010). It also helps people change depressive behaviors by scheduling regular activities and engaging in pleasurable activities. CBT can include stress management, relaxation techniques, and sleep management.

- **Interpersonal psychotherapy (IPT)** helps people to resolve conflicts with other people, deal with grief or changes in their relationships, and develop better relationships (Peeters et al., 2013). Treatment consists of several sessions where the person works toward identifying stressors and begins the process of managing interpersonal distress.

- **Supportive counseling**. Supportive counseling involves being a good listener and providing emotional support. The therapist also may give information about depression and teach problem-solving skills. This type of treatment is most appropriate for mild depression.

- **Mindfulness practice/mindfulness-based cognitive therapy (MBCT)** uses mindfulness and accepting the present moment to encourage individuals with depression to pay attention to their experiences and disengage from triggering or stressful factors moment by moment (Lu, 2015). The approach incorporates elements of CBT.

- **Trauma-focused cognitive behavioral therapy** incorporates elements of cognitive behavioral and family therapy.

- **Wraparound care** is a team approach that involves all individuals who are relevant to the well-being of the person (such as family members, teachers, and social service providers) in setting goals with the person and developing an individualized set of services and supports. Wraparound services and supports are usually provided in the person's home.

- **Family support and therapy** tries to help all family members change their patterns of communication and their behaviors so that their relationships are more supportive, and less conflict occurs.

- **Problem-solving therapy** involves meeting with a therapist to clearly identify problems, think of different solutions for each problem, choose the best solution, develop and carry out a plan, and then see whether this solves the problem.

Research shows that there is an even better outcome when psychological therapy is given in combination with antidepressant medication.

Medical treatment

In addition to therapy, medical treatment may be used to treat depression. Here are some examples:

- **Antidepressant medications** have proven effective for adults who have moderate to severe depression.

- **Antipsychotic medications** may be used to treat people with bipolar disorder. They are also sometimes used to treat people with severe depression in combination with antidepressants where other treatments have not worked.

- **Mood stabilizers** can help people with bipolar disorder by reducing the swings from one mood to another. They are also sometimes used in long-term depression.

- **Electroconvulsive therapy (ECT)** is a procedure done under general anesthesia, usually in a hospital setting. Controlled electric currents are passed through the brain. It is used to treat severe depression and sometimes severe bipolar disorder.

- **Brain stimulation therapies** are used to treat medicine-resistant depression. Some of these therapies include repetitive transcranial magnetic stimulation (rTMS) and vagus nerve stimulation (VNS).

People respond to medications in different ways, so the right type of medication depends on the person. Sometimes people need to try different types of medicine to see which are best for them.

A Note About First Aiders And Medication

First Aiders should never advise anyone to stop medication without a doctor's help. Stopping medication suddenly can be dangerous, and it can worsen mental disorders such as depression.

First Aiders should not advise people about medication. First Aiders can encourage people to talk about all available treatment options, including medication, with a medical professional.

ACTION E: Encourage Self-help and Other Support Strategies

You can help the person consider resources in addition to professionals and choose what they prefer.

Other people who can help

Encourage the person to consider other available support, such as family, friends, faith communities, support groups, or others who have experienced depression (peer counselors).

Some people who experience depression find it helpful to meet with others who have had similar experiences. There is some evidence that these mutual help groups can help with recovery from depression and anxiety (Bryan & Arkowitz, 2015).

Self-help strategies

Many health professionals believe self-help strategies are helpful for someone with depression. It is a good idea to discuss the appropriateness of self-help strategies with a mental health professional. Some strategies include:

- **Self-help books based on CBT.** As an example, researchers have sought to develop a CBT-based guided self-help intervention for adults with intellectual disability. It may prove useful for adults with an intellectual disability who also have depression or other mental health challenges for which CBT has been shown to be helpful (McQueen et al., 2018). See the Helpful Resources section.

- **Computerized therapy.** Self-help treatment programs delivered over the internet or on a computer; some are available free of charge. See the Helpful Resources section.

- **Relaxation training.** Teaching a person to relax voluntarily by tensing and relaxing muscle groups; some programs are available for free download from the internet. See the Helpful Resources section.

- **Light therapy.** Bright light exposure to the eyes, often in the morning.

You should not be too forceful when encouraging the person to use self-help strategies.

Scientific studies of complementary therapies such as acupuncture, meditation, mindfulness, yoga, exercise, dietary supplements, etc., for depression have shown that these therapies do not make a difference for depression (Haller et al., 2019).

Many alternative medicine approaches are not approved by the U.S. Food and Drug Administration (FDA).

People taking herbal remedies should tell their doctor about what they take. Caution must be used when combining herbal remedies with any other medications.

Encouraging appropriate professional help and self-help strategies are ways to help a person to recovery and well-being.

SUMMARY

The goal of this chapter of the Mental Health First Aid manual is to serve as a guide for understanding depression. As a First Aider, you can encourage help-seeking skills and behaviors. You can also be a bridge to professional assessment and treatment planning that can lead to recovery and well-being. As a First Aider, you DO NOT diagnose or treat yourself or others. However, you are a vital link to early intervention which is important in reducing future episodes of depression. You can also respond to a person at immediate risk to themselves or others in order to prevent harm. Finally, as a First Aider, you can be a positive role model for others by showing understanding, support, and patience.

DISA TURNER, *Vanishing Act*

I've had anxiety since childhood and stubbornly recurring depression since my early teens. Some days, it's a mild annoyance. Other days, though, it's so utterly exhausting that I feel like I'm fading, evaporating ("Vanishing Act").

CHAPTER 5: ANXIETY

WHAT IS ANXIETY?

Everybody experiences anxiety at some time. Anxiety is a common feeling that causes increased alertness, fear, and physical signs, such as a rapid heart rate.

When people describe their anxiety, they may use terms such as anxious, stressed, freaking out, panicky, wound up, nervous, on edge, worried, tense, overwhelmed, or hassled. Although everyday anxiety is an unpleasant state, it can be quite useful in helping a person avoid dangerous situations and motivate them to solve everyday problems.

Anxiety can vary in severity from mild uneasiness to a terrifying panic attack. Anxiety can also vary in how long it lasts — from a few moments to many years.

An anxiety disorder differs from everyday anxiety in the following ways:

- It is more severe.
- It is persistent.
- It interferes with the person's activities, studies, and family and social relationships.
- If not treated, it continues to cause real pain and distress, and it can lead to poor work or academic performance, impaired social functioning, and other negative outcomes.

Some anxiety symptoms that are quite common are worry in general, but particularly worry about what others might think; fear in social situations; anxiety about bad things happening; and anxiety about past events or perceived misdeeds.

Anxiety at any age is characterized by:

- High levels of distress and fear.
- Avoidance of feared situations or objects.

People with anxiety disorders overestimate the threat from a situation that they fear. They also tend to underestimate their ability to handle these situations. Each individual with anxiety can have a different range of worries and responses to anxiety.

Anxiety symptoms and anxiety disorders can also increase a person's risk for depression; depression is serious.

Anxiety related disorders, especially panic disorder, are associated with suicide attempts. The risk increases if the person also has a depressive or substance use disorder.

Anxiety disorders may increase the risk for nonsuicidal self-injury. Nonsuicidal self-injury may be a coping mechanism for feelings of unbearable anxiety.

Anxiety disorders tend to be more common in women than men, with 54 percent of women and 46 percent of men experiencing anxiety disorder (NIMH, Jul 2018).

See Chapter 2: Mental Health First Aid, for more information about culture and mental disorders.

Co-Occurring Mental Disorders

Many people with anxiety disorders do not fit neatly into a particular type of anxiety disorder. It is common for people to have some symptoms of several anxiety disorders.

A high level of anxiety over a long period will often lead to depression, so many people have a mixture of anxiety and depression.

People with anxiety disorders frequently use substances as a form of self-medication to help cope. This can lead to substance use disorders. Furthermore, heavy use of alcohol and other drugs can lead to increased anxiety (Robinson et al., 2004).

Prevalence Of Anxiety Disorders

Approximately 18 percent of adults between the ages of 18 to 54 in the United States report having an anxiety disorder in any given year (NIMH, Jul 2018).

Anxiety disorders tend to begin in childhood, adolescence, or early adulthood.

> **Remember:**
>
> As a First Aider, it is important to recognize your own biases. If these biases interfere with your ability to be an effective First Aider, it may be helpful to explore and try to understand the person's experiences, values, or belief systems.

The table shows the prevalence of several anxiety disorders.

TYPE OF MENTAL DISORDER	ADULTS
Specific phobia	10.1%[1]
Social anxiety disorder (formerly social phobia)	8.0%[5]
Post-traumatic stress disorder	4.7%[2]
Generalized anxiety disorder	2.9%[5]
Panic disorder	3.1%[5]
Obsessive-compulsive disorder	1.2%[3]
Agoraphobia (without panic)	1.7%[5]
Any anxiety disorder	21.3%[5]

[1] Bandelow, B., & Michaelis, S. (2015). Epidemiology of anxiety disorders in the 21st century. Dialogues in Clinical Neuroscience, 17(3), 327-35.

[2] Goldstein, R. B., Smith, S. M., Chou, S. P., Saha, T. D., Jung, J., Zhang, H., Pickering, R. P., Ruan, W. J., Huang, B., ... Grant, B. F. (2016). The epidemiology of DSM-5 posttraumatic stress disorder in the United States: Results from the National Epidemiologic Survey on Alcohol and Related Conditions-III. Social Psychiatry and Psychiatric Epidemiology, 51(8), 1137-48.

[3] Kessler, R. C., Petukhova, M., Sampson, N. A., Zaslavsky, A. M., & Wittchen, H.-U. (2012). Twelve month and lifetime prevalence and lifetime morbid risk of anxiety and mood disorders in the United States. International Journal of Methods in Psychiatric Research, 21(3), 169-184.

Prevalence Of Panic Attacks

According to the National Institute of Mental Health, more than one in four people have a panic attack at some time in their lives. Few go on to have repeated attacks, and fewer still go on to develop panic disorder or agoraphobia.

SIGNS AND SYMPTOMS OF ANXIETY AND ANXIETY DISORDERS

HOW ANXIETY AFFECTS THE WAY A PERSON THINKS, FEELS, BEHAVES, AND APPEARS

Thoughts

- Mind racing or going blank
- Decreased concentration
- Decreased memory
- Indecisiveness
- Confusion
- Vivid dreams

Emotions

- Unrealistic or excessive fear and worry about past and future events
- Irritability
- Impatience
- Anger
- Feeling on edge
- Nervousness
- Having a sense of impending danger, panic, or doom

Behaviors

- Avoidance of situations
- Obsessive or compulsive behavior
- Distress in social situations
- Sleep disturbance
- Increased use of alcohol or other drugs
- Avoiding people, places, or situations that trigger anxiety
- Engaging in rituals, sometimes repeated, designed to protect the person from the fear or worry

Appearance and Well-being

- Restlessness or tension with inability to relax
- Increased heart rate (pounding heart, chest pain)
- Shortness of breath and rapid breathing (hyperventilation)
- Sweating, dizziness, numbness
- Trembling or shaking
- Gastrointestinal problems
- Muscle aches and pains (especially neck, shoulders, and back), restlessness, tremors, and shaking

Types Of Anxiety Disorders

The various types of anxiety disorders differ from each other by the types of situations or things that the person feels anxious about and the kind of beliefs they have that increase their anxiety. The main types are post-traumatic stress disorder (PTSD), social anxiety disorder (social phobia), agoraphobia, generalized anxiety disorder, and panic disorder (American Psychiatric Association, 2013). It is not unusual for a person to have more than one of these disorders.

Many people diagnosed with anxiety have symptoms that do not fit neatly into one particular type of disorder. Medical professionals may find it challenging to diagnose anxiety disorder, for two reasons. One, it is not unusual for a person to have more than one anxiety disorder. Two, some anxiety symptoms are common in other mental and physical illnesses.

Anxiety disorders can occur for no apparent reason or without cause.

Generalized anxiety disorder

Some people experience ongoing and persistent anxiety as they experience various types of events and activities. This anxiety, called generalized anxiety disorder (GAD), interferes with their lives.

People with this disorder will have overwhelming, unfounded worry.

They worry about work, family issues, health, money, appearance, relationships, and performance in sports or other activities, even when there are no signs of trouble. People with generalized anxiety disorder may be perfectionists and may seek approval or reassurance more than others do. They worry about things that may go wrong or their inability to cope, often related to their performance at work or in school. They will have several physical and psychological symptoms of anxiety or tension.

People with generalized anxiety disorder may have poor problem-solving skills, may not be able to tolerate uncertainty, and may believe that worry is a helpful way to deal with problems. They can appear keyed-up or on edge, are often fatigued at the end of the day, and their moods may be irritable and tense.

The anxiety is difficult for the person to control or tolerate. Generalized anxiety disorder can make it difficult for people to concentrate and function at home.

Panic disorder

Some people have short periods of extreme anxiety called panic attacks. A panic attack is an abrupt surge of intense apprehension, fear, or even terror. These attacks can begin suddenly and develop rapidly. This intense fear is inappropriate for the circumstances. A range of physical symptoms can appear, including rapid heart rate, sweating, sensations of shortness of breath, nausea, and feelings of being detached from reality.

Around one-quarter of the population has a panic attack at some stage in their life (Bystritsky et al., 2010). However, having one or many panic attacks does not necessarily mean that a person will develop panic disorder.

Someone who experiences at least two unexpected panic attacks and then is persistently worried about possible future panic attacks or about losing control can be diagnosed with panic disorder.

The person may avoid exercise or other activities that may produce physical sensations similar to those of a panic attack. They may avoid places where panic attacks have occurred.

Panic disorder is more likely to occur after age 20.

Agoraphobia

Agoraphobia involves avoiding situations in which the person fears they may have a panic attack and avoids certain situations for fear of a panic attack occurring. The focus of the anxiety is that it will be difficult or embarrassing to get away from the place if a panic attack occurs or that there will be no one present who can help.

Some people with agoraphobia may avoid only a few situations, such as parties or being in a car, or certain places, such as shopping malls. Others may avoid leaving home altogether.

Most people believe that agoraphobia is a fear of open spaces or a fear of leaving the house. However, a person cannot be said to have agoraphobia unless they have a fear of panic attacks.

Social anxiety disorder

A person with social anxiety disorder fears situations in which they may be observed and judged by others. Usually the person is afraid of behaving in a way that is embarrassing or humiliating or might lead to rejection. This disorder often develops in shy children as they move into adolescence. Commonly feared situations include speaking or eating in public, dating, and social events.

Specific phobias

Specific phobias are intense fears of specific objects or situations. A person will exhibit exceptional fear of something not normally considered dangerous, and avoiding the object of that fear will cause significant impairment to their ordinary function. To be diagnosed with specific phobia, the fear or anxiety must occur nearly every time the person encounters the object or situation, but the response may vary in intensity, from anticipatory dread to a panic attack (NIMH, Nov 2017).

Among people who have anxiety, it's common to have multiple specific phobias, each triggered by a different stimulus.

Specific phobias are commonly classified in five categories:

- Animal Type, if the phobia concerns animals or insects.

- Natural Environment Type, if the phobia concerns objects such as storms, heights or water.

- Blood-Injection-Injury Type, if the phobia concerns receiving an injection or seeing blood or an injury.

- Situational Type, if the phobia concerns a specific situation like flying, driving, tunnels, bridges, enclosed space, or public transportation.

- Other Type, if the phobia concerns other stimuli such as loud sounds, clowns, choking, or vomiting.

Anxiety And Distress As Symptoms Of Obsessive-Compulsive Disorder

Obsessive-compulsive disorder (OCD) comes with anxiety and distress but is not classified in the DSM-5 as an anxiety disorder. In the DSM-5, OCD is grouped with body dysmorphic disorder, hoarding, excoriation (skin picking disorder), and trichotillomania (hair pulling disorder).

People with OCD struggle with either obsessions or compulsions or both. Obsessions are recurrent and unwanted thoughts, images, or urges that are experienced as intrusive and inappropriate. Obsessions cause marked anxiety and distress.

Obsessive thoughts may concern contamination or illness, safety concerns, sexual or taboo impulses, fears of harm or aggression, religious or moral preoccupations, or need for symmetry and exactness.

Compulsions are repetitive behaviors or mental acts that the person feels driven to perform to reduce the distress caused by an obsession. Common compulsive behaviors include washing, cleaning, checking, repeating, ordering, counting, or seeking reassurance.

OCD can be a very disabling condition. OCD symptoms often begin during childhood. About half of OCD cases occur before adulthood.

Due to the distressing or embarrassing nature of the obsessions or compulsions, some people with OCD do not want to share the true nature of their worries with others. This may explain why OCD is often underdiagnosed or misdiagnosed.

When family members or caregivers join in or tolerate time-consuming OCD behaviors or offer the person reassurance for their extreme fears coming from obsessions, it can cause the OCD symptoms to continue.

WHAT CAUSES ANXIETY DISORDERS?

Anxiety has no single cause and often involves the interaction of various biological, psychological, and social factors. The changes in behavior, emotions, thinking, and well-being that make up the signs of an anxiety disorder occur for many reasons, including the effect of trauma and abuse. Anxiety, like other mental disorders, is connected with changes in neurotransmitters. Neurotransmitters send messages from one nerve cell to another in the brain, and these messages regulate thinking and emotions related to anxiety. Other biological, psychological, and social causes are still being researched.

Risk Factors For Anxiety

Anxiety is a reaction to perceived threats in the environment, but some people are more likely than others to develop an anxiety disorder (Zbozinek et al., 2012). Those most at risk include those who:

- Are more sensitive to people, places, and events around them; traumatic experiences affect their emotional and physical sense of safety and security more deeply.
- Tend to see the world as threatening.
- Have a history of anxiety in childhood or adolescence, including marked shyness.
- Are female.
- Misuse alcohol.
- Have had a traumatic experience.

Adverse childhood experiences (ACEs) may increase risk of anxiety. See Chapter 6: Trauma and Trauma-related and Stressor-related Disorders to review ACEs.

Some family factors may increase risk for anxiety disorders:

- A difficult childhood (for example, physical, emotional, or sexual abuse; neglect; or over-strictness).
- A family background that involves poverty or a lack of job skills.
- A family history of anxiety disorders.
- Parental alcohol use.
- Separation and divorce.

Anxiety symptoms also can result from:

- Some medical conditions, such as hyperthyroidism, arrhythmias, chronic obstructive pulmonary disease, and vitamin B12 deficiency.

- Side effects of certain prescription drugs such as corticosteroids, some asthma medications, and medications for hypothyroidism. Other prescription medications may trigger or worsen anxiety.

- Intoxication with alcohol, amphetamines, caffeine, nicotine, cannabis, cocaine, hallucinogens, and inhalants.

- Withdrawal from alcohol, cocaine, sedatives, and anti-anxiety medications.

- No apparent reason.

Some people develop ways of reducing anxiety that actually cause further difficulties. For example, people with phobias avoid anxiety-provoking situations. This avoidance reduces their anxiety in the short-term but can limit their lives in significant ways. Similarly, people with compulsions reduce their anxiety by repetitive acts such as frequent hand washing. These compulsions become issues in themselves. Some people will use drugs or alcohol to cope, which can increase anxiety in the long term.

Trauma And Anxiety Disorders

Trauma is very closely related to anxiety, although not everyone with an anxiety disorder has a history of trauma. Trauma can trigger anxiety, and past associations with trauma, especially ACEs, can re-trigger the symptoms throughout a person's life.

The most common reactions to trauma relate to some form of anxiety, and traumatic experiences lead to ongoing anxiety disorders more than to other mental health and substance use disorders. See Chapter 6: Trauma and Trauma-related and Stressor-related Disorders.

Stigma Around Anxiety

There is stigma associated with mental disorders like anxiety. Stigma can lead people to hide their issues and delay seeking help. People are often ashamed to discuss their symptoms of anxiety with family, friends, teachers, and/or work colleagues and may be reluctant to seek treatment and support because of concerns about what others will think.

Stigma around certain anxiety disorders can be especially harmful when the person is teased, bullied, or shunned in their social group. People who have phobias about specific situations can be easily identified and suffer the stigma, making it harder to overcome, or even to ask for help.

IMPORTANCE OF EARLY INTERVENTION FOR ANXIETY DISORDERS

It is important that anxiety disorders are recognized and treated early. Anxiety disorders often develop in childhood and adolescence. Untreated anxiety can lead to the onset of other mental illnesses, reduced educational achievement, and early parenthood.

Many people with anxiety disorders do not realize there are treatments that can help. In the U.S., only around 37 percent of the people who experience generalized anxiety disorder in the past year received professional help (Skarl, S., 2015). Even when people finally seek help, a delay of 10 years or more is not unusual. These delays can cause serious consequences in the person's life, limiting social and occupational opportunities and increasing the risk for depression and drug and alcohol disorders (CDC, 2016).

> Only around 37 percent of those who had generalized anxiety disorder in the past year received professional help.

THE MHFA ACTION PLAN FOR ANXIETY DISORDERS

See Chapter 2: Mental Health First Aid to read about how to use ALGEE. In this section, we discuss each step briefly and add information about treatments for anxiety.

ALGEE is a useful way to remember the steps of the action plan you can use to help a person with signs and symptoms of mental disorders. Not every step must be done, and they don't have to be done in order.

Special Considerations for Anxiety in People with Developmental Disabilities

If you know the person's family, caregiver, or legal guardian, you may wish to first engage with them to talk about your concerns and see if they have noticed similar concerns. However, recall that you must ask the person whether it is okay to speak with the family member. If the person does not have the capacity to make their own health care treatment decisions, you will find out who is permitted to give consent for these decisions for the person.

If you are able to speak with the family, caregiver, or legal guardian, you might listen nonjudgmentally, provide reassurance and information, and then help them connect to professional help or other resources to get help for the person. The way that you engage with the person's family will depend on your role and relationship.

When navigating consent to care, it is important to consider the individual's capacity to make their own health care treatment decisions, known as decisional capacity. When adults with developmental disabilities have incomplete decisional capacity, consent is obtained from a surrogate (such as a family caregiver who serves as a legal guardian) and assent, uncoerced willingness to undergo treatment, from the individual.

If you are the parent or relative, you might be talking directly to your adult relative using the relevant ALGEE action steps. If the person appears to be at risk of self-harm and says that they intend to die, call 911 and do not leave the person alone.

Figure 12

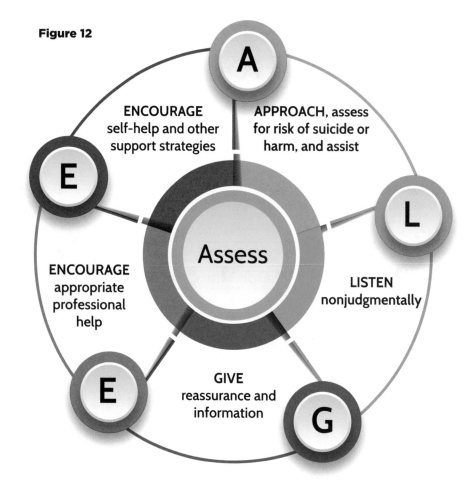

ACTION A: Assess for Risk of Suicide or Harm

See Chapter 2: Mental Health First Aid for a discussion of Action A.

If you think that a person may have anxiety and be in need of help, approach them about your concerns.

As you talk with the person, be on the lookout for any indications that they may be in crisis.

The main crises associated with anxiety are:

- The person experiences an extreme level of anxiety such as a panic attack.
- The person has severe anxiety following a traumatic event.
- The person has suicidal thoughts and behaviors.
- The person is engaging in nonsuicidal self-injury.

Encourage people to talk about their feelings, symptoms, and what is going on in their mind. Be alert for any of the warning signs of suicide. See Chapter 12: Suicide.

If you have no concerns that the person is in crisis, you may ask them how they are feeling and how long they have been feeling that way, then move on to Action L.

Heart attack or panic attack?

Symptoms of a panic attack sometimes resemble a heart attack or other medical issue. This is especially challenging if it is the first time a person is experiencing these symptoms. The symptoms are similar, and as a First Aider, you should always call 911 or refer a person to a medical professional who will be able to monitor the person for a heart attack. Of course, always involve the person in this decision-making.

How to approach

The approach that is helpful for someone with anxiety disorders is very similar to that for someone experiencing depression. See Chapter 4: Depression for more information. The key points are to:

- Approach the person about your concerns about their anxiety.

- Find a suitable time and space where you both feel comfortable.

- If the person does not initiate a conversation with you about how they are feeling, you should say something to them.

- Respect the person's privacy and confidentiality.

How to assess and assist in a crisis

If you are concerned that the person may be having a panic attack, learn how to assess and assist in Chapter 13: First Aid for Mental Health Crises, Mental Health First Aid for Panic Attacks.

For the following concerns, see Chapter 13 to learn how to assess and assist: .

- The person has experienced a traumatic event.

- You are concerned that the person may be having suicidal thoughts.

- You are concerned that the person may be engaging in nonsuicidal self-injury.

If you determine the person is not in crisis, you can ask how they are feeling, how long they have been feeling that way, and move on to Action L.

ACTION L: Listen Nonjudgmentally

Take time to listen before you try to discuss possible courses of action.

Refer to Chapter 2: Mental Health First Aid to read more about how to listen nonjudgmentally, including how to convey an attitude of acceptance, genuineness, and empathy, and what verbal and nonverbal skills are effective.

ACTION G: Give Support and Information

The assurance and information helpful to someone with troublesome anxiety is similar to that given to someone with depression, so look back at Chapter 4: Depression. Recall that once a person with a mental health challenge feels that they have been heard, it can be easier to offer support and information.

ACTION E: Encourage Appropriate Professional Help

Offer the person support to manage their feelings — either as a listener or by providing suggestions for where they could seek professional help. Make sure the person expresses a willingness to ask for help. If they ask for help, respond as follows:

- Discuss appropriate professional help and effective treatment options.

- Encourage the person to use these options.

- Offer to help them seek out these options.

- Encourage the person not to give up seeking appropriate professional help.

Information about mental health professionals can be found in Chapter 1: Mental Health in the United States**.**

If the person is uncertain about what to do, encourage them to see their doctor first, so the doctor can check for an underlying physical health cause for the anxiety and refer the person to the appropriate specialized help.

Treatments available for anxiety disorders

Research shows that medication combined with psychotherapy is an effective treatment approach for anxiety disorders (Gautam et al., 2017). Treatment involving psychotherapy or medication alone can also produce positive outcomes.

Psychotherapy

The treatment of choice for many anxiety disorders is some type of psychotherapy. The person with the anxiety disorder can learn specific techniques and apply them when symptoms of the anxiety disorder are triggered.

Psychological therapies

The following have the strongest evidence for effectiveness:

- CBT, or cognitive behavioral therapy, is the most effective treatment for anxiety disorders.

- There are several different elements to CBT, depending on the type of anxiety disorder that is being treated.

- CBT helps people recognize and change distorted and unhelpful thoughts and actions that maintain anxiety. It helps individuals learn to tolerate their distress about anxiety-provoking situations with helpful coping strategies.

- CBT can be delivered by a therapist working one-on-one or in a group of people with similar issues. It can be accomplished by an individual systematically working through a self-help book or a self-help website. Useful self-help books and websites are listed in the Helpful Resources section.

- Exposure and response prevention (also known as exposure therapy) is a specialized form of CBT. It involves gradually exposing the person to the things that make them anxious. This helps individuals learn that they can reduce their fears without avoiding them and that their fears about situations often do not come true or are not as bad as they thought.

Medical treatments

Scientific evidence supports the effectiveness of several medications. Antidepressant medications are effective for most anxiety disorders. Other types of medication such as beta-blockers can also be of help, particularly for generalized anxiety disorder.

As with depression, the person may not want to seek professional help, but you can find out if there are specific reasons why and help them understand what is possible. You may be able to help the person overcome worry about seeking help. Some ideas include:

- Encouraging the person to talk with a trusted individual.

- Remaining patient, friendly, and open.

- Asking them whether more pressing circumstances might make them feel that they could need help.

- Respect the person's privacy and confidentiality.

TRAUMA AND TRAUMA-RELATED AND STRESSOR-RELATED DISORDERS

RUBY PEARL, *Untitled*

Ruby Pearl is a self-taught artist who uses paint to create worlds that she would like to inhabit. Art has been a constant in Pearl's life, bringing her peace and balance despite suffering past abuse and homelessness. For Pearl, art is like breathing. "Each stroke of my brush not only validates who I am from the darkness of my childhood, but also celebrates who I've become. I've finally been loved — loved by myself," said Pearl.

Pearl lives with post-traumatic stress, bipolar, and severe anxiety disorders, which she manages through prescription medications, weekly therapy, a positive attitude, and support from friends, fellow artists, and staff from the vocational art therapy program she attends.

CHAPTER 6: TRAUMA AND TRAUMA-RELATED AND STRESSOR-RELATED DISORDERS

This chapter first defines trauma and the impact of trauma on the mental disorders described in this manual. Next, it describes trauma-related and stressor-related disorders and some of their symptoms, causes, and treatments.

WHAT IS TRAUMA?

A trauma is a shocking and dangerous event that someone sees or that happens to them. Trauma is associated with levels of stress that can harm physical or mental health.

The following are examples of traumas that can happen to individuals:

- Verbal, physical, or sexual abuse.
- Emotional or physical neglect.
- Exposure to violence, including domestic violence.
- Alcohol/drug exposure.
- Exposure to mental illness and suicide.
- Having a household member in prison.
- Serious accident or illness; medical trauma.
- Traumatic grief/separation, significant loss.
- Poverty.
- Divorce/parental separation.
- Bullying, racism, or discrimination based on:
  - Body type.
  - Sexual orientation.
  - Physical or developmental disability.
  - Ethnic, racial, or religious affiliation.
  - Social media attacks.

Mental Health First Aid USA has added this chapter to make the material relevant for the United States. This additional content has been added with input from mental health experts.

Mass traumatic events include terrorist attacks, mass shootings, fleeing civil unrest, torture, combat, home displacement, and severe weather events (such as hurricane, tsunami, or forest fire).

Historical trauma is cumulative emotional and psychological wounding during the lifespan and across generations, originating from massive group trauma experiences.

Complex trauma is trauma that happens repeatedly and over extended periods of time; it usually involves a person of authority or a caregiver. Both the betrayal by a person who should be trusted and the experience of the trauma itself are harmful. Complex trauma happens to children and adults.

Just one event can have a lifetime impact on a person's overall well-being and their capacity to cope.

Sometimes a series of traumatic events occur before anyone identifies that the person's well-being and their capacity to cope were negatively affected.

Trauma was previously used to describe physical injuries or the impact of war or combat (NIMH, Feb 2017). But in the latter part of the 20th century it came to include psychological impacts such as abuse.

WHAT IS THE IMPACT OF TRAUMA?

For some people, reactions to stress interfere with their daily life and ability to function and interact with others. Traumatic stress refers to reactions that persist and affect a person's daily life after they have experienced a traumatic event and the event has ended.

Traumatic reactions can include intense and ongoing emotional upset, depressive symptoms or anxiety, behavioral changes, difficulties with self-regulation, problems relating to others or with forming attachments, loss of previously acquired skills, attention and academic difficulties, nightmares, difficulty sleeping and eating, and physical symptoms such as aches and pains. People may use alcohol or other drugs, behave in risky ways, or engage in unhealthy sexual activity.

Researchers are studying the long-term impact of traumatic experiences. Much of what we know about the long-term consequences of traumatic experiences comes from the Adverse Childhood Experiences (ACE) Study that began in 1995. Conducted by CDC, the ACE Study included over 17,000 participants ranging in age from 19 to 90. Researchers gathered medical histories and information about the subjects' exposure to 10 ACEs, including emotional abuse and other traumas.

The study showed that the rate of exposure to ACEs was high: Nearly 64 percent of participants experienced at least one exposure, and of those, 69 percent reported two or more. The study found that adults who had at least four ACEs were much more likely to have a range of psychological and medical problems.

The ACE Study showed that repeated exposure to traumatic events during childhood can affect the brain and nervous system and increase health-risk behaviors such as smoking, eating disorders, substance use, and high-risk activities. Living in a near-constant state of fight or flight, with stress hormones like cortisol and adrenaline flowing even when there is no real threat, is harmful.

Figure 13 Impact of Childhood Trauma shows how a person may be affected throughout their life by trauma.

Adult survivors of traumatic events may also have difficulty establishing fulfilling relationships and maintaining employment. In a SAMHSA Treatment Improvement Protocol from 2014 the following facts about trauma appear:

- 64 percent of adult suicide attempts are attributable to adverse childhood experiences.
- 80 percent of people in psychiatric hospitals have experienced physical or sexual abuse.
- 66 percent of people in substance abuse treatment report childhood abuse or neglect.
- 90 percent of women with alcoholism were sexually abused or suffered severe violence from parents.

WHO IS AT HIGH RISK FOR SYMPTOMS OF TRAUMATIC STRESS?

People vary in how they respond to traumatic experiences.

The majority of people are resilient in the aftermath of traumatic experiences. However, some people need more help over a longer period of time in order to heal, and may need continuing support from family and friends and/or mental health professionals. Anniversaries of or media reports about the event may cause the person to have a recurrence of symptoms, feelings, and behaviors.

SIGNS AND SYMPTOMS IN THOSE WHO HAVE EXPERIENCED TRAUMA

Victims of and witnesses to traumatic event are affected by what they see and feel; they may have symptoms ranging from complete withdrawal and paralysis to uncontrolled grief and inability to stand still. They may shiver, talk to themselves, be confused about time and place, and feel numb.

HOW TRAUMA AFFECTS THE WAY A PERSON THINKS, FEELS, BEHAVES, AND APPEARS

Thoughts

- Experiencing an altered sense of reality
- Recurrent or intrusive memories of the event
- Recurrent or distressing dreams
- Not being able to remember important aspects of the traumatic event

Emotions

- Dissociation (feeling as if the traumatic event is happening in the moment when it is not)
- Having a hard time feeling positive emotions
- Intense or prolonged psychological distress or intense physiological reactions to internal or external cues that are somewhat like the traumatic event

Behaviors

- Trying to avoid distressing memories, thoughts, or feelings of the event
- Avoiding people, places, or things associated with the traumatic event
- Experiencing irritability or angry outbursts
- Experiencing hypervigilance
- Elevated heart rate and blood pressure

Appearance and Well-being

- Shaken or disoriented
- Startling very easily
- Difficulty with sleep, including falling asleep, sleeping through the night, or experiencing restless sleep
- May have physical injuries

WHAT ARE TRAUMA-RELATED AND STRESSOR-RELATED DISORDERS?

Trauma- and stressor-related disorders are a group of emotional and behavioral problems.

When diagnosing, mental health professionals look for specific signs or symptoms called "diagnostic criteria"; these must be present for a diagnosis. For trauma- and stressor-related disorders, a diagnostic criterion is exposure to a traumatic or stressful event.

Types Of Trauma- And Stressor-Related Disorders

Acute stress disorder

The symptoms of acute stress disorder occur within the first month after exposure to trauma. The person has significant distress and may be unable to engage in social activities, relationships, and employment (this is referred to by mental health professionals as being "impaired"). The person may experience guilt about not having prevented the traumatic event. In addition, the person may have dissociative symptoms, flashbacks to the trauma, and nightmares. They may react to triggers of the trauma in everyday life with avoidance or withdrawal (O'Donnell et al., 2016).

For most people experiencing acute stress disorder, support from family and friends and some professional intervention will resolve their symptoms within a month.

The danger is that acute stress disorder can develop into PTSD. Prompt treatment and appropriate social support can reduce the risk of acute stress disorder developing into PTSD.

HOW ACUTE STRESS DISORDERS AFFECTS THE WAY A PERSON THINKS, FEELS, BEHAVES, AND APPEARS

 Thoughts
- Experiencing an altered sense of reality
- Recurrent or intrusive memories of the event ("flashbacks")
- Recurrent or distressing dreams
- Not being able to remember important aspects of the traumatic event

 Emotions
- Dissociation (feeling as if the traumatic event is happening in the moment when it is not)
- Having a hard time feeling positive emotions
- Intense or prolonged psychological distress or experiencing intense physiological reactions to internal or external cues that are somewhat like the traumatic event
- Guilt
- Anger

 Behaviors
- Trying to avoid distressing memories, thoughts, or feelings of the event
- Avoiding people, places, or things associated with the traumatic event
- Irritability or angry outbursts
- Hypervigilance
- Elevated heart rate and blood pressure

 Appearance and Well-being
- Shaken or disoriented
- Startling very easily
- Difficulty with sleep, including falling asleep, sleeping through the night, or experiencing restless sleep
- May have physical injuries

Post-traumatic stress disorder

PTSD differs from acute stress disorder in that the symptoms persist for at least one month. Symptoms can persist for months or years and interfere with the person's work, home, and social life. Often, people are diagnosed with PTSD years after the experience(s) occur. PTSD has less emphasis on dissociative symptoms as compared with acute stress disorder (O'Donnell et al., 2016).

Symptoms of PTSD fit into four categories: (U.S. Department of Veterans Affairs, 2016)

- Reliving the event.
  - Recurrent dreams.
  - Flashbacks.
  - Intrusive memories.
  - Unrest in situations that bring back memories of the original trauma.
- Avoiding situations that are reminders of the event.
  - Visual associations.
  - Smells.
  - Sounds.
  - Physical surroundings similar to the traumatic event.
- Negative changes in beliefs and feelings.
  - Feelings of numbness.
  - Withdrawal from those around them.
  - Reduced interest in others and the outside world.
- Hyperarousal.
  - Constant watchfulness.
  - Irritability.
  - Jumpiness.
  - Being easily startled.
  - Outbursts of rage.
  - Insomnia.

Often, a person who should be diagnosed with PTSD is instead diagnosed with depression or anxiety disorder or a different mental disorder. This can occur because the person and the mental health professional do not make the connection between the event or series of events and the current issue because the event was long before the person got diagnosed.

Prevalence Of Trauma-Related Disorders

About 7 to 8 percent of the U.S. population will experience a traumatic disorder at some point in their lives (U.S. Department of Veterans Affairs, 2016).

Approximately 3.5 percent of the population is diagnosed with PTSD.

WHAT CAUSES TRAUMA?

Risk Factors For Trauma-Related Disorders And Impact Of Trauma On Other Behavioral Health Disorders

Trauma occurs when the person responds to an experience in a way that harms their overall health and well-being. Among people with minimal risk factors for trauma, some can return to their usual level of functioning with no long-lasting effects from a traumatic event.

Some specific traumas may affect overall health and well-being, and others may not. Researchers have looked into why this is.

Individuals respond differently to different traumas. Certain factors affect whether trauma affects a person's overall health and well-being. For example, the type of support the person receives at the time of the trauma plays a role, as does the way that they personally handled the trauma at the time. In addition, their personality traits play a role, including their level of resilience.

Among clinicians and researchers seeking to explain why people react differently to trauma, there is strong interest in the concept of resilience.

Stigma Around Trauma

Some mental health conditions are due to trauma. Stigma associated with mental illnesses can lead people to hide their issues and delay seeking help. People, especially older men, are often ashamed to discuss their symptoms or experiences of trauma with family, friends, teachers, or work colleagues and may be reluctant to seek treatment and support because of concerns about what others will think (Shrivastava, Johnston, & Bureau, 2012).

Better understanding of the experiences of people with mental illness can reduce stigma and discrimination.

Navigating life with a mental disorder can be tough, and the isolation, blame, and secrecy that stigma brings can cause people not to reach out, get needed support, and recover. Learning how to avoid and address stigma is important for everyone, and especially for First Aiders.

Researchers asked people whether they worry about others judging them when they say they have sought mental health services (Cohen Veterans Network and National Council for Behavioral Health, 2018). The results showed that people do indeed worry about this. Broken down by age group, the percentages of people who worry about others judging them for seeking mental health services are:

- Gen Z (ages 0–21): 49%
- Millennials (ages 22–37): 40%
- Gen X (ages 38–53): 30%
- Boomers (ages 54–72): 20%

Experiencing discrimination due to racism, sexism, religious persecution, and homophobia has been shown to be traumatic for some people, and can lead to poor health outcomes and increased substance use (Gone et al., 2019).

Even though most people can be successfully treated, in 2017, among the 46.6 million adults with any mental illness, only 42.6 percent received mental health services in the past year (SAMHSA, 2018).

According to the American's Mental Health 2018 study, nearly one-third of Americans have worried about others judging them when they told them they have sought mental health services, and over a fifth have even lied to avoid telling people they were seeking mental health services.

The Importance Of Early Intervention For Trauma

Supporting a person immediately after a traumatic event and providing ongoing support can prevent symptoms that cause acute distress and lifelong physical, mental, and emotional challenges. Asking a person about their current situation and life experiences without judgment or blame can open a conversation that can be life changing. Find out if they are still being harmed or are safe.

THE MHFA ACTION PLAN FOR TRAUMATIC STRESS OR EVENTS

See Chapter 2: Mental Health First Aid to read about how to use ALGEE. In this section, we discuss each step briefly and add information about treatments for trauma.

ALGEE is a useful way to remember the steps of the action plan you can use to help a person with signs and symptoms of mental disorders. Not every step must be done, and they don't have to be done in order.

Special Considerations For Traumatic Stress In People With Developmental Disabilities

If you know the person's family, caregiver, or legal guardian, you may wish to first engage with them to talk about your concerns and see if they have noticed similar concerns. However, recall that you must ask the person whether it is okay to speak with the family member. If the person does not have the capacity to make their own health care treatment decisions, you will find out who is permitted to give consent for these decisions for the person.

If you are able to speak with the family, caregiver, or legal guardian, you might listen nonjudgmentally, provide reassurance and information, and then help them connect to professional help or other resources to get help for the person. The way that you engage with the person's family will depend on your role and relationship.

When navigating consent to care, it is important to consider the individual's capacity to make their own health care treatment decisions, known as decisional capacity. When adults with developmental disabilities have incomplete decisional capacity, consent is obtained from a surrogate (such as a family caregiver who serves as a legal guardian) and assent, uncoerced willingness to undergo treatment, from the individual.

If you are the parent or relative, you might be talking directly to your adult relative using the relevant ALGEE action steps. If the person appears to be at risk of self-harm and says that they intend to die, call 911 and do not leave the person alone.

Figure 14

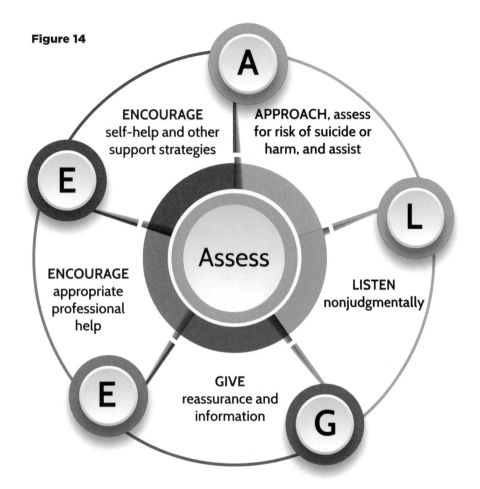

Action A: Assess for Risk of Suicide or Harm

See Chapter 2: Mental Health First Aid for a in-depth discussion of Action A.

If you think that a person may have had trauma and is in need of help, approach them about your concerns.

Because trauma survivors are often hyper-vigilant and sensitive to how others approach them, choosing a non-intrusive time and a quiet and calm environment will be very helpful. Offer the person choices and options about when and where so they feel a sense of control.

As you talk with the person, be on the lookout for any indications that they may be in crisis.

Crises that may be associated with trauma include:

- The person experiences an extreme level of anxiety, such as a panic attack.
- The person has severe anxiety following a traumatic event.
- The person has suicidal thoughts and behaviors.
- The person is engaging in nonsuicidal self-injury.

Encourage the person to talk about their feelings, symptoms, and what is going on in their mind. Be alert for any of the warning signs of suicide. See Chapter 12: Suicide**.**

If you have concerns that the person may be having suicidal thoughts, call 911.

If the person you are helping is engaging in nonsuicidal self-injury and is also suicidal, call 911. Suicidal thoughts or behaviors are an emergency and must be considered as such.

If you have concerns that the person may be engaging in nonsuicidal self-injury but is not suicidal, see Chapter 11: Nonsuicidal Self-injury.

If the person has experienced a traumatic event, find out how to assess and assist this person in Chapter 13: First Aid for Mental Health Crises, Mental Health First Aid Following a Traumatic Event.

If you have no concerns that the person is in crisis, you may ask them how they are feeling and how long they have been feeling that way, then move on to Action L.

Action L: Listen Nonjudgmentally

If you believe the person is not in a crisis, you can engage them in conversation.

Trauma survivors are often overwhelmed by their feelings and other types of sensations. Keeping yourself as calm and centered as much as you can is reassuring in itself. Keeping your voice calm and modulated without speaking down to the person makes a difference. Speaking slowly and clearly conveys a sense of purpose to the conversation.

Take time to listen before you try to discuss possible courses of action.

See Chapter 2: Mental Health First Aid to read more about how to listen nonjudgmentally, including how to convey an attitude of acceptance, genuineness, and empathy, and what verbal and nonverbal skills are effective.

Action G: Give Support and Information

A person who has experienced trauma might not have had the experience of reassurance or support in the past. Helping a person understand that they are not alone is reassuring.

After you have listened attentively and sensitively to the person and given them a chance to fully express and explore their issue, you can begin to discuss possible courses of action.

Doing what you say you are going to do and being honest in your interactions and communications is very important, especially when a trauma survivor has been misled by those who offered to help or who should have helped.

Action E: Encourage Appropriate Professional Help

Information about professionals can be found in Chapter 1: Mental Health in the United States.

Treatments available for trauma

Many treatments and therapies are available to help someone recover from trauma. Some proven treatments include:

- **Trauma-focused cognitive behavioral therapy (TF-CBT).** TF-CBT draws on what a person thinks and how they feel and behave. Trauma can impact all of these and can shape a person's worldview as well as their sense of self. CBT is based on the idea that individuals can change how they think, which helps them change how they feel and develop new behaviors based on those changes. TF-CBT also helps people understand how trauma has impacted them in all areas.

- **Eye movement desensitization reprocessing (EMDR) therapy.** EMDR therapy uses eye movement to help the person focus on external stimuli and allow for internal processing of traumatic memories. The treatment is done in small doses over time and has been shown to be highly effective for individuals whose distress has not been responsive to other therapies.

- **Prolonged exposure (PE) therapy.** Many people who have experienced trauma have adapted by avoiding anything related to or reminding them of the trauma. This avoidance often gets in the way of recovering from the traumatic event or events. Gradually confronting the memories of the avoided situations and exploring the thoughts and feelings associated with them can help reduce the distress a person feels when confronted with those situations.

- **Dialectical behavioral therapy (DBT).** DBT is a clinical intervention that has been very effective for adolescents and adults who struggle with trauma response. DBT teaches skills to help the person recognize patterns of thoughts, emotions, and behaviors, and learn techniques to regulate intense difficult emotions before they result in unhealthy or self-harm behaviors.

- **Somatic experiencing.** Somatic experiencing is a therapy that focuses on what a person experiences in their body and how physical sensations are correlated to thoughts, emotions, actions, memories, and mental images. It is a gentle approach that allows a person to go at their own pace. It is very effective in addressing the common negative effect of trauma that makes people dissociate, appear "checked out," or feel ungrounded.

- **Medications.** Medicine can help treat serious symptoms of PTSD and help people cope with daily activities while being treated.

If a person is hospitalized because of trauma, it is very important that the doctors and nurses at the hospital know that the person is a trauma survivor. Your support and advocacy for the individual can make a big difference in how a person is treated.

Action E: Encourage Self-help and Other Support Strategies

A First Aider can also help someone identify people, programs, or activities that can help them reduce or manage symptoms of mental health challenges. These can be different for every person depending on their social networks, the resources available in their community, and their interests. A person with trauma can benefit from self-help and other support strategies discussed below. They have proven to be very helpful in reducing the symptoms and response to past trauma.

Other people who can help

Encourage the person to turn to family, friends, and support groups. The power of knowing that one is not alone in a struggle and that other people have felt the same way can make a tremendous difference. Connecting people with others who have experienced PTSD or other trauma-related challenges can be helpful. This has been shown through research on veterans with PTSD, who benefitted greatly from the power of peer support and mutual self-help (Hundt et al., 2015). Being able to share experiences and hear how others have managed their challenges can provide an opportunity for growth and change.

Self-help strategies

Self-help strategies are frequently used by people with trauma. You should not be too forceful when trying to encourage the person to use self-help strategies.

Several skills training interventions have been shown to help a person learn new ways of managing trauma response and how to create safety within their environments and in their lives. Some of those interventions are:

- Seeking Safety (www.seekingsafety.org), which can be provided by therapists as well as peer supporters.

- Wellness Recovery Action Planning (WRAP; http://mentalhealthrecovery.com/wrap-is/) for trauma is normally provided by peer supporters and has been beneficial in supporting a person's development of intentional planning and creating support networks for dealing with trauma.

- Center for Mind-Body Medicine's global trauma relief programs (www.cmbm.org).

- 12-step groups.

Self-help and recovery for a person who has experienced trauma also includes re-establishing a claim to their identity. It is important for the First Aider to recognize that cultural, historical, and gender issues can play a large part in healing and moving forward in a person's life. Being able to reclaim and name one's history, often to reunite with others who have had similar experiences, can be helpful.

Encouraging appropriate professional help and self-help strategies are ways to help a person to recovery and well-being.

See the Introduction for more information on recovery and well-being.

DANIEL KASPERICK, *In the Beginning*

In 1988, I was diagnosed with bipolar disorder. This painting is one of my abstracts: "Hope." It is difficult to tell what is going on there. As an abstract, they are about the expression itself.

Themes of weariness and suffering are softened by ideas of peace and brotherhood. I look forward to continuing my art, as I find solace and expression in the artistic process.

CHAPTER 7: BIPOLAR DISORDER

WHAT IS BIPOLAR DISORDER?

Previously known as manic-depressive disorder, bipolar disorder involves bouts of major depression and periods of mania (euphoria, poor judgment, and extreme risk-taking activity) in a cycle. Bipolar disorder usually begins in adolescence or early adulthood (NIMH, Apr 2016).

People with bipolar disorder sometimes feel very happy or "up" and are much more energetic and active than usual. This is called a manic episode. Sometimes people with bipolar disorder feel very sad and "down," and are much less active than usual. This is called depression or a depressive episode.

It is not unusual for people with bipolar disorder to become psychotic during depressive or manic episodes. Psychosis involves delusions and hallucinations. Delusions are beliefs with no basis in reality. Hallucinations involve seeing or hearing things that others do not see or hear (Toh, Thomas, & Rossell, 2015).

See Chapter 8: Psychosis for additional information on bipolar disorder with psychosis.

A person is not diagnosed with bipolar disorder until they have experienced an episode of mania (American Psychiatric Association, 2013). It may, therefore, take many years before they are diagnosed correctly and get the most appropriate treatment.

Bipolar disorder is not the same as "ups and downs." Bipolar symptoms are more powerful than that. The mood swings are extreme and are accompanied by changes in sleep, energy level, and the ability to think clearly. Bipolar symptoms are so strong, they can make it hard for someone to do well at work or to get along with friends and family members.

Bipolar disorder can be dangerous in that it increases the risk of suicide (American Foundation for Suicide Prevention, 2018). Bipolar disorder may account for one-quarter of all completed suicides (American Psychiatric Association, 2013).

Bipolar disorder is a lifelong and recurrent illness. People with the disorder need long-term treatment to maintain control of their symptoms.

Bipolar disorder may affect the person so much that they become an active risk of harm to self or others. In these cases, a professional can determine if they require hospitalization.

Co-Occurring Mental Disorders

Nonsuicidal self-injury is a significant risk for people with bipolar disorder. And people with bipolar disorder are more likely to have trouble with intoxication and withdrawal from alcohol and other drugs that can mimic depressive episodes.

Prevalence Of Bipolar Disorder

Approximately 2.8 percent of U.S. adults have experienced bipolar disorder in the past year (NIMH, Apr 2016).

SIGNS AND SYMPTOMS OF BIPOLAR DISORDER

The side by side tables show how bipolar disorder may affect how a person thinks, feels, behaves, and appears.

HOW A PERSON WITH BIPOLAR DISORDER THINKS, FEELS, BEHAVES, AND APPEARS DURING A DEPRESSIVE PHASE

Thoughts

- Difficulty concentrating or making decisions
- Thinking often about death, wishing to be dead, or having a specific plan for hurting oneself

Emotions

- An unusually sad mood
- Feeling worthless
- Feeling guilty though not really at fault
- Loss of enjoyment and interest in activities that used to be enjoyable

Behaviors

- Crying spells
- Withdrawal from others
- Slowing down
- Neglect of work or family
- Not taking care of oneself
- Loss of interest in personal appearance and hygiene, such as wearing dirty clothes and not bathing or washing

Appearance and Well-being

- Lack of energy and tiredness
- Moving more slowly or sometimes becoming agitated and unable to settle
- Having sleeping difficulties or sometimes sleeping too much
- Changes in eating habits: either weight loss or weight gain
- Wearing dirty clothes and not bathing or washing

HOW A PERSON WITH BIPOLAR DISORDER THINKS, FEELS, BEHAVES, AND APPEARS DURING A **MANIC PHASE**

Thoughts

- Grandiose delusions: very inflated self-esteem, a belief of being superhuman, especially talented, or an important religious figure
- Rapid thinking

Emotions

- Elevated mood: Feelings of being high, happy, full of energy, on top of the world, and invincible
- Lack of insight: The person is so convinced that their manic delusions are real that they do not realize they are ill
- Lack of inhibitions: doing risky things, extreme spending, provocative attire, or being very sexually active

Behaviors

- Rapid speech
- Irritability, especially if others disagree with unrealistic plans or ideas
- Overactivity

Appearance and Well-being

- Increased energy
- Need less sleep than usual; can go for days with very little sleep

Bipolar Disorder With Psychotic Features

A person with bipolar disorder with psychotic features may have hallucinations, delusions, or disordered thinking during either a depressive or manic episode.

Bipolar Disorder With Mania That Is Not Severe

A person with bipolar disorder may experience less severe symptoms of mania. This state is known as hypomania. People who experience hypomania need treatment to avoid the risk of more severe symptoms.

Bipolar Disorder With Depression And Restlessness

Some people with bipolar disorders experience a mixed state, in which they feel depressed but also restless.

WHAT CAUSES BIPOLAR DISORDER?

It appears that there is no single cause of bipolar disorder, but rather that both genes (heredity) and other factors play a role. Additional factors that researchers are looking at include brain injuries and complications during pregnancy and childbirth.

Research shows that a certain genetic makeup can make some people more likely than others to develop bipolar disorder. Brain structure and function in people with the disorder may be different. Research on the cause of bipolar disorder continues.

Trauma And Bipolar Disorder

Trauma may affect the degree to which bipolar disorder disrupts a person's life (Marshall et al., 2018).

Stigma Around Bipolar Disorder

There is stigma associated with mental illness such as bipolar disorder. But people with bipolar disorder deserve understanding, respect, and knowledge of the facts about their illness. Bipolar disorder has been both romanticized and demonized throughout history. This has led to distortions in our understanding of people who have bipolar disorder.

People in a manic state may behave in a way that is unlike their "regular" behavior. Their actions while manic may have a negative effect on relationships or their reputation. They may feel ashamed because of their actions while ill. Family, friends, and co-workers can help ease the shame by understanding the behaviors as part of the person's disorder, not a moral flaw.

Stigma may greatly affect whether someone with bipolar disorder seeks treatment. In those who do seek treatment, stigma may be partially responsible when they do not follow their doctor's recommended treatment.

Perceived stigma has also been shown to be related to reduced social functioning in people with bipolar disorder.

Stigma can lead to negative feelings about oneself, including shame, worthlessness, feelings of incompetence, and overall low self-esteem (Lazowski et al., 2012).

Understanding the illness and knowing there are effective treatments can help reduce stigma.

IMPORTANCE OF EARLY INTERVENTION FOR BIPOLAR DISORDER

Early intervention for people with bipolar disorder is most important. If left untreated, bipolar disorder usually becomes worse and more difficult to treat (Ghio et al., 2014). Research has shown that the earlier a person begins treatment from the first onset of symptoms, the more likely the person is to respond well to treatment. Delays in treatment increase that person's personal, social, or work-related troubles.

THE MHFA ACTION PLAN FOR BIPOLAR DISORDER

See Chapter 2: Mental Health First Aid to read about how to use ALGEE. In this section, we discuss each step briefly and add information about treatments for bipolar disorder.

ALGEE is a useful way to remember the steps of the action plan you can use to help a person with signs and symptoms of mental disorders. Not every step must be done, and they don't have to be done in order.

Special Considerations For Bipolar Disorder In People With Developmental Disabilities

If you know the person's family, caregiver, or legal guardian, you may wish to first engage with them to talk about your concerns and see if they have noticed similar concerns. However, recall that you must ask the person whether it is okay to speak with the family member. If the person does not have the capacity to make their own health care treatment decisions, you will find out who is permitted to give consent for health care treatment decisions for the person.

If you are able to speak with the family, caregiver, or legal guardian, you might listen nonjudgmentally, provide reassurance and information, and then help them connect to professional help or other resources to get help for the person. The way that you engage with the person's family will depend on your role and relationship.

When navigating consent to care, it is important to consider the individual's capacity to make their own health care treatment decisions, known as decisional capacity. When adults with developmental disabilities have incomplete decisional capacity, consent is obtained from a surrogate (such as a family caregiver who serves as a legal guardian) and assent, uncoerced willingness to undergo treatment, from the individual.

If you are the parent or relative, you might be talking directly to your adult relative using the relevant ALGEE action steps. If the person appears to be at risk of self-harm and says that they intend to die, call 911 and do not leave the person alone.

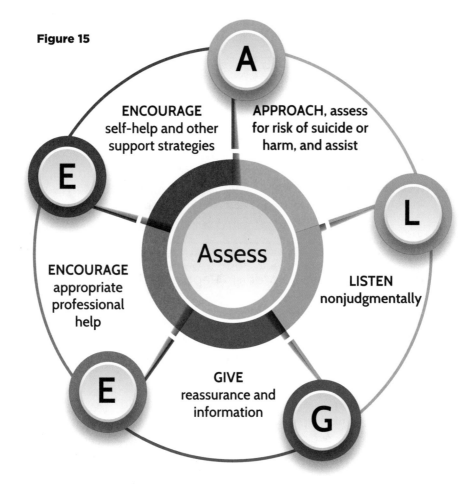

Figure 15

ACTION A: Assess for Risk of Suicide or Harm

See Chapter 2: Mental Health First Aid for an in-depth discussion of Action A.

If you think that a person may have bipolar disorder and is in need of help, approach them about your concerns.

As you talk with the person, be on the lookout for any indications that they may be in crisis.

The potential crises that may be associated with bipolar disorder are:

- The person has suicidal thoughts and behaviors.
- The person is engaging in nonsuicidal self-injury.
- The person is aggressive.
- The person is showing signs of psychosis.

If the person appears to be at risk of self-harm and says that they intend to die, or you think the person may be having suicidal thoughts, call 911 and do not leave the person alone.

If the person you are helping is engaging in nonsuicidal self-injury and is also suicidal, call 911. Suicidal thoughts or behaviors are an emergency and must be considered as such.

If you have concerns that the person may be engaging in nonsuicidal self-injury but is not suicidal, see Chapter 11: Nonsuicidal Self-Injury.

If you have concerns that the person may become aggressive or is experiencing psychosis, find out how to assess and assist in Chapter 13: First Aid for Mental Health Crises.

If you determine the person is not in crisis, you can ask how they are feeling and how long they have been feeling that way, and move on to Action L.

ACTION L: Listen Nonjudgmentally

If you believe the person is not in a crisis, you can engage them in conversation.

Take time to listen before you try to discuss possible courses of action.

Refer to Chapter 2: Mental Health First Aid to read more about how to listen nonjudgmentally, including how to convey an attitude of acceptance, genuineness, and empathy, and what verbal and nonverbal skills are effective.

ACTION G: Give Support and Information

As you provide support and information, consider these tips for what not to do:

- Don't tell someone to "snap out of it" or to "get over it."
- Do not adopt an overinvolved or overprotective attitude.
- Do not use a patronizing tone of voice or a facial expression that shows an extreme look of concern.
- Do not ignore, disagree with, or dismiss the person's feelings by attempting to say something positive like, "You don't seem that bad to me."

ACTION E: Encourage Appropriate Professional Help

Offer the person support to manage their feelings — either as a listener or by providing suggestions for where the individual could seek professional help. If help is needed, then respond as follows:

- Discuss appropriate professional help and effective treatment options.
- Find out if they have received treatment in the past.
- Encourage the person to use these options.
- Offer to help them seek out these options.
- Encourage the person not to give up seeking appropriate professional help.

Treatment of bipolar disorder

There is evidence that the following treatments help people with bipolar disorder:

- **Medications.** Medications are essential to help people with bipolar disorder. They can reduce the swings from one mood to another.
- **Psychoeducation** involves providing information to the person about bipolar disorder and its treatment and about how to manage its effect on their life. Psychoeducation has been found to reduce relapses when used with medication.
- **Psychotherapy.** Two therapies that research has found to be helpful are CBT and interpersonal and social rhythm therapy. CBT helps people monitor mood swings, overcome thinking patterns that affect mood, and function better. Interpersonal and social rhythm therapy covers potential problem areas in the person's life (grief, changes in roles, disputes, and interpersonal deficits) and helps them regulate social and sleep rhythms.

- **Family therapy.** Educating family members on how they can support the person with bipolar disorder and avoid negative interactions that can trigger relapses has proven to be helpful for people with bipolar disorder.

If the person is uncertain about what to do, encourage them to first see a doctor who can check for an underlying physical health cause for symptoms and refer them to the appropriate specialized help.

What if the person doesn't want help?

The person may not want to seek professional help. You should find out if there are specific reasons why. For example, the person might be concerned about the cost of the service or not having a doctor they like. You may be able to help the person overcome their worry about seeking help.

If the person still doesn't want help after you have explored their reasons with them, let them know that if they change their mind in the future about seeking help, they can contact you. You must respect the person's right not to seek help unless you believe that they are at risk of harming self or others.

ACTION E: Encourage Self-Help and Other Support Strategies

Other people who can help

Encourage the person to consider other available support, such as family, friends, faith communities, or people who have also experienced bipolar disorder (peer supporters). There is evidence that mutual support groups may be helpful for people with bipolar disorder.

Self-help strategies

People with bipolar disorder can benefit from self-help strategies. Many of the self-help strategies recommended for depression and anxiety are also appropriate for people with bipolar disorder.

People with bipolar disorder may benefit from an exercise regime but should be wary when there are warning signs of a manic episode. If exercise appears too stimulating during those times, decreasing the frequency or intensity of exercise until the warning signs or episode have passed may be a good idea.

Getting enough sleep and avoiding alcohol and substances may also be beneficial.

CHAPTER 8: PSYCHOSIS

WHAT IS PSYCHOSIS?

Psychosis describes a mental health challenge in which a person has lost some contact with reality. The person may have hallucinations and delusions and severe disruptions in thinking, emotions, and behavior.

The person can have difficulty with relationships, work, school, other usual activities, and activities of daily living such as bathing, personal hygiene and grooming, dressing, and eating.

Psychosis is a syndrome, or a collection of symptoms, rather than a diagnosis.

Recovery from psychosis is possible, especially with early intervention. Effective treatment is available.

Psychosis occurs in episodes, known as psychotic episodes. An episode usually involves three different phases, as shown in Figure 16. Not all people will experience clear symptoms of all three phases; each person's experience will differ.

Prodromal phase. In this phase symptoms can be quite subtle, and a person or their family or friends may not notice the early signs and symptoms of a psychotic episode. Some of these may include depressed mood, anxiety, reduced concentration, social withdrawal, idiosyncratic thinking, and sleep disturbances.

If not addressed, early warning signs may increase in severity and lead to behavior that escalates to a point of crisis.

Acute phase. As the person becomes unwell, they may start showing psychotic symptoms such as delusions, hallucinations, and disorganized thinking. The acute phase can be very distressing, especially if the person is having these kinds of symptoms for the first time.

Recovery phase. The recovery phase occurs after the psychotic episode. In this phase, the person starts an individual journey to return to their normal, everyday lives. Appropriate professional support can help them sustain their recovery.

Psychotic disorders involve a high risk for suicide. More than 30 percent of people with a psychotic disorder will attempt suicide at some point in their lives, and one in five people with a psychotic disorder considered suicide over the last two weeks (Taylor, Hutton, & Wood, 2015).

Approximately 5 percent of people with schizophrenia die by suicide (Palmer, Pankratz, & Bostwick, 2005). Having concurrent depression or a substance use disorder increases this risk (Beyer & Weisler, 2016).

Psychosis often starts between when a person is a teen through their mid-20s (NIMH, 2015).

Figure 16

Phases of Psychosis

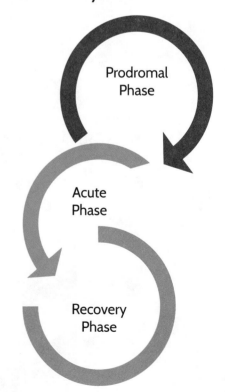

Prodromal Phase

Acute Phase

Recovery Phase

Prevalence Of Psychosis Among U.s. Adults

Three out of 100 people will experience psychosis in their lives (NIMH, 2015).

SIGNS AND SYMPTOMS OF PSYCHOSIS OR A PSYCHOTIC DISORDER

HOW PSYCHOSIS AFFECTS HOW A PERSON THINKS, FEELS, BEHAVES, AND APPEARS

Thoughts

- Difficulty concentrating or paying attention in conversations
- Expressing unusual ideas; voicing strange feelings. For example, believing that other people are controlling them or plotting to do harm to them. These beliefs may involve the authorities, such as the FBI or police. The person may express their ideas in a way that is not appropriate and is overly intense.
- Having difficulty in naming the correct day of the week or month of the year, identifying government leaders, or interpreting the meaning of common phrases
- Reporting an unusual perceptual experience — for example, heightened or reduced sensitivity or intensity of smell, sound, or color

Emotions

- Depressed
- Anxious and overwhelmed
- Irritable
- Suspicious and fearful (at times, about something about to happen to them, the community, local institutions, or the government)
- Having limited, flat, or inappropriate emotions (for example, laughing hysterically during sad situations or showing no emotion at all)

Behaviors

- Talking to themselves or talking to someone who is not present
- Inappropriate behavior for a situation (for example, loud shouting about a special mission during a quiet ceremony)
- Unusual sleep disturbances, particularly the loss of a regular sleep schedule and/or insomnia
- Social isolation or withdrawal
- Confused or disorganized manner or speech
- Changes in appetite
- Reduced energy
- A decrease in grades or work performance

Appearance and Well-being

- Decline in self-care or personal hygiene
- Showing no facial expressions, limited facial expressions, or inappropriate facial expressions
- Dressing inappropriately for the weather, with too much or too little clothing

Hallucinations are things a person sees, hears, feels, or smells that others do not see, hear, feel, or smell.

Most hallucinations involve hearing voices either in the external world or inside the person's head. Noises, voices, and sounds are called auditory hallucinations.

Other hallucinations that are rarer include:

- Seeing shadows, shapes, or visions of people, animals, or supernatural creatures (visual hallucinations).
- Bodily sensations, including feelings on the skin or inside the body, smells, or tastes (tactile, olfactory, or gustatory hallucinations).

The person experiencing a psychotic episode believes that these experiences are very real. The person often finds the experiences frightening and upsetting and describes the voices making negative comments about them or plotting harm against them. They may hear more than one voice or may experience many different types of hallucinations.

Delusions are strong beliefs that are not consistent with the person's culture, are unlikely to be true, and may seem irrational to others, such as:

- Believing external forces are controlling thoughts, feelings, and behaviors.
- Believing that trivial remarks, events, or objects have personal meaning or significance.
- Believing that people are talking about them, following them, or plotting against them.
- Thinking that they have special powers, are on a special mission, or even that they are God.

Delusions are fixed; they do not change even when there is conflicting evidence. Some delusions are bizarre, others are not.

People experiencing the early stages of psychosis often go undiagnosed for a year or more before receiving treatment. A major reason for this is that psychosis often begins in late adolescence or early adulthood, and the early signs and symptoms involve behaviors and emotions that are common in this age group.

Many young people will have some of these symptoms without developing psychosis. Others showing these symptoms will eventually be diagnosed as having one of the disorders discussed below.

TYPES OF DISORDERS IN WHICH PSYCHOSIS MAY BE PRESENT

Disorders that can come with psychosis (like schizophrenia and bipolar disorder) are serious. They can derail a person's social, academic, and vocational development. These disorders can be disabling.

Psychosis can be present in schizophrenia, PTSD, psychotic depression, bipolar disorder, schizoaffective disorder, and drug-induced psychosis. Several of these disorders are discussed below, while PTSD is discussed in Chapter 6: Trauma and Trauma-related and Stressor-related Disorders.

Schizophrenia

Contrary to common belief, schizophrenia does not mean "split personality." The term schizophrenia refers to changes in mental function in which the person has unusual or disorganized ways of thinking.

Symptom onset usually begins in late adolescence or early adulthood. It is rare to develop schizophrenia after age 45 (NIMH, 2015).

Schizophrenia may be hard to distinguish in its early phases. Many of the symptoms are similar to the symptoms of depression, bipolar disorder, or other illnesses. As a result, misdiagnosis is common.

Men and women have schizophrenia at similar rates, but there are differences:

- Onset is later in women than in men.

- Men with schizophrenia tend to have more cognitive impairment, social withdrawal, substance abuse, and "blunted affect" (when a person's face does not show emotions). Women with schizophrenia have more affective changes (changes to their emotions), mood disturbance, and depressive symptoms.

- Women with schizophrenia are more responsive to treatment than men and have 50 percent fewer hospitalizations (Prat et al., 2018).

People with schizophrenia have a higher risk for co-occurring medical conditions such as cardiovascular and respiratory diseases, leading to a mortality rate that is higher than that of the general population. Some factors contributing to this increased risk are smoking and not getting enough physical activity (Olfson et al., 2015).

Schizophrenia is one of the top 15 leading causes of disability worldwide (NIMH 2015).

Prevalence of schizophrenia

Between .25 percent and .64 percent of people in the United States have schizophrenia. NIMH researchers find it difficult to obtain an exact number because schizophrenia is difficult to diagnose, and it overlaps with other disorders and is often combined with other psychotic disorders in estimates (NIMH, 2015).

Co-occurring mental disorders

Approximately half the people with schizophrenia have co-occurring mental and/or behavioral health disorders (Tsai & Rosenheck, 2013).

Signs and symptoms of schizophrenia

HOW A PERSON WITH SCHIZOPHRENIA MAY THINK, FEEL, BEHAVE, AND APPEAR	
Thoughts	• Vivid and bizarre thoughts and ideas • Trouble discerning dreams from reality • Confused thinking • Memory loss • Trouble paying attention
Emotions	• Severe anxiety and fearfulness • Extreme moodiness • Feeling that people are out to get them • Inappropriate emotions • Limited or reduced feelings of pleasure in everyday life
Behaviors	• Unusual body movements • Difficulty beginning and sustaining activities • Peculiar behavior • Seeing things and hearing voices that are not real • Confusing television or movies with reality • Reacting with anger or laughter when these are not appropriate • Severe problems in making and keeping friends
Appearance and Well-being	• Speaking in a monotone voice • Lack of facial expressions or gestures • Lack of eye contact • Less attention paid to self-care • Appearing unaware of the things around them

Major Depressive Disorders With Psychotic Features

Depression may be so severe that it causes psychotic symptoms. For example, people with depression may experience delusions involving feeling very guilty about something that is not their fault, believing that they are severely physically ill, or believing that they are being mistreated or observed. Some people may also experience hallucinations, most commonly hearing voices.

Bipolar Disorder

A person experiencing mania may exhibit a very inflated sense of self-esteem, even to the point of believing that they are superhuman, especially talented, or an important religious figure.

Schizoaffective Disorder

A person with schizoaffective disorder has symptoms of psychosis and elevated or depressed mood or both but is not diagnosed with bipolar disorder. (Bipolar disorder can come with elevated or depressed mood.)

Substance- Or Medication-Induced Psychotic Disorder

This psychosis is brought on by intoxication with or withdrawal from alcohol or other drugs. Research shows that a first episode of substance-induced psychotic disorder means that the person is at more risk of a long-lasting psychotic illness not directly related to substance use.

Both prescribed medications and illegal drugs can contribute to an episode of psychosis. According to the DSM-5, for between 7 percent and 25 percent of those having a first episode of psychosis, it is substance-induced (American Psychiatric Association, 2013).

Substance- or medication-induced psychosis usually appears quickly and lasts a short time (from a few hours to a few days) until the effects of the substance wear off. The most common symptoms are visual and/or tactile hallucinations, disorientation, and memory problems.

WHAT CAUSES PSYCHOSIS AND PSYCHOTIC DISORDERS?

The exact cause of disorders that involve psychosis is not fully understood. Researchers believe that psychosis is caused by a combination of factors, including genetics, biochemistry, and the effects of extreme trauma or stress. Biological factors could be genetic vulnerability, changes in the brain, or a dysfunction in the neurotransmitters in the brain. Stress may trigger psychotic symptoms in vulnerable people.

In people with schizophrenia, the brain undergoes biochemical changes. One of the major known changes is to the neurotransmitter dopamine (Brisch et al., 2014). Antipsychotic medications used for schizophrenia work by altering dopamine levels in the brain.

The risk factors for bipolar disorder are covered in Chapter 7: Bipolar Disorder.

Trauma And Psychotic Disorders

An individual who experiences trauma has a higher risk of developing a disorder that can involve psychosis.

Further, experiencing a psychotic episode may cause trauma. People with psychotic disorders experience multiple traumas, such as involuntary hospitalization or being placed in restraints; being mistreated by authorities due to a lack of understanding of mental illness; and victimization. High rates of trauma lead to high rates of PTSD (Alsawy et al., 2015).

If trauma is addressed and appropriate treatment and supports are provided sooner than later, a person's chance of recovering is much greater.

When more people in society understand that trauma may have played a role in the development of schizophrenia or bipolar disorder for some people, stigma and discrimination against people with mental illness can be reduced.

Stigma Around Psychotic Disorders

There is stigma associated with people talking to themselves and not being responsive to social norms.

Teasing; bullying; discrimination in social, family, and work situations; and mistreatment by law enforcement can result from stigma associated with psychosis (Corrigan & Shah, 2017).

Negative stereotypes lead to prejudice or discrimination against a person with a psychotic disorder. One such stereotype is the belief that a person with psychosis is dangerous. In reality, a very small percentage of people experiencing psychosis may threaten violence. Only 4 percent of violence in the United States is attributable to people diagnosed with mental illness (U.S. Department of Health and Human Services, 2017). In fact, violence may be directed against the person themselves due to their disorder. And they are a threat to themselves.

An additional negative stereotype leading to prejudice or discrimination against a person with a psychotic disorder is the belief that people with psychosis are incompetent or cannot lead a normal life. But people with psychotic disorders may be able to function in daily life using coping skills.

One negative stereotype against the person's family is a belief that they are incompetent (Corrigan & Shah, 2017).

IMPORTANCE OF EARLY INTERVENTION FOR PSYCHOSIS

Getting the right treatment within the first two to three years after the first episode of psychosis has been shown to decrease episodes of psychosis by more than 50 percent. It prevents much of the disability associated with a psychotic illness (Jordan et al., 2014). Research has shown that the earlier a person begins treatment from the first episode of psychosis, the more likely the person is to respond well to treatment (NIMH, 2015).

If a person is experiencing several symptoms of psychosis, encourage them to see a mental health professional. It is important not to ignore or dismiss such warning signs, even if they appear gradually or are unclear.

THE MHFA ACTION PLAN FOR PSYCHOSIS

See Chapter 2: Mental Health First Aid to read about how to use ALGEE. In this section, we discuss each step briefly and add information about treatments for psychosis.

ALGEE is a useful way to remember the steps of the action plan you can use to help a person with signs and symptoms of mental disorders. Not every step must be done, and they don't have to be done in order.

Special Considerations for Psychosis in People with Developmental Disabilities

If you know the person's family, caregiver, or legal guardian, you may wish to first engage with them to talk about your concerns and see if they have noticed similar concerns. However, recall that you must ask the person whether it is okay to speak with the family member. If the person does not have the capacity to make their own health care treatment decisions, find out who is permitted to give consent for health care treatment decisions for the person.

If you are able to speak with the family, caregiver, or legal guardian, you might listen nonjudgmentally, provide reassurance and information, and then help them connect to professional help or other resources to get help for the person. The way that you engage with the person's family will depend on your role and relationship.

When navigating consent to care, it is important to consider the individual's capacity to make their own health care treatment decisions, known as decisional capacity. When adults with developmental disabilities have incomplete decisional capacity, consent is obtained from a surrogate (such as a family caregiver who serves as a legal guardian) and assent, uncoerced willingness to undergo treatment, from the individual.

If you are the parent or relative, you might be talking directly to your adult relative using the relevant ALGEE action steps. If the person appears to be at risk of self-harm and says that they intend to die, call 911 and do not leave the person alone.

Figure 17

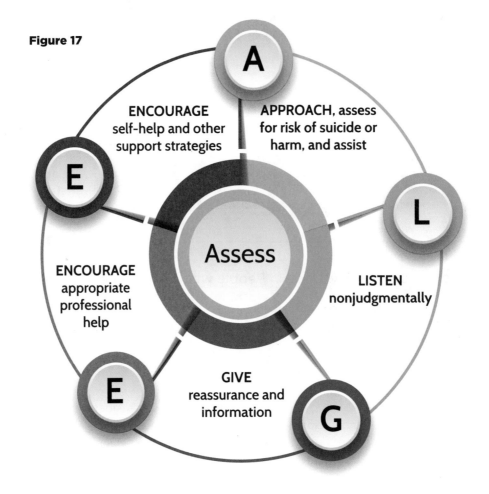

ACTION A: Assess for Risk of Suicide or Harm

See Chapter 2: Mental Health First Aid for a discussion of Action A.

If you think that a person may be experiencing psychosis and in need of help, approach them about your concerns.

As you talk with the person, be on the lookout for any indications that they may be in crisis.

The main crises associated with psychosis are:

- The person is at risk of harm to self (suicidal thoughts and behaviors).
- The person is at risk of harming others.
- The person is experiencing an acute psychotic state and may act upon delusions or hallucinations or is engaging in violence/aggressive behavior.

If the person appears to be at risk of self-harm and says that they intend to die, call 911 and do not leave the person alone.

Encourage the person to talk about their feelings, symptoms, and what is going on in their mind. Be alert for any of the warning signs of suicide. See Chapter 12: Suicide.

People developing psychosis do not often reach out for help. They may try to keep their symptoms a secret because they are scared or embarrassed.

You should state the specific behaviors you are concerned about and should not speculate about the person's diagnosis. Allow the person to talk about their experiences and beliefs if they want to. As much as possible, let the person set the pace and style of the interaction. You should recognize that they may be frightened by their thoughts and feelings.

If you have concerns that the person may be having suicidal thoughts, call 911.

If the person you are helping is engaging in nonsuicidal self-injury and is also suicidal, call 911. Suicidal thoughts or behaviors are an emergency and must be considered as such.

If you have concerns that the person may be engaging in nonsuicidal self-injury but is not suicidal, see Chapter 11: Nonsuicidal Self-Injury.

If you have concerns that the person is experiencing an acute psychotic state, see Chapter 13: First Aid for Mental Health Crises, Mental Health First Aid for Psychotic States. Someone in this state can be a victim of crime or unintentional harm.

If you have concerns that the person is showing aggressive behavior, find out how to assess and assist this person in Chapter 13: First Aid for Mental Health Crises, Mental Health First Aid for Aggressive Behaviors.

If you have no concerns that the person is in crisis, you may ask them how they are feeling and how long they have been feeling that way, then move on to Action L.

ACTION L: Listen Nonjudgmentally

The person may be behaving and talking in a manner that is different than usual due to symptoms of psychosis. Talking with someone who may be in and out of touch with reality requires you to:

- Understand the symptoms for what they are: a product of a medical illness.
- Empathize with how the person feels about their beliefs and experiences. For example, you might say, "That must be horrible for you," or "I can see that you are upset."
- Avoid confronting the person or criticizing or blaming them.
- Never threaten the person with hospitalization.
- Not state any judgments about the person's beliefs and experiences.
    - Do not dismiss the delusions or hallucinations.
    - Do not act alarmed, horrified, embarrassed, or amused by the person's delusions or hallucinations.
    - It is not safe to state that you agree that someone's fear is real when it isn't actually real. For example, someone with psychosis might be afraid of someone poisoning their food.

Dealing with communication difficulties

People experiencing symptoms of psychosis are often unable to think or communicate clearly. When someone speaks to you in a disorganized way:

- Respond in an uncomplicated and succinct manner.
- Repeat things if necessary.
- Give the person plenty of time to process the information and respond to what you have said.

Be aware that even if the person is showing a limited range of feelings, that does not mean that the person is not feeling anything.

Do not assume the person cannot understand what you are saying, even if their response is limited.

ACTION G: Give Support and Information

When a person is in a severe psychotic state, it is difficult and inappropriate to give information about psychosis. When the person is in touch with reality, you could ask if they would like some information about psychosis.

Try to find out what type of assistance they need by asking what will help them feel safe and in control. If possible, offer the person choices of how you can help them so that they are in control.

Find out if they have received treatment in the past. Do not make any promises that you cannot keep; this can create an atmosphere of distrust and add to the person's distress.

First Aiders can provide hope that treatment can help address any current difficulties and can also help prevent more serious problems in the future. Remind the person that what they are experiencing is a disorder.

See Action G in Chapter 4: Depression for more advice about giving reassurance and information.

ACTION E: Encourage Appropriate Professional Help

Information about mental health professionals can be found in Chapter 1: Mental Health in the United States.

Treatments available for people with psychotic disorders

A range of treatments have good evidence of effectively treating psychosis. Most people recover from psychosis and are able to lead satisfying and productive lives.

The pattern of recovery from psychosis varies from person to person.

Medications

The following categories of medications are effective:

- **Antipsychotic medications** are essential for treating psychosis, particularly for people with schizophrenia, because most will not get better without medication.
- **Antidepressant medications.** People with schizophrenia may have symptoms of depression as well. Antidepressants are effective for treating these symptoms.

Psychological treatment

The following treatments are effective for people with schizophrenia:

- **Cognitive behavioral therapy.** This type of psychological therapy can help reduce psychotic symptoms by helping the person develop alternative explanations of schizophrenia symptoms, reducing the impact of the symptoms, and encouraging the person to take their medication.

- **Psychoeducation.** Psychoeducation refers to education and empowerment of the person and their family about their illness and how best to manage it. Empowering the individual and their family/support system with knowledge and skills can help reduce relapse as family and friends become aware of signs and of developing symptoms. Psychoeducation may also help reduce family tension.

- **Coordinated specialty care (CSC).** This recovery-oriented treatment program connects individuals who have experienced first episode psychosis (FEP) with a team of specialists who work with the patient to create a personal treatment plan toward recovery. The aim is to initiate support as early as possible following the first episode. A treatment plan can include some of the following: psychotherapy, medication management, family education and support, case management, and work or education support, depending on the individual's needs and preferences.

- **Peer counseling.** It can be helpful for the person to work with someone with experience of a psychotic disorder who is trained to work with others with the disorder.

- **Social skills training.** This training is used to improve social and independent living skills.

- **Supported employment and education (SEE).** SEE services are an important part of coordinated specialty care and offer a way to help individuals return to work or school. A SEE specialist helps people develop the skills they need to achieve their personal school and work goals, further supporting their recovery.

- **Assertive community treatment (ACT).** ACT is an approach for people experiencing more severe, chronic, and persistent symptoms of psychotic disorders. The person's care is managed by a team of health professionals, such as a psychiatrist, nurse, psychologist, and social worker. Care is available 24 hours a day and is tailored to the person's individual needs. Support is provided to family members as well. ACT has been found to reduce relapse and the need for hospitalization.

- **Adult day treatment.** Adult day treatment is a program that provides social skills, training, group and individual counseling, medication evaluations, and occupational or vocational therapy for person in a structured daily program.

- **Partial hospitalization.** Partial hospitalization provides the comprehensive staffing and programming of inpatient hospitalization for people who are not at immediate risk of harm to self and others and who can go to a stable and supportive living environment at the end of the day.

- **Emergency psychiatric services.** Emergency psychiatric services provide immediate assessment, crisis counseling, and referral for people at immediate risk of harm to self or others. Often this service precedes admission to inpatient hospitalization, but most people who seek emergency psychiatric services stabilize and can return to their community setting after the evaluation.

- **Hospitalization.** A person experiencing severe psychosis may benefit from a short hospital stay in order to keep them safe, stabilize their symptoms, and help them connect to appropriate treatment options in the community.

People with psychotic disorders need a stable support network at home to prevent relapses. When family members are emotionally over-involved, critical, or hostile, the person has a higher likelihood of a relapse into psychosis (López et al., 2009). When this is an accepted communication style in a family, it can be harmful.

What if the person doesn't want help?

The person may refuse to seek help even if they realize they are unwell. Their confusion and fear about what is happening to them may lead them to deny that anything is wrong. Or they may refuse to seek help because they lack insight that they are unwell.

If the person's psychosis is severe, they are at risk of harming self or others, and they are unwilling to get help, then involuntary commitment (placing a person in a psychiatric hospital against their will) may be necessary. A person who is experiencing severe psychosis may require and benefit from a stay in the hospital to ensure safety and to enter or return to a recovery pathway.

States have different laws and procedures for involuntary commitment, but almost all would require that there be evidence that the person has a mental illness and is a danger to self or others or cannot take care of themselves.

If the person is not at risk of harming themselves or others, you should remain patient, as people experiencing psychosis often need time to develop insight regarding their illness. Remain friendly and open to the possibility that they may want your help in the future. You can encourage the person to talk to someone they trust.

ACTION E: Encourage Self-help and Other Support Strategies

The environment surrounding a person with schizophrenia or with another psychotic disorder is an important aspect of their recovery. Treatments may be more effective when they have stable housing and a meaningful role in society and when family members and friends are supportive.

Other people who can help

Try to determine whether the person has a supportive social network, and if they do, encourage them to use these supports.

Family and friends can help by:

- Listening to the person without judging or being critical.
- Checking if the person is feeling suicidal and taking immediate action if they are.
- Being aware of specific stressors that can trigger the exacerbation of symptoms — this can vary individual to individual.
- Encouraging the person to get appropriate treatment and support.
- Providing the same support as they would for a physically ill person — these might include sending get-well cards, flowers, phoning or visiting the person, and helping out if they feel they cannot manage.
- Learning about and/or having a supportive understanding about psychotic disorders.
- Looking for assistance from a support group.

Self-help strategies

Many people experiencing psychosis also have a depressive or anxiety disorder. Many of the self-help strategies recommended for depression and anxiety are also appropriate for people with psychosis. However, mental health professionals must be consulted.

Not all self-help strategies are suitable for all people with psychotic illnesses; for example, certain natural remedies may trigger mania in people with bipolar disorder, while exercise may be too stimulating during a manic period.

People experiencing psychosis should reduce stress and social demands. They should also avoid alcohol, cannabis, and other drugs. People sometimes take drugs as a way of coping with a developing psychotic illness, but these drugs can make the symptoms worse, initiate relapse, and make the disorder difficult to diagnose (Ouellet-Plamondon, Abdel-Baki, Salvat, & Potvin, 2017). For example, the use of cannabis can slow recovery (Harrison et al., 2008).

CHAPTER 9
EATING DISORDERS

AMY KERR, *I Am More*

While in the depths of depression, the phrase, "I am more than this," popped into my head, and a fully formed public art and writing project seemed to download into my brain: "I Am More." It combines my portraits in pastel and colored pencil with the writing of the portrait subject describing how they are more than their challenges. Subjects from ages 15 to 79 are pictured in the location of their choice and they describe how they are more than their depression, grief, PTSD, eating disorders, addiction, cancer diagnosis, and more.

CHAPTER 9: EATING DISORDERS

WHAT ARE EATING DISORDERS?

Eating disorders are illnesses in which people have severe disturbances in their eating behaviors and distorted thoughts and emotions about how their body looks or feels.

People with eating disorders typically become preoccupied with food and their body weight (NIMH, 2018). A person with an eating disorder can be underweight or overweight or fall within the healthy weight range.

Eating disorders are serious and potentially life-threatening illnesses. Many people with eating disorders may also have another mental disorder. Eating disorders are associated with a higher lifetime risk for suicide (NIMH, Nov 2017).

Eating disorders can go untreated because the people around the person with an eating disorder believe that willpower alone can change the course of the disorder. Or, they might believe that the eating disorder is about food, weight, and appearance rather than being a medical condition.

Most people with eating disorders have distress that causes significant disruption to their life. Yet many do not receive treatment.

Health professionals recognize a number of different types of eating disorders, including anorexia nervosa, bulimia nervosa, and binge eating disorder. This manual does not cover all types of eating disorders.

Disordered eating refers to dieting, fasting, and bingeing.

Prevalence Of Eating Disorders Among U.s. Adults

Eating disorders affect approximately 30 million people in the United States (20 million women and 10 million men) (Wade, Keski-Rahkonen, & Hudson, 2011).

Eating disorders are more common in women than men. They most often affect women between the ages of 12 and 35. Half the people with bulimia nervosa and anorexia nervosa first show signs of the disorders at age 18 (NIMH, Nov 2017).

Research shows that cultural stereotypes can affect whether a doctor diagnoses someone with an eating disorder. White women who show symptoms of an eating disorder are more quickly identified than women who are Black or Hispanic with the same symptoms, not just by their physicians (Becker et al., 2003), but also by their peers (Sala et al., 2013).

Latinx, Asians, Blacks, and Whites have around the same rates of eating disorders, although bulimia is more common in Blacks and Latinx than in Whites. Binge eating disorder appears at a higher rate in all minority groups than among Whites (Marques et al., 2011).

Lesbian, gay, bisexual, transgender, queer or questioning, or intersex (LGBTQI+) people face unique challenges that may put them at greater risk of developing an eating disorder. Research shows that beginning as early as age 12, gay, lesbian, and bisexual teens may be at higher risk of binge eating and purging than heterosexual peers.

Co-Occurring Mental Disorders

Eating disorders frequently co-occur with depression, anxiety disorders, and substance use disorders (NEDA, 2018a).

SIGNS AND SYMPTOMS OF AN EATING DISORDER

Some warning signs may be difficult to detect. This is because people with an eating disorder may feel shame, guilt, and distress about their eating or exercising behaviors, and they may hide these behaviors. They may find it difficult to ask for help from family and friends.

HOW AN EATING DISORDER AFFECTS THE WAY A PERSON WITH AN EATING DISORDER THINKS, FEELS, BEHAVES, AND APPEARS

Thoughts

- Preoccupation with food, body shape, and weight
- Rigid thinking (for example, labeling of food as either good or bad)
- Distorted body image (for example, complaining of being, feeling, or looking fat when actually at a healthy weight or underweight)

Emotions

- Extreme body dissatisfaction
- Heightened anxiety around mealtimes
- Depression, anxiety, or irritability
- Sensitivity to comments or criticism about exercise, food, body shape, or weight
- Low self-esteem (for example, negative opinions of self; feelings of shame, guilt, or self-loathing)

Behaviors

- Dieting behaviors (for example, fasting, counting calories or carbohydrates, adhering to the keto diet, and avoidance of food groups or types)
- Evidence of binge eating (for example, disappearance or hoarding of food)
- Evidence of deliberate vomiting or laxative use (purging), such as trips to the bathroom during or immediately after meals, or evidence of use of diuretics or enemas
- Excessive, obsessive, or ritualistic exercise patterns (for example, exercising when injured or in bad weather, over exercising, feeling compelled to perform a certain number of repetitions of exercises, or experiencing distress if unable to exercise)
- Changes in food preferences, such as refusing certain fatty or unhealthy foods, cutting out entire food groups such as meat or dairy, claiming to dislike foods previously enjoyed, a sudden concern with healthy eating, or replacing meals with fluids
- Development of rigid patterns around food selection, preparation, and eating (for example, cutting food into small pieces and eating very slowly)

HOW AN EATING DISORDER AFFECTS THE WAY A PERSON WITH AN EATING DISORDER THINKS, FEELS, BEHAVES, AND APPEARS

Behaviors

- Not eating meals, especially when in a social setting (for example, skipping meals by claiming to have already eaten or to have an intolerance or allergy to particular foods)
- Lying about the amount or type of food consumed or not answering questions about eating and weight
- Behaviors focused on body shape and weight, such as interest in weight-loss websites, books, and magazines or in images of thin people
- Development of repetitive or obsessive behaviors relating to body shape and weight (for example, body checking such as pinching waist or wrists, repeated weighing of self, and excessive time spent looking in mirrors)
- Social withdrawal or avoidance of previously enjoyed activities
- New dietary sensitivity (for example, going gluten free)
- Engaging in self-harm such as cutting

Appearance and Well-being

- Weight loss or noticeable weight fluctuations
- Sensitivity to cold or feeling cold most of the time, even in warm temperatures
- Changes in menstruation
- Changes in sleeping patterns
- Swelling around cheeks or jaw, calluses on knuckles, dental discoloration from vomiting, dental problems
- Fainting and/or dizziness
- Gastrointestinal complaints
- Difficulty concentrating
- Impaired immune system

Types Of Eating Disorders

Health professionals recognize several different types of eating disorders, including anorexia nervosa, bulimia nervosa, and binge eating disorder.

Anorexia nervosa

The main characteristics of anorexia nervosa (anorexia) are:

- Focusing on body shape and weight as the main measure of self-worth.
- Maintaining a very low body weight or failing to gain appropriate weight.
- Having an intense fear of gaining weight or becoming fat.

Extreme weight-loss strategies can include dieting; fasting; over exercising; using diet pills, diuretics, or laxatives; and vomiting. Diuretics increase the amount of water and salt expelled as urine.

Anorexia is not common. A national survey showed that less than 0.6 percent of people had experienced anorexia at some time in their life. Most people with anorexia are female (National Eating Disorders Association 2018). The disorder often starts in adolescence with dieting that becomes out of control.

For some people, the disorder is brief, but in others it can become a long-term health issue, and there is a risk of death. Ten percent of people with the disorder die of it (NEDA, 2018b).

People who get help early in the course of anorexia tend to have a better outcome.

Approximately one-third of people with anorexia got treatment specifically for their eating disorder (NIMH, Nov 2017).

Bulimia nervosa

A person may have bulimia nervosa if they have recurrent episodes of uncontrolled eating or eating unusually large amounts of food and feel a lack of control over the eating. This over-eating is followed by purging, fasting, and/or excessive exercising to make up for the binge (NIMH, Nov 2017).

Bulimia usually starts with dieting that becomes out of control, but bingeing prevents severe weight loss. A person with bulimia can be slightly underweight or overweight or fall within the healthy weight range.

The main characteristics of bulimia nervosa are:

- Judging self-worth by body shape or weight.

- Repeated episodes of uncontrolled overeating (binge eating) at least once a week for three months or more.

- Extreme weight control behavior, such as extreme dieting, frequent use of vomiting or laxatives to control weight, diuretic and enema abuse, or excessive exercise.

- Not meeting the characteristics and symptoms of anorexia nervosa (American Psychiatric Association, 2013).

Bulimia is more common than anorexia. A national survey of adults found that 1 percent had experienced bulimia at some time in their lives.

Females are more likely than males to develop bulimia. A national survey of young adult females found that 1 to 1.5 percent had bulimia nervosa in the previous year and 1 percent had it sometime in their life (Smink, van Hoeken, & Hoek, 2012).

People with bulimia are typically ashamed of their eating behaviors and attempt to conceal their symptoms. For this and other reasons, only a minority get treatment. A recent study showed that only 43.2 percent of those with bulimia nervosa got treatment specifically for their eating disorder (NIMH, Nov 2017).

Binge eating disorder

Binge eating disorder occurs when a person has regular episodes of eating an unusually large amount of food in a short period of time and continues to eat beyond the point of feeling comfortably full. They have a sense of having a lack of control during these binges. These binges occur at least once per week over three months or more.

The person with binge eating disorder may have a normal body weight or may be overweight or obese.

The person with binge eating disorder may have feelings of guilt, embarrassment, or disgust and may binge eat alone to hide the behavior (Smink, van Hoeken, & Hoek, 2012). They are generally quite distressed about their binge eating.

RISKS ASSOCIATED WITH EATING DISORDERS

Eating disorders have the highest rate of death of any mental disorder (Smink, van Hoeken, & Hoek, 2012).

The most common complications that lead to death are cardiac arrest and electrolyte and fluid imbalances.

Death by suicide can also result (Udo et al., 2018). One out of every five deaths for someone with anorexia nervosa is caused by suicide (Arcelus et al., 2011).

A person who has an eating disorder is at increased risk of a medical emergency, including potentially fatal complications such as organ failure, electrolyte imbalances, and bleeding in the digestive tract. This is due to malnutrition and other complications of the eating disorder.

Bulimia is less frequently a cause of death than anorexia; however, heart failure and death from other causes can occur in either disorder.

Serious health consequences associated with eating disorders include severe malnutrition, brain dysfunction, and heart or kidney failure.

Eating disorders increase the risk of nonsuicidal self-injury. People with eating disorders and people who engage in nonsuicidal self-injury report having overwhelming feelings (Suokas, et al., 2014). These feelings may be relieved in the moment by bingeing, purging, over-exercising, or by engaging in nonsuicidal self-injury.

Some eating disorders can lead to severe weight loss. Severe weight loss can cause hair and nails to grow brittle, skin to dry out and become yellow, and a covering of soft hair to develop. It can also cause the slowing of growth and delay of puberty. There can be muscle and cartilage deterioration, loss of bone density that may lead to osteoporosis and fractures, irregular or slow heartbeat, anemia, swollen joints, light-headedness, and fainting.

Repeated vomiting can cause tooth decay (because of the acid in vomit), a chronically inflamed and sore throat, severe dehydration, stomach and intestinal ulcers, and inflammation of the esophagus.

Because some people with eating disorders are overweight and obese, it is important to acknowledge the dangers of being overweight or obese. Being overweight and obese is associated with illness and premature death. In the long term, there is a risk of cardiovascular disease, type 2 diabetes, arthritis, and many other chronic illnesses.

RISK FACTORS FOR DEVELOPING AN EATING DISORDER (NEDA, 2018-D)

As with mental disorders, there is no single cause of eating disorders. A range of biological, psychological, and social factors may be contributing factors.

The following factors increase a person's risk of developing an eating disorder:

Biological

- Obesity (increases risk for bulimia and anorexia).
- Childhood obesity (increases risk for bulimia and anorexia).
- Early start of periods in girls (age 12 or younger increases risk for bulimia and anorexia).
- Family members with an eating disorder.
- Family members with other mental illnesses, such as depression, anxiety, or substance use disorders.

Psychological

- Dieting.

- Low self-esteem.

- Perfectionism.

- Anxiety.

- Temperament, including harm avoidance and low novelty seeking.

Social

- Conflict in the home; low contact with or high expectations held by parents or caregivers.

- Physical or emotional abuse or neglect; emotional abuse or emotional neglect; sexual abuse.

- Teasing or bullying, especially about weight.

- Family history of dieting.

- Parental obesity.

Trauma And Eating Disorders

An individual who experiences trauma has a higher risk of developing an eating disorder. In fact, according to the ACE Study, the risk increases for each additional adverse childhood experience.

A recent study indicate that rates of eating disorders are generally higher in people who have experienced trauma and PTSD (Mitchell et al. 2012). Approximately one in four people with an eating disorder has symptoms of PTSD.

Stigma Around Eating Disorders

People with an eating disorder are often ashamed to discuss their symptoms and issues related to eating or body image. They may not seek treatment and support because of their concern about what others will think.

Weight stigma, also known as weight bias, is discrimination or stereotyping based on a person's weight. Among overweight and obese adults, those who experience weight-based stigmatization engage in more frequent binge eating, are at increased risk for eating disorder symptoms, and are more likely to have a diagnosis of binge eating disorder (Tomiyama, 2014).

Weight stigma can increase dissatisfaction with one's body; this is a risk factor in the development of eating disorders. The idealization of thinness in the United States is a contributor to the development of eating disorders.

IMPORTANCE OF EARLY INTERVENTION

Eating disorders often start in adolescence. Early detection and treatment will help prevent the thoughts, feelings, and behaviors associated with eating disorders from becoming more entrenched.

Research has shown that the sooner treatment is started, the more likely the person is to recover (Fukutomi et al., 2020). If a young person gets to adulthood without treatment, recovery becomes more difficult. With anorexia, there is also a much higher risk of death.

THE MHFA ACTION PLAN FOR EATING DISORDERS

See Chapter 2: Mental Health First Aid to read about how to use ALGEE. In this section, we discuss each step briefly and add information about treatments for eating disorders.

ALGEE is a useful way to remember the steps of the action plan you can use to help a person with signs and symptoms of mental disorders. Not every step must be done, and they don't have to be done in order.

Before you approach the person, learn as much as you can about eating disorders. Do this by reading books, articles, and brochures or gathering information from a reliable source, such as an eating disorder support organization or a health professional specialist. Do not approach the person in situations that may lead them to become sensitive or defensive, such as when either of you is feeling angry, emotional, tired, frustrated, or is drinking, having a meal, or in a place surrounded by food.

Special Considerations for Eating Disorders in People with Developmental Disabilities

If you know the person's family, caregiver, or legal guardian, you may wish to first engage with them to talk about your concerns and see if they have noticed similar concerns. However, recall that you must ask the person whether it is okay to speak with the family member. If the person does not have the capacity to make their own health care treatment decisions, you will find out who is permitted to give consent for these decisions for the person.

If you are able to speak with the family, caregiver, or legal guardian, you might listen nonjudgmentally, provide reassurance and information, and then help them connect to professional help or other resources to get help for the person. The way that you engage with the person's family will depend on your role and relationship.

When navigating consent to care, it is important to consider the individual's capacity to make their own health care treatment decisions, known as decisional capacity. When adults with developmental disabilities have incomplete decisional capacity, consent is obtained from a surrogate (such as a family caregiver who serves as a legal guardian) and assent, uncoerced willingness to undergo treatment, from the individual.

If you are the parent or relative, you might be talking directly to your adult relative using the relevant ALGEE action steps. If the person appears to be at risk of self-harm and says that they intend to die, call 911 and do not leave the person alone.

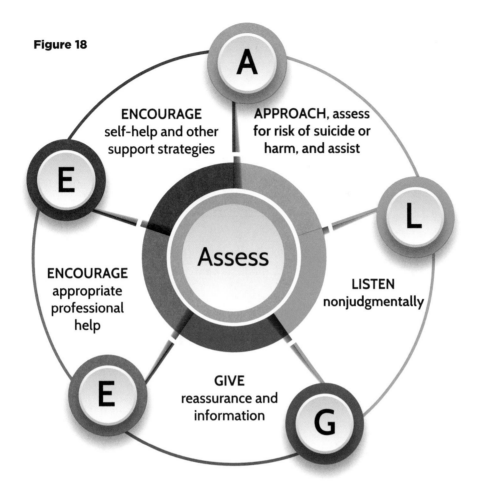

Figure 18

ACTION A: Assess for Risk of Suicide or Harm

The three main crises associated with eating disorders are:

- The person has a medical emergency.
- The person has suicidal thoughts.
- The person is engaging in nonsuicidal self-injury.

If you have concerns that the person may be having a medical emergency (which might include potentially fatal complications such as organ failure, electrolyte imbalances, and bleeding in the digestive tract), call 911.

Encourage the person to talk about their feelings, symptoms, and what is going on in their mind. Be alert for any of the warning signs of suicide. See Chapter 12: Suicide.

If you have concerns that the person may be having suicidal thoughts, call 911.

If the person you are helping is engaging in nonsuicidal self-injury and is also suicidal, call 911. Suicidal thoughts or behaviors are an emergency and must be considered as such.

If you have concerns that the person may be engaging in nonsuicidal self-injury but is not suicidal, see Chapter 11: Nonsuicidal Self-injury.

If you have no concerns that the person is in crisis, you may ask them how they are feeling and how long they have been feeling that way, then move on to Action L.

How to approach
It is common to feel nervous when approaching someone about their eating and exercising. Do not avoid talking to them because you fear it might make them angry or upset or make their issue worse. Speaking to the person may give them a sense of relief at having someone acknowledge their dilemmas, or they may find it helpful to know that someone cares about them and has noticed that they are not coping.

Initially, focus on displaying empathy and not on changing the person or their perspective. Try not to just focus on weight or food. Focus on the eating behaviors that are concerning you. Do not comment positively or negatively on the person's weight or appearance.

Allow the person to discuss other concerns that are not about food, weight, or exercise.

ACTION L: Listen Nonjudgmentally

Listen to the person's concerns. There may be issues in their life that need to be identified. They may discuss symptoms of depression and anxiety.

Understand that the person's behavior is related to their illness.

Be aware that you may find it tough to listen to what the person has to say, especially if you do not agree with what they are saying about themselves and food. Don't get drawn into a discussion about their appearance or weight or express disagreement with their beliefs.

ACTION G: Give Support and Information

Offer to get information about eating disorders and available help. Emphasize that a qualified professional is the best resource so they can get the right services.

If you become aware the person is visiting "pro-ana" or "pro-mia" websites (websites that promote anorexia and bulimia, respectively), discourage further visits, as the websites can encourage destructive behavior. Be aware, however, that it is important not to mention these sites if the person is not already aware of them.

Supporting a person who reacts negatively
Understand that the person may react negatively. If this happens, it is important not to take the reaction personally. There are many reasons a person may react negatively, including that they:

- Are not ready to make a change.
- Do not know how to change without losing their coping strategies.
- Have difficulty trusting others.
- Think you are being pushy, nosy, coercive, or bullying.
- Do not see their eating habits as an illness.

Try hard not to express disappointment or shock if the person responds with denial, anger, aggression, tears, or defensiveness. Resist the temptation to respond angrily, as this may escalate the situation. Instead, be willing to repeat your concerns and remind the person that even if they don't agree, your support is still offered, and they can come and talk with you again in the future if they want to.

ACTION E: Encourage Appropriate Professional Help

Eating disorders are complex mental disorders, and people experiencing them benefit from professional help.

Explain that you think their behavior may indicate there is a problem that needs professional attention. Offer to assist them in getting the help they need.

It is best to encourage the person to seek help from a professional with specific training in eating disorders. Treatment can be provided by the various professionals listed below:

Primary care physicians can diagnose an eating disorder, provide a physical check-up, give information on the physical health consequences of the disorder, refer to specialists, and link to community supports. Not all doctors are formally trained in detecting and treating eating disorders, so the person may need to see a specialist.

Psychiatrists, specialty-trained nurse practitioners, and other mental health professionals can help the person address psychological and behavioral components of the illness.

Nutritional counselors can provide education about nutritional needs, meal planning, and monitoring eating choices.

Successful treatment involves both physical and mental aspects; therefore, eating disorders are best treated by multidisciplinary teams, generally consisting of a primary care physician, a mental health professional, and a dietitian or nutritionist. Sometimes allied health professionals (such as occupational therapists and mental health nurses) who have specific training in managing eating disorders may also be involved.

Eating disorders are not always recognized by health professionals. It may take some time to get the right diagnosis and treatment. When the person sees a professional, it can help if they are told that the person may have an eating disorder.

Treatments available for eating disorders

Successful treatment involves medical and psychological components. Treatment is often long-term and intensive, depending on the severity of the eating disorder. The following treatments have shown evidence of effectiveness for eating disorders:

- **Anorexia.** There has been little research on which treatments work best. However, the first goal for any intervention and treatment is to ensure the person's physical health, which involves restoring the person to a healthy weight. Sometimes it is necessary to admit the person to a hospital when the weight loss is dangerous. There are no medications proven to work with anorexia.

- **Bulimia.** CBT is generally the most effective treatment. It aims to change eating habits and weight control behaviors, as well as the person's preoccupation with body shape and weight. Interpersonal psychotherapy (IPT) aims to help the person to identify and change interpersonal problems that contribute to an eating disorder. Antidepressants can also help with bulimia but are not as effective as CBT.

- **Binge eating disorder.** CBT is effective for binge eating disorder. Interpersonal psychotherapy and antidepressants can also help, but the evidence for their effectiveness is not as strong as the evidence for CBT.

What if the person doesn't want help?

People with an eating disorder may refuse professional help. Understand that the person may resist help for several reasons, including that they:

- Feel ashamed of their behavior.

- Fear gaining weight or fear losing control over their weight.

- Are afraid of acknowledging that they are unwell.

- Don't think they are ill.

- Believe that there are benefits to their disordered eating or exercising. For example, they might find that controlling their weight makes them feel better about themselves or gives them a sense of accomplishment.

Be sensitive toward the person's fears about seeking help. You may find it helpful to get advice from an organization that specializes in eating disorders on how to get a resistant person to professional help.

Eating disorders are long-term problems that are not easily overcome. Although you may feel frustrated by the person's behavior, do not threaten to end or alter your relationship with them, and don't give up on them. Instead, continue to be supportive while waiting for them to accept the need to change.

Being supportive includes encouraging their strengths and interests that are unrelated to food or physical appearance. Acknowledge the person's positive attributes, successes, and accomplishments.

ACTION E: Encourage Self-help and Other Support Strategies

Other people who can help

You can suggest that the person surround themselves with supportive people.

Some organizations that provide information and support for people with eating disorders are listed in Helpful Resources.

Self-help strategies

Self-help books based on CBT can help bulimia and binge-eating disorders (Linardon, et al., 2017. It is best to work through these books under the guidance of a therapist, but there is also benefit in using these books as self-help (Smolak, et al., 2013).

Encouraging appropriate professional help and self-help strategies are ways to help a person get to recovery and well-being. (See the Introduction to learn more about recovery and well-being.)

SUBSTANCE USE DISORDERS

CHAPTER 10: SUBSTANCE USE DISORDER

WHAT ARE SUBSTANCE USE DISORDERS AND ADDICTION?

Substance use disorders are problematic patterns of using alcohol or another substance that result in impairment in daily life or noticeable distress. Repeated use of and dependence on the substance will result in tolerance, withdrawal, and a pattern of compulsive use.

Substance use can have harmful effects on mental health; it can result in injury or accidental death or suicide. And substance use can develop into a substance-related disorder. Substance use disorders and substance-induced disorders (such as substance-induced psychosis) are dangerous.

Alcohol use disorder, sedative use disorder, opioid use disorder, and cannabis use disorder are examples of specific diagnoses in the DSM-5.

With young adults, the fact that substance use can harm the developing brain is a concern, because the brain is still developing until age 26.

Addiction is the most severe substance use disorder and is a medical illness caused by repeated misuse of a substance or substances.

National Institute on Drug Abuse defines addiction as "a brain disorder that occurs when repeated drug use leads to changes in the function of multiple brain circuits that control pleasures/reward, stress, decision-making, impulse control, learning and memory, and other functions. These changes make it harder for those with an addiction to experience pleasure in response to natural rewards — such as food, sex, or positive social interactions — or to manage their stress, control their impulses, and make the healthy choice to stop drug seeking and use."

Well-supported scientific evidence shows that addiction to alcohol or drugs is a chronic brain disease with a course that includes relapse and potential for recovery (Kelly, Saitz, & Wakeman, 2016).

Substance use disorders and addiction are treatable. Research-based treatments help people stop using alcohol and other drugs and resume productive lives, also known as being in recovery.

Yet many people with substance use disorders do not receive any treatment. Among young adults who need treatment, 92.3 percent did not receive treatment at a specialty facility in the past year. Among adults ages 26 or older who need treatment, 87.7 percent did not receive treatment at a specialty facility in the past year. These statistics do not include individuals who go directly to support groups (Lipari, Park-Lee, & Van Horn, 2016).

When Do Substance Disorders Begin?

Substance use usually begins in adolescence or early adulthood. Seventy-five percent of those with substance use disorder develop it by age 27.

What Substances Do People Use And How Does Addiction Start?

Substance use disorders occur with legal and illegal substances.

Legal substances include alcohol, nicotine, and prescribed medications. When prescription medicines used to treat illness or pain are used in higher doses or for longer periods than prescribed, a substance use disorder can result.

Illegal drugs include heroin, fentanyl, prescription medications obtained by means other than a prescription, and several others discussed below (Grant et al., 2010).

People vary in how much of a substance (including alcohol or other drugs) they need to use to get the desired effect. And over time, the person needs to use increasing amounts to get the desired effect, or they get less effect with the same amount of the substance. This is called increased tolerance. When they use increasing amounts, overdose is more likely.

Frequent and increasingly heavy alcohol use can result in dependence, so that when drinking is abruptly halted, the person shows evidence of withdrawal and is at risk of physical harm.

Is It A Substance Use Disorder?

Not all use of alcohol or other drugs becomes a problem. And when a person develops a tolerance to a medication their doctor has prescribed, this does not mean a person has a substance use disorder. Similarly, if they experience withdrawal from a medication their doctor has prescribed, this does not mean they have a substance use disorder.

When you see that someone has had repeated problems (legal problems, relationship problems, or other) resulting from episodes of drinking or using substances, consider that it could be a substance use disorder.

PREVALENCE OF SUBSTANCE USE DISORDERS

In 2018 in the United States, approximately 20.3 million people ages 12 or older had a substance use disorder in the past year.

Of these 20.3 million people with a substance use disorder in the past year:

- 14.8 million had an alcohol use disorder.
- 8.1 million had an illicit drug use disorder.

The most common illicit drug use disorder was marijuana use disorder (4.4 million people).

An estimated 2 million people had an opioid use disorder, which includes 1.7 million people with a prescription pain reliever use disorder and 500,000 people with a heroin use disorder.

The rate of substance use disorders in 2018 was similar to what was seen from 2015 to 2017. But the rates of pain reliever use disorder, opioid use disorder, and alcohol use disorder were lower in 2018 than in 2015.

Co-Occurring Mental Health And Substance Use Disorders

Many people with substance use disorders have co-occurring mental health challenges.

Of the 18.3 percent of adults ages 18 or older with a mental illness (approximately 44.7 million adults), 3.4 percent (8.2 million adults) have both a substance use disorder and a mental illness (Hartz et al., 2014).

One reason is that many people use alcohol or other drugs to try to reduce symptoms of anxiety, depression, or psychosis, sometimes called "self-medication," even though it rarely is effective and rarely works for long.

For those whose substance use disorder developed before age 26, the odds of developing a mood disorder increase (Lai et al., 2015).

Impact Of Substance Use Disorders

Among the potential consequences of substance use disorders are:

- **Death from motor vehicle crashes.** Alcohol is a factor in 28 percent of all deaths from motor vehicle crashes in the United States. In 2016, 10,497 people died in alcohol-impaired driving crashes (CDC, 2016).

- **Physical injuries.** These can result when people drive while intoxicated or high, get into a car with an intoxicated driver, do dangerous stunts, get into fights, or take other risks.

- **Aggression and antisocial behavior,** such as getting into fights or engaging in criminal activity, including vandalism or theft.

- **Legal trouble.**

- **Sexual risk taking.** People may consent to sexual activity that they would not agree to while sober. They are more likely to engage in unsafe sex or sex with multiple partners while affected by substances. Unwanted pregnancy or sexually transmitted infections can result.

- **Being a victim of crime.** While affected by alcohol and other drugs, a person is at increased risk of being a victim of violent crime, including physical or sexual assault. They are more susceptible to date rape.

- **Suicide and self-injury.** When intoxicated or high, people are more likely to act on suicidal thoughts or to injure themselves. This is because most illicit substances increase feelings of anxiety, depression, and anger; reduce the fear of pain; reduce inhibitions; and cause people not to use more effective coping strategies (Pompili, et al., 2010).

- **Long-term negative effects** on physical health, relationships, educational and financial status, and job prospects.

SIGNS AND SYMPTOMS OF A SUBSTANCE USE DISORDER

The table shows how a substance use disorder affects the way a person thinks, feels, behaves, and appears. When substance use becomes more frequent, the signs may become more noticeable over time.

HOW A SUBSTANCE USE DISORDER AFFECTS THE WAY A PERSON THINKS, FEELS, BEHAVES, AND APPEARS

Thoughts

- Constantly thinking about the substance
- Difficulty concentrating or focusing
- Forgetting things
- Continued use despite knowing that they have a mental or physical health challenge caused by the substance

Emotions

- Frequent craving (a strong urge) to use the substance
- Desire to cut down use but difficulty doing so
- Guilt or remorse about actions taken to get the substance or while on the substance
- Mood swings

Behaviors

- Spending an increasing amount of time seeking, obtaining, or using the substance or recovering from its effects
- Taking the substance in larger amounts or for a longer period than intended
- Neglecting important duties at work, school, or in the home
- Arguing or fighting and/or trouble with law enforcement
- Using substances in situations where it is physically hazardous, like driving a car, boating, swimming, or using machinery
- If actively using the substance, showing physical signs of intoxication

Appearance and Well-being

- Glazed or bloodshot eyes
- Dilated or constricted pupils
- Noticeable changes in weight
- Increased tolerance for the substance
- If they have developed a dependence over time and then stopped using in the past 12–36 hours, they will show signs of physical withdrawal and some psychological signs related to craving (anxiety, irritability, fatigue, nausea/vomiting, hand tremor, or, in the case of alcohol, seizure)
- Disrupted sleep cycles, with periods of too much or too little sleep

COMMONLY MISUSED SUBSTANCES

Figure 19 shows substance use disorders in the United States and how often with occur in a single year.

Alcohol

People use alcohol in part because in small quantities, it causes them to relax and lower their inhibitions. They may feel more confident and act more extroverted.

When people say that someone who is arrested for drunk driving "blew a .08," they are referring to the legal limit of alcohol consumption as measured by blood alcohol concentration. Blood alcohol concentration is the percentage of alcohol in a person's blood stream measured in grams of alcohol per 100 milliliters of blood.

For adults, the legal limit of alcohol is 0.08 percent. With a blood alcohol concentration of 0.08 percent or above, users have:

- Poor muscle coordination.
- Loss of balance.
- Slower reaction time.
- Slurred speech.
- Difficulty in detecting danger.
- Impaired judgment and concentration.
- Impaired memory.

Figure 19

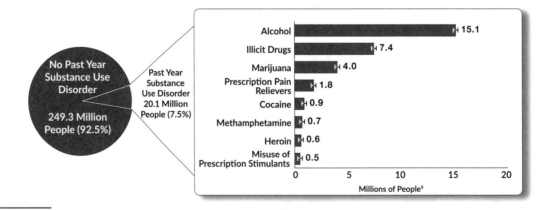

Number of People Aged 12 or Older with a Substance Use Disorder During the Past Year: 2016 (SAMHSA)[8]

[8] Estimated numbers of people refer to people aged 12 or older in the civilian, noninstitutionalized population in the United States. The numbers do not sum to the total population of the United States because the population for the National Survey on Drug Use and Health (NSDUH) does not include people under 12; people with no fixed household address, for example, homeless or transient people not in shelters; activea-duty military personnel; and residents of institutional group quarters, such as correctional facilities, nursing homes, mental institutions, and long-term care hospitals (Center for Behavioral Health Statistics and Quality, 2017).

[9] The estimated numbers of people with substance use disorders are not mutually exclusive because people can have use disorders for more than one substance.

Contrary to popular belief, it is the amount of alcohol present in the bloodstream that affects a person's ability to function, not the type of alcoholic drink consumed.

If a person is feeling suicidal, they are more likely to attempt suicide when under the influence of alcohol. In fact, as compared with other drugs, opioids and alcohol bring the greatest risks of suicidal behavior.

Alcohol can:

- Intensify feelings of anxiety, depression, and anger.

- Inhibit the use of effective coping strategies.

- Make a person more likely to act on suicidal and self-injury feelings.

Those who use alcohol over the long term are more likely to have diseases of the liver and pancreas, cardiovascular diseases, certain cancers, diabetes, neuropsychiatric disorders, and infectious diseases (because of alcohol's effects on the immune system and a harsher disease course).

With heavy and prolonged use, alcohol can cause family conflict, unemployment, dropping out of school, and social isolation (Darvishi et al., 2015).

People who suffer from anxiety or depressive disorders and drink heavily can show rapid improvement in their mood when they cut out alcohol.

Opioid Drugs

Opioids are a class of molecule that can bind to receptors on the brain and throughout the body. Opioid binding results in a number of effects: decreased pain, decreased respiratory rate, and cough suppression are some of the most notable. Opioid binding also results in a pleasurable feeling.

Opioids come from a variety of sources. The human body produces natural opioids called endorphins that are important for normal functioning.

Opioid drugs include the illicit drugs heroin and opium, as well as methadone, buprenorphine, and prescription pain relievers oxycodone, hydrocodone, hydromorphone, and morphine. Hydrocodone products, for example, are commonly prescribed in the United States for relief from dental pain and pain from injuries.

Synthetic opioids are for pain relief. They mimic naturally occurring opioids such as codeine and morphine. Fentanyl and carfentanyl are synthetic opioids. In 2017, more than 28,000 deaths involving synthetic opioids (other than methadone) occurred in the United States, which is more deaths than from any other type of opioid.

Side effects of opioids include constipation, nausea, and drowsiness. With an overdose, the person stops breathing.

A drug that can save a life in the case of opioid overdose is naloxone. First Aiders who know someone with signs of opioid disorder should have naloxone on hand. We discuss naloxone and the importance of having it at all times to respond to an opioid overdose in Chapter 13: First Aid for Mental Health Crises.

Intentional suicide and death by accidental overdose are grave dangers for people with opioid disorder. One study found that opiates were present in 20 percent of suicide deaths.
When a person takes too much of an opioid, they can experience depressed or slowed breathing, confusion, lack of oxygen to the brain, and death.

Opioid overdoses may happen in several ways. Some of those ways are:

- When alcohol or sedatives are present.

- When a combination of prescription opioids is present.

- In instances of recreational drug use.

- When a person accidentally or intentionally takes too much of their prescription medication.

- When a person mixes certain types of prescribed medicines, especially medicines that are used to treat anxiety.

- After a person stops taking opioids, but then takes them again and uses the dose they had been accustomed to taking.

Trends In Opioid Use

In the late 1990s, health care providers began to prescribe opioid pain relievers to treat chronic, non-cancer pain. This was done despite a lack of evidence about the long-term effects of opioids, particularly regarding the risk of addiction, misuse, and overdose. Opioids have been prescribed at higher rates over the past 15 years for treatment of moderate to severe pain (NIDA, 2018). Unfortunately, drug misuse and addiction have risen over this period.

Every day, more than 172 Americans die after overdosing on opioids, averaging seven people per hour. Between 2011 and 2015, overdose deaths in the United States from opioids tripled (Hedegaard, Warner, & Miniño, 2017).

Heroin, chemically similar to prescribed opioids, is an example of an illicit drug that is an opioid. Four out of five new heroin users started by misusing prescription drugs (Jones, 2013). In a 2014 survey of people in treatment for opioid addiction, 94 percent of respondents said they use heroin because prescription opioids were "far more expensive and harder to obtain" (Cicero, Ellis, & Surratt, 2014).

Most people who become dependent on opioids experience secondary effects of use, such as losing their job and criminal behavior.

When someone stops taking an opioid, they can experience withdrawal. Symptoms of opioid withdrawal are similar to the flu: chills, nausea, vomiting, diarrhea, and muscle aches. Withdrawal can cause significant impairment and distress. Even after withdrawal symptoms have subsided, individuals who took opioids for a long period of time can experience increased sensitivity to pain that can last much longer.

Stimulants Such As Amphetamine, Methamphetamine, Mdma (Ecstasy), And Cocaine

Stimulants increase a person's alertness, attention, and energy and also increase blood pressure, heart rate, and respiration. Stimulants cause increased activity in the body. Some impacts of stimulants are listed:

- As the effect of a stimulant wears off, a person may experience a range of problems, including depression, irritability, agitation, craving, increased appetite, and sleepiness.

- High doses of amphetamine use can lead to aggression, intense anxiety, paranoia, and psychotic symptoms.

- Withdrawal symptoms can include temporary depression.

Types Of Stimulants

Amphetamines (including methamphetamine)

Amphetamines are stimulant drugs. Amphetamines come in many shapes and forms and are taken in many ways. They can be in the form of powder, tablets, capsules, crystals, or liquid.

As the effect of amphetamines wears off, a user may experience depression, irritability, agitation, increased appetite, or sleepiness. High doses of amphetamine can lead to substance-induced psychosis. With substance-induced psychosis, the person may experience aggression, intense anxiety, paranoia, delusions, and hallucinations. They may recover as the drug wears off, but they may have substance-induced psychosis if the drug is used again. Withdrawal symptoms can include temporary depression.

Some types of amphetamines are prescribed for attention-deficit/hyperactivity disorder (ADHD) and a few other medical conditions, such as depression in the elderly. People may obtain these medications and use them for the effects (for example, in hopes of improving their performance at work or school). These types of amphetamines cause some of the same substance use disorder problems as other stimulants.

Amphetamine psychosis, also called speed psychosis, is a symptom of stimulant use. The person may experience hallucinations, delusions, and uncontrolled violent behavior. The person will recover as the drug wears off but is vulnerable to further episodes of substance-induced psychosis if the drug is used again.

Methamphetamine

Methamphetamine (also called meth, crystal meth, or crystal) is a white, odorless, bitter-tasting crystalline powder that easily dissolves in water or alcohol and is taken by mouth, through the nose, by needle injection, or by smoking (NIDA, 2010).

Methamphetamine has a chemical structure similar to that of amphetamine, but it has stronger effects on the brain. The effects of methamphetamine can last six to eight hours. After the initial rush, the person may be in a state of agitation, which can sometimes lead to violent behavior.

Methamphetamine use is a significant threat to public safety. Methamphetamine use is associated with domestic violence, assault, child abuse and neglect, burglaries, and violent behavior.

Cocaine

Cocaine is a highly addictive stimulant drug. Cocaine produces very strong euphoria.

Cocaine is a white powder referred to on the street as coke, C, snowflake, and blow. The act of consuming cocaine is called doing bumps, doing lines, or skiing.

After using it even for a short time, people can develop a need for increased amounts of cocaine for the effects they once experienced, as well as withdrawal symptoms when they cannot use it.

With long-term use, mental health challenges can develop, such as paranoia, aggression, anxiety, and depression. Some people have a genetic makeup that makes them more likely to have mental health challenges, and using cocaine is particularly risky for them. Cocaine can also cause substance-induced psychosis.

A 2016 national survey showed that 0.7 percent of people ages 12 or older used cocaine in the past month (SAMHSA, 2014).

Hallucinogens

Hallucinogens are drugs that affect a person's perceptions of reality. Some hallucinogens also produce rapid, intense emotional changes.

A particular problem associated with hallucinogens is flashbacks, during which users re-experience some of the perceptual effects of the drug without using it. Some hallucinogens are LSD, which has the street name acid; hallucinogenic mushrooms; and DMT.

MDMA (ecstasy)

Methylenedioxymethamphetamine (MDMA) is a stimulant drug that has hallucinogenic properties. MDMA is commonly known as ecstasy or molly. MDMA appears in capsule, tablet, or powder form.

Ecstasy is commonly mixed with other substances. This means that users do not know how much they will need to get the effect they want. The amount of pure MDMA and other chemicals varies greatly across products.

The effects of MDMA can last between three and six hours. Users report that they feel emotionally close to others when using MDMA. Some young people use it at dance parties.

When coming off ecstasy, users often experience depressed mood.

The National Institute of Drug Abuse reports that while using MDMA, a person may feel:

- Increased energy.
- Increased heart rate and blood pressure.
- Changes in mood, appetite, and other biological functions.
- Nausea.
- Muscle cramping.
- Involuntary teeth clenching.
- Blurred vision.
- Chills.
- Sweating.

Overheating or dehydration can occur with ecstasy unless the person drinks enough water.

The long-term effects of using ecstasy are of particular concern. Research shows that these effects include:

- Arrythmia (irregular heartbeat) and heart damage.
- Irritability.
- Depression.
- Impulsivity.
- Impaired attention and memory.
- Anxiety.
- Aggression.
- Sleep disturbances.
- Concentration difficulties.
- Lack of appetite.
- Heart disease.
- Decreased cognitive function.

Cannabis (Marijuana)

Cannabis is a mind-altering drug. Cannabis comes from the dried leaves, stems, seeds, and flowers of the hemp plant. Cannabis has many other names, such as marijuana, flower, bud, pot, herb, weed, grass, ganja, and chronic. It can be smoked, vaped (using devices called vape pens that use cartridges), or consumed by ingestion (edibles). Vaping uses battery-powered vaporizers that simulate the action and sensation of smoking. Vaping cannabis does not cause an odor of cannabis. Vaporizers are also known as vapes, e-cigs, e-hookahs, e-pipes, tanks, and mods.

Cannabis is by far the most commonly used drug in the United States.

Cannabis is considered a Schedule IV drug, meaning that there are no legitimate medical uses for the drug. However, as of 2019, 33 states and the District of Columbia have legalized cannabis use for medical purposes. Twelve states have legalized it for recreational use for adults 21 years and older (Berke & Gould, 2019).

Use of cannabis can interfere with motivation and intellectual performance at work or at school. It interferes with concentration and may lead to increased risk of accidents if used while driving.

SAMHSA reports that the overall percentage of people who report being current cannabis users in 2016 was higher than percentages from 2002 to 2015.

Impact of cannabis use on mental health

Cannabis use is associated with mental health challenges. People who use cannabis are more likely to have a mood disorder.

Synthetic cannabis

Synthetic cannabis, known on the street as spice or K2, is made of manmade chemicals. It can be toxic. CDC states that "These seemingly innocent little packages of 'fake weed' can cause serious side effects that are very different from those of marijuana." Users can experience rapid heart rate, vomiting, agitation, confusion, and hallucinations and may require emergency care or intensive care.

Tobacco

People who have mental health challenges have a higher rate of tobacco use than people without mental health challenges. Nearly a third of adults with any mental illness report using tobacco, compared to a quarter of adults without mental illness (Lipari & Van Horn, 2017)

People with mental illness may use tobacco as a coping mechanism to deal with mental health challenges. Nicotine has mood-altering effects that can temporarily relieve symptoms of mental illness. For some people, tobacco products are more affordable in the short-term than care for their mental health challenges.

In this section, we discuss two methods that people use to consume tobacco: e-cigarettes and smoking.

E-Cigarettes (Vaping)

The act of using an e-cigarette is called vaping. Brand names such as Juul are popular ("juuling").

Nearly all e-cigarettes contain nicotine.

Nicotine e-cigarettes cause serious health problems. These can be immediate and long term. With daily nicotine e-cigarette use, a person can expect to experience:

- Coughing.
- Shortness of breath.
- Frequent headaches.
- Increased phlegm production.
- Respiratory illnesses.
- Worse cold and flu symptoms than non-vapers.
- Reduced physical fitness.
- Physical addiction to nicotine.

According to the CDC, about 3.7 percent of adults use e-cigarettes every day or some days.

Men and women use e-cigarettes at about the same rate (Schoenborn & Gindi, 2014).

To researchers, one important question to ask about vaping is whether it affects the rate of smoking. Another is whether non-smokers take up vaping. In one study, researchers compared two groups who had tried vaping nicotine at least once — non-smokers ages 18–24 and non-smokers 25 and over. The results were alarming. The non-smokers ages 18–24 tried vaping nicotine at a much higher rate — 10 percent of them had, compared to 4 percent for the non-smokers ages 25 and over (Schoenborn & Gindi, 2014). See Figure 20.

Figure 20

IS VAPING APPEALING TO NON-SMOKERS? One study showed that it is. Non-smokers ages 25+ 4% had tried vaping. Non-smokers ages 18-24 10% had tried vaping. (Schoenborn & Gindi, 2014)

Smoking

Cigarette smoking causes serious health problems, both immediate and long term. With daily cigarette smoking, a person can expect to experience:

- Coughing.
- Shortness of breath.
- Frequent headaches.
- Increased phlegm production.
- Respiratory illnesses.

- Worse cold and flu symptoms than non-smokers
- Reduced physical fitness.
- Physical addiction to nicotine.

Long-term serious health problems include:
- Early heart disease.
- Significantly increased risk for stroke and transient ischemic attack.
- Oral decay, gum disease, and tooth loss.
- Chronic lung diseases such as chronic obstructive pulmonary disease (COPD) and emphysema.
- Vision problems and hearing loss.

Caffeine

Use of caffeine does not qualify as a substance whose excessive use can become a disorder. Caffeine is in coffee, teas, and energy drinks. It is mentioned because it can cause a form of intoxication and withdrawal symptoms.

RISK FACTORS FOR SUBSTANCE USE DISORDERS (CENTER ON ADDICTION, 2017)

The likelihood of developing an addiction differs from person to person, and no single factor determines whether a person will become addicted to alcohol or other drugs. In general, the more risk factors a person has, the greater the chance that taking drugs will lead to drug use and addiction.

The following are risk factors for substance use disorders:
- Genetic predisposition.
- Certain brain characteristics that can make someone more vulnerable to addictive substances than the average person.
- Psychological factors such as stress, personality traits like high impulsivity or sensation seeking, depression, anxiety, eating disorders, personality disorders, and other mental disorders.
- Environmental influences such as:
  ◦ Exposure to physical, sexual, or emotional abuse or trauma.
  ◦ Substance use or addiction in the family or among peers.
  ◦ Access to an addictive substance.
  ◦ Attitudes toward substance use and its dangers.
  ◦ Exposure to popular culture references that encourage substance use.
- Starting alcohol or other drug use or nicotine use at an early age.
- Deviant peer relationships, peer pressure and popularity, bullying, and affiliation with gangs (Whitesell et al. 2013).

Protective Factors

Research suggests that specific protective factors can reduce the risk of developing a substance use disorder. First Aiders can encourage specific resources and types of supports to increase the protective factors a person has in their life. These include:
- Having a good social support system.
- Positive self-talk.

- Having good, problem-focused coping skills.
- High self-esteem.
- Emotional well-being, which may include receiving effective treatment for another mental illness or emotional problems.
- Community bonding.
- Community-sponsored substance use prevention efforts and programs.
- Availability of positive things to do for fun.
- Reinforcement for positive social involvement.
- No tobacco and no other substance use in their family.
- Regular work or school attendance.

Having a supportive, connected family, including an extended family network, is also a protective factor.

Risk Factors For Alcohol Use Disorder

There are many factors that increase a person's chances of developing alcohol use disorder (Yang et al., 2018). These include:

- **Availability and tolerance of alcohol in society.** Where alcohol is readily available and socially acceptable, alcohol use disorders are more likely to develop. This applies not only to society, but also to social groups within a society.
- **Alcohol use in the family.** People who grow up in families where alcohol use is acceptable, where parents model use of alcohol and alcohol is readily available, are more likely to develop an alcohol use disorder.
- **Social factors.** Certain groups are more prone to alcohol use disorders, including men, people with low education and income, people who have had a relationship breakup, and certain occupations with a drinking culture.
- **Genetics.** People who have a biological parent with an alcohol use disorder are more likely to develop the disorder, even if adopted into a family with no alcohol use disorder.
- **Alcohol sensitivity.** Some people are physiologically less sensitive to the effects of alcohol than others, and these people are more likely to drink heavily and develop an alcohol use disorder.
- **Enjoyment from drinking.** People can learn a habit of heavy drinking. This habit is maintained because alcohol has been associated with pleasant effects or a reduction of stress.
- **Other mental illnesses.** People who have other mental health challenges may use alcohol because they believe it is helpful for these issues. But what might work in the short term may cause serious harm in the long term.

Risk Factors For Substance-Related Disorders

A risk factor is something that increases the chances of a person being less able to cope with daily activities and lead to substance use. Examples of individual factors that may put someone at risk for developing a substance use disorder include:

- **Genetics.** 40 to 60 percent of an individual's chance of developing a substance use disorder is based on genetics (NIDA, 2010). External influences such as stress, trauma, or other substances may also alter an individual's genetics.
- **Alcohol or drug sensitivity.** Some people are initially physiologically less sensitive to the effects of alcohol than others, and these people are more likely to drink heavily and develop an alcohol use

disorder. Other people report that they knew from their first taste of alcohol or their first use of an opioid that they were "hooked."

- **Environmental factors.** External factors such as stress, trauma, and childhood trauma may increase a risk for substance use disorders and mental illness (Khoury et al., 2010).

Risk Factors For Co-Occurring Substance Use Disorder And Mental Illness

There are three possible explanations for the fact that some people have both substance use disorder and mental illness.

First of all, a person with risk factors for both mental illness and substance use disorder may develop both. Secondly, mental illness can lead to substance use and addiction. And thirdly, substance use and addiction can lead to the development of mental illness.

Trauma And Substance Use

Consider the following facts about trauma and substance use disorders:

- Up to 59 percent of abuse and/or violent trauma survivors develop substance misuse issues (Khoury et al., 2010).
- Traumatic experiences that occur in childhood lead to an increased risk of substance use disorders (Khoury et al., 2010).
- Survivors of accidents, illness, or natural disasters have 10 to 33 percent higher rates of addiction.
- A diagnosis of PTSD increases the risk of developing alcohol misuse.
- Female trauma survivors face increased risk for an alcohol use disorder.
- Male and female sexual abuse survivors experience a higher rate of addiction.
- The more adverse childhood experiences, the more likely the individual will use tobacco as an adult.

Stigma Around Substance Use Disorders

Stigma and shame can lead people to hide their struggles with substances and delay seeking help.

Better understanding of substance use disorders can reduce stigma and discrimination. Addiction is a chronic brain disorder. It is not a moral failing, irresponsibility, or pleasure seeking. For some people, addiction occurred when the person was trying (through substances) to manage distress associated with traumatic life events.

Substance Use And Incarceration

Rates of incarceration for drug-related crimes vary across races. Black people are more than 2.7 to 6 times as likely as White people to be incarcerated for drug related crimes, despite similar rates of drug sales and substance use (The Hamilton Project, 2016).

See Chapter 2: Mental Health First Aid for more information about culture and mental disorders.

IMPORTANCE OF EARLY INTERVENTION FOR SUBSTANCE USE DISORDERS

It is easier for someone to recover from a substance use disorder if it is treated early.

Intervening quickly regarding alcohol and drugs also reduces the possibility of serious problems such as death from a motor vehicle crash, physical injuries, aggression, and more.

THE MHFA ACTION PLAN FOR SUBSTANCE USE DISORDERS

See Chapter 2: Mental Health First Aid to read about how to use ALGEE. In this section, we discuss each step briefly and add information about treatments for the most prevalent type of substance use disorder in the United States: alcohol use disorder (SAMHSA, 2017). The information can be generalized to help people with problems with other substances.

ALGEE is a useful way to remember the steps of the action plan you can use to help a person with signs and symptoms of mental disorders. Not every step must be done, and they don't have to be done in order.

Special Considerations for Substance Use Disorders in People with Developmental Disabilities

If you know the person's family, caregiver, or legal guardian, you may wish to first engage with them to talk about your concerns and see if they have noticed similar concerns. However, recall that you must ask the person whether it is okay to speak with the family member. If the person does not have the capacity to make their own health care treatment decisions, find out who is permitted to give consent for these decisions for the person.

If you are able to speak with the family, caregiver, or legal guardian, you might listen nonjudgmentally, provide reassurance and information, and then help them connect to professional help or other resources to get help for the person. The way that you engage with the person's family will depend on your role and relationship.

When navigating consent to care, it is important to consider the individual's capacity to make their own health care treatment decisions, known as decisional capacity. When adults with developmental disabilities have incomplete decisional capacity, consent is obtained from a surrogate (such as a family caregiver who serves as a legal guardian) and assent, uncoerced willingness to undergo treatment, from the individual.

If you are the parent or relative, you might be talking directly to your adult relative using the relevant ALGEE action steps. If the person appears to be at risk of self-harm and says that they intend to die, call 911 and do not leave the person alone.

Figure 21

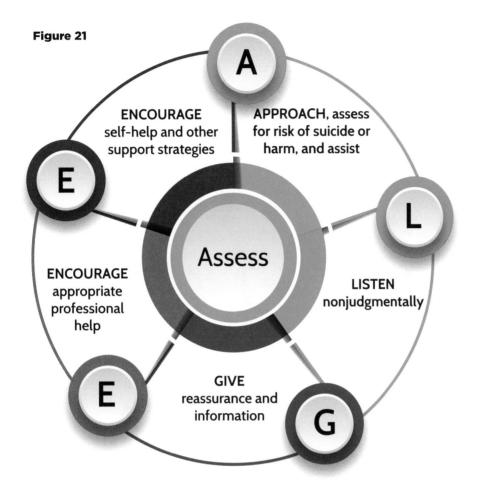

If the person is under the influence of alcohol or other drugs or showing signs of physical withdrawal, first ensure their physical well-being. After they are safe and not under the influence of alcohol or drugs, you can discuss treatment, educate them about substance use disorders, or discuss their history.

ACTION A: Assess for Risk of Suicide or Harm

Have the phone number for alcohol and other drug helplines and perhaps the address of a reputable website with you to offer them (see the Helpful Resources section).

Look for indications that the person may be in crisis. If you have concerns that the person may be having suicidal thoughts, call 911.

If the person you are helping is engaging in nonsuicidal self-injury and is also suicidal, call 911. Suicidal thoughts or behaviors are an emergency and must be considered as such.

If you have concerns that the person may be engaging in nonsuicidal self-injury but is not suicidal, see Chapter 11: Nonsuicidal Self-injury.

If the person has overdosed or you suspect alcohol poisoning or severe withdrawal, call 911. See Chapter 13: First Aid for Mental Health Crises, Mental Health First Aid for Severe Effects from Alcohol Use.

If the person has severe effects from alcohol or drug intoxication, overheating, or dehydration, or is aggressive, agitated, has bizarre behavior, or is psychotic, see Chapter 13: First Aid for Mental Health Crises.

If there is no crisis, and the person appears to be under the influence of alcohol or drugs, ask them if they are intoxicated. If they are under the influence, tell them you want to postpone the discussion. Make sure they will not drive or do any other unsafe activity.

If there is no crisis and the person is not intoxicated, let them know that you are concerned and willing to help. Consider the following:

- **The person's own perception of their substance use.** Ask them about their substance use (for example, about how much of the substance they are using and how often) and if they are aware of any consequences.

- **The person's readiness to talk.** Ask about areas of their life that the substance use may be affecting, for example, their mood, work performance, and relationships. Be aware that the person may deny or might not recognize or be willing to accept that they have a substance use problem. Trying to force the person to admit they have a problem may cause conflict.

- **Use "I" statements.** Express your point of view by using "I" statements, for example, "I am concerned about how much you've been drinking lately" rather than "you"' statements such as "You have been drinking too much lately." Provide specific examples of the consequences of substance use, such as missing work, arguments with a spouse or loved one, or incidents of violence.

- **Rate the act, not the person.** Identify and discuss the person's behavior and do not criticize their character. For example, you might say, "Your drug use seems to be getting in the way of your friendships" rather than "You're a druggie."

- **The person's recall of events.** Bear in mind that events that occurred while they were using may not be easy for the person to recall or to recall accurately.

- **Stick to the point.** Focus on the person's substance use and do not get drawn into arguments or discussion about other issues.

ACTION L: Listen Nonjudgmentally

This conversation might be the first time the person has thought about their substance use as a problem. Here are some specific points that apply to talking with someone with a potential substance use disorder.

- Treat the person with respect and dignity.

- Do not threaten, confront, or lecture them.

- Listen to the person without judging them as bad or immoral.

- Do not express moral judgments about their substance use.

- Do not label the person. For example, don't call them a "druggie" or "alcoholic."

- Try not to express your frustration at the person for having a substance use problem.

Chapter 2: Mental Health First Aid offers additional tips on nonjudgmental listening.

ACTION G: Give Support and Information

Ask the person if they would like information about substance use disorders and any associated risks. If they agree, provide them with relevant information.

Find out if they have received treatment in the past. Try to find out whether the person wants help to change their substance use problem. If they do, offer your help and discuss what you are willing and able to do.

Treat the person with respect and dignity

Interact with the person in a supportive way rather than threatening, confronting, or lecturing the person.

Have realistic expectations for the person

Do not expect a change in the person's thinking or behavior right away. Major behavior changes take time to achieve and often involve the person going through a number of stages. The stages of change as developed by Prochaska are described in the box. Keep in mind that:

- Changing substance use habits is not easy.

- Willpower and self-resolve alone are not enough to stop substance use.

- Advice alone will not help the person change their behavior.

- A person may try to change or stop their substance use more than once before they are successful. Relapse is part of the recovery from substance use disorders.

- If abstinence from drinking or using drugs is not the person's goal, reducing the quantity of alcohol or other drugs consumed is still a worthwhile objective.

- For opiate use disorders, medication-assisted treatment (MAT) uses methadone, buprenorphine, and naltrexone to help people abstain from substance use.

- For alcohol dependence, medication-assisted treatment can involve disulfiram or naltrexone. When used as a treatment for alcohol dependency, naltrexone blocks the euphoric effects and feelings of intoxication (SAMHSA, 2019).

If the person is unwilling to change their substance use behavior, do not:

- Join in drinking or drug use with the person.

- Try to control the person by bribing, nagging, threatening, or crying.

- Make excuses for the person or cover up their drinking or drug use or behavior.

- Take on the person's responsibilities, except if not doing so would cause harm to them or others.

- Feel guilty or responsible for the person's substance use.

If the person says that they do want to change, tell them what you are willing and able to do to help. This may range from simply being a good listener to organizing professional or peer-based help.

The Stages of Change

A person who has a substance problem may not be ready to change. Major behavior changes take time and often involve the person going through a number of stages. There are five stages of change, and the person may move back and forth between the stages at different times. The information and support you offer can be tailored to their level of readiness as shown below:

Stage 1: Pre-contemplation – The person does not think they have a problem.
- Give the person information about the substance and how it might be affecting them. Discuss less harmful ways of using the substance and how to recognize overdose.

Stage 2: Contemplation – The person thinks their substance use might be a problem.
- Encourage the person to keep thinking about quitting, talk about the pros and cons of changing, give information, and refer them to a professional.

Stage 3: Preparation – The person has decided to make a change.
- Encourage the person, support their decision to change, and help them plan the steps they will take to stop using substances. For example, one step may be to talk to a substance use counselor or to their doctor.

Stage 4: Action – Making the change.
- Provide support by helping the person develop strategies for saying "no" and for avoiding people who use substances, and to do other things when they feel like using substances. Help them find other ways to cope with distress. Encourage them to get periodic health checks.

Stage 5: Maintenance – Keeping up the new habits.
- Support the person to keep up the new behavior. Focus on the positive effects of not using substances and praise their achievements.

Explore ideas for harm reduction

If the person wants to change their drinking behavior, help them realize that only they can take responsibility for reducing their alcohol intake and that although changing drinking patterns is difficult, they should not give up trying. Encourage and assist the person to find some information on how to reduce the harm associated with their problem drinking.

If appropriate, inform the person that alcohol may interact with other drugs (illicit, prescribed, or over-the-counter) in unpredictable ways that may lead to a medical emergency.

Managing social pressure to drink

There is often social pressure to get drunk when drinking. Encourage the person to be assertive when they feel pressured to drink more than they want or intend to.

Tell the person that they have the right to refuse alcohol. Tell them that they can say "No thanks" without explanation. You can suggest different ways they can say "no" such as "I don't feel like it," "I don't feel well," or "I am taking medication." Encourage the person to practice different ways of saying "no."

Suggest that saying "no" to alcohol gets easier the more they do it and that the people who care about them will accept their decision not to drink or to reduce the amount that they drink.

Supporting The Person Who Does Not Want To Change

If a person does not want to reduce or stop their substance use, you cannot make them change. It is important that you maintain a good relationship with the person, as you may be able to have a beneficial effect on them. Let the person know you are available to talk in the future.

You can speak with a health professional who specializes in substance use disorders to determine how to best approach the person about your concerns, or you could consult with others who have dealt with such problems.

If the person continues to have a substance use problem, continue with ALGEE and in particular encourage them to seek out information. Have a helpline phone number or the web address of a reputable website with you to give to the person (see the Helpful Resources section).

If the person is using or planning to use alcohol or other drugs while pregnant or breastfeeding, encourage them to consult their doctor.

ACTION E: Encourage Appropriate Professional Help

Tell the person that you will support them in getting professional help. If they are willing to seek professional help, give them information about local options and encourage them to make an appointment.

See Chapter 1: Mental Health in the United States for information about professionals who can help.

The treatments for substance use disorders will vary based on the degree of dependence, how motivated the person is to change, and the presence of co-occurring mental disorders and physical problems.

If the person is physically dependent on alcohol, opiates, or other drugs, the first treatment will be a safe withdrawal through detoxification ("detox") under professional supervision.

Detox should be combined with counseling and self-help to reduce the risk of relapse, engage the person in a commitment to recovery, and promote abstinence. Treatment is only the initial part of the recovery process, and many lifestyle changes are required to change drinking behaviors.

The following treatments are known to be effective (Willenbring, Massey, & Gardner, 2009):

- **Brief intervention.** Brief counseling by a health care professional can help someone reduce or stop drinking. If the person develops a substance use disorder, it can help to motivate them to enter more intensive treatment.

  This type of intervention generally takes four or fewer sessions, each lasting from a few minutes up to an hour. The health care professional determines how much the person is drinking, gives information about risks to their health, advises them to cut down, discusses options for how to change, motivates the person to act by emphasizing personal responsibility, and monitors progress. In doing these things, the health care professional adopts an empathic rather than a coercive approach.

- **Treatment for substance use disorders.** If the person has a substance use disorder, then treatment aims to do several things:
    ○ Address and seek to overcome any physiological dependence on substances.
    ○ Overcome psychological dependence, such as using substances to help the person cope with anxiety or depression.
    ○ Overcome habits that have been formed, such as a social life that revolves around substances.
- **Psychological treatments.** These include:
    ○ CBT, which teaches the person how to cope with cravings and how to recognize and cope with situations that might instigate a return to using.
    ○ Motivational enhancement therapy, which helps motivate and empower a person to change.
    ○ Individual and group supportive counseling.
- **Medications.** Following withdrawal, the use of medications can serve the following purposes:
    ○ Disulfiram and naltrexone are prescribed for alcohol dependence. If a person takes disulfiram and drinks, they have severe physical side effects.
    ○ Medication-assisted treatment removes the craving for some substances. It involves a medically supervised prescription regimen involving methadone, buprenorphine, or naltrexone.

The best treatment for alcohol use disorder is a combination of both medication and psychological treatment.

ACTION E: Encourage Self-Help and Other Support Strategies

Inform the person of supports they may find useful and allow the person to decide which they prefer.

Numerous groups that support people recovering from substance use. Twelve-step programs, such as Alcoholics Anonymous (AA) and Narcotics Anonymous (NA), are self-help groups in which people work to follow steps to recovery. Mutual aid groups such as Rational Recovery and Celebrate Recovery are alternatives to 12-step groups.

Family and friends

Family and friends can play an important role in the recovery of a person with a substance use problem. Encourage the person to reach out to friends and family who support their efforts to change their substance use behaviors and to spend time with supportive non-using friends and family.

Family and friends can help the person seek treatment and support to change their substance behavior. They can also help reduce the chances of a relapse after a person has stopped substance use. People are more likely to start using again if there is an emotional upset in their life, and family and friends can try to reduce this possibility.

Research has shown that people are more likely to recover if they have:

- Stable family relationships.
- Approval and sympathy expressed by their families.
- Supportive friends.
- Friends who don't use alcohol or other drugs and who encourage the person not to use.
- Peer support (Moos, 2007).

Not all family and friends will be supportive of a person's efforts, so it is useful to discuss this with the person so they will be realistic.

Encourage the person to reach out to friends and family who are able to support their efforts to change their drinking behaviors and to spend time with supportive nondrinking friends or family.

Family members of the person can attend support groups such as Al-Anon, Alateen, Adult Children of Alcoholics, and Nar-Anon. They follow the same 12 steps and recovery process as Alcoholics Anonymous.

Self-help strategies

There are websites that allow a person to screen themselves for alcohol problems and encourage the person to change (see the Helpful Resources section). There is evidence that such websites can be effective (White et al., 2010).

NONSUICIDAL SELF-INJURY

KURT VON BEHRMANN, *Cutter*

Being an artist who likes to discuss "difficult topics," I opted to talk about my own experience with cutting in art. The arm with the horizontal lines represents the cutting side of mental illness. The opposite, lighter side represents the energy of mania. The eagle is symbolic of the soul being split in half by mania and depression. Instead of eagle eyes, this eagle has human ones.

"Cutter" is a deeply symbolic painting. Elements represent themselves while representing so much more. The thrust of the work is a discussion of bipolar, cutting, and the feeling of being split in half by mania and depression while trying to remain complete.

CHAPTER 11: NONSUICIDAL SELF-INJURY

WHAT IS NONSUICIDAL SELF-INJURY?

Nonsuicidal self-injury (NSSI) refers to situations in which the self-injury is intentional but is not a suicide attempt. Many terms are used to describe self-injury, including self-harm and self-mutilation.

It is not always easy to tell the difference between nonsuicidal self-injury and a suicide attempt. When you ask a person directly if they are suicidal, you should assume the person is being truthful.

If the person is engaging in nonsuicidal self-injury and is also suicidal, refer to Chapter 12: Suicide.

It is possible that the same person is at times suicidal and at other times self-injuring without the intent to die by suicide.

Nonsuicidal self-injury is not a distinct diagnosis but rather a behavior (Peterson et al., 2008). It is a common behavior in both people diagnosed with various mental disorders and people without any specific psychiatric diagnosis.

Cutting, scratching, hitting or banging, burning, carving, and skin-picking are the ways that people most frequently self-harm. Women are more likely to engage in cutting, while men are more likely to engage in intentional bruising or having others hurt them (Mereish, O'Cleirigh, & Bradford, 2014).

Although some people may feel some relief following the act of harming themselves, this is often only temporary.

People of every ethnicity, educational history, and household income engage in nonsuicidal self-injury. Some facts about nonsuicidal self-injury in specific groups include:

- More people who are unmarried engage in nonsuicidal self-injury than do people who are married.
- Sexual minorities are more likely to engage in nonsuicidal self-injury; almost half of all bisexual women engage in nonsuicidal self-injury (DeAngelis, 2015-a).
- Women are 1.5 times more likely to report engaging in nonsuicidal self-injury than men (Bresin & Schoenleber, 2015).
- A study of adolescents and adults shows that males are less likely than females to report their nonsuicidal self-injury as problematic; this may contribute to lower rates of diagnosis in males (Victor et al., 2018).
- Nonsuicidal self-injury can occur at any age. However, it is most common in young adults and adolescents. The median age of onset of self-injury is 16 years (Klonsky, 2011).
- About 17 percent of adolescents have engaged in nonsuicidal self-injury at least once (Mereish, O'Cleirigh, & Bradford, 2014).

Mental Health First Aid USA has added this chapter to make the material relevant for the United States. This additional content has been added with input from mental health experts.

Prevalence Of Nonsuicidal Self-Injury

Nonsuicidal self-injury occurs in approximately 5.5 percent of adults in the United States (Swannell et al., 2014).

Fifteen percent of young adults engage in nonsuicidal self-injury (Kerr, Muehelekamp, & Turner, 2010).

Co-Occurring Mental Disorders

Nonsuicidal self-injury is common among people who have been diagnosed with major depressive disorder. Among adults age 18 to 35 who engage in nonsuicidal self-injury, 72.5 percent had major depressive disorder at some point in their life (Gratz et al., 2015).

Nonsuicidal self-injury is common among people who have been diagnosed with borderline personality disorder (Kerr, Muehelekamp, & Turner, 2010). NIMH describes borderline personality disorder this way: "Borderline personality disorder is an illness marked by an ongoing pattern of varying moods, self-image, and behavior. These symptoms often result in impulsive actions and problems in relationships. People with borderline personality disorder may experience intense episodes of anger, depression, and anxiety that can last from a few hours to days."

SIGNS AND SYMPTOMS IN A PERSON WHO ENGAGES IN NONSUICIDAL SELF-INJURY

HOW A PERSON WHO ENGAGES IN NONSUICIDAL SELF-INJURY MAY THINK, FEEL, BEHAVE, AND APPEAR	
Thoughts	• Thinking there is no way out of a bad situation • Thinking that people don't care about you or your problems
Emotions	• Feeling unbearable anguish • Feeling depressed or desperate • Feeling a need to relieve stress, pressure, or tension
Behaviors	• Cutting, scratching, or pinching skin enough to cause bleeding or a mark that remains on the skin • Banging or punching objects to the point of bruising or bleeding • Ripping and tearing skin • Carving words or patterns into the skin • Burning skin with cigarettes, matches, hot water, or other heating tools • Pulling out large amounts of hair • Deliberately overdosing on medications when this is not meant as a suicide attempt • Viewing websites, photos, and online video about self-injury or talking about photos or videos on how to self-injure • Hiding the behaviors associated with self-injury

HOW A PERSON WHO ENGAGES IN NONSUICIDAL SELF-INJURY MAY THINK, FEEL, BEHAVE, AND APPEAR

Appearance and Well-being

- Cuts or bruises in various stages of healing
- May wear inappropriate clothing for the weather to hide injuries, like turtlenecks in the summer
- Blood on clothing
- First aid supplies being used up more quickly than expected
- Changing eating or sleeping habits

WHAT CAUSES NONSUICIDAL SELF-INJURY?

This section looks at reasons people engage in this behavior and risk factors for doing so.

Why Do People Engage In Nonsuicidal Self-Injury?

People self-injure for many reasons. The main reasons include:

- Managing feelings of distress and negative emotions (self-soothing).
- Punishing themselves.
- Communicating personal distress to others.
- Escaping a situation of responsibility (Cipriano, Cella, & Cotrufo, 2017).

Many people who self-injure report a sensation of immediate relief during the process (American Psychiatric Association, 2013). For some the process is like an addiction.

Recent studies suggest that people who self-injure have self-beliefs about being "bad" and deserving criticism. As Harvard University researcher Jill Hooley wrote, "The worse people feel about themselves, the more inclined they will be to try [painful] methods of mood regulation that most other people would not even consider" (DeAngelis, 2015-b).

Risk Factors For Nonsuicidal Self-Injury

While it can be difficult to know why people self-injure, and although there is no one single cause of self-injury, there are some important risk factors that may increase someone's risk of engaging in self-injury.

Psychological risk factors

- Depression, anxiety disorders, PTSD, eating disorders, borderline personality disorder, and substance use disorder.
- Alcohol or drug misuse.
- Previous nonsuicidal self-injury or suicide attempts.
- Lack of optimism.
- Low self-esteem.
- Ineffective coping or problem-solving skills.
- Reduced ability to tolerate distress.
- A heightened sense of perfectionism.

Negative life events and family adversity

- Childhood trauma, maltreatment, or neglect.

- Emotional, physical, or sexual abuse in childhood.

- Unstable or dysfunctional family background.

- Family or friend self-injury or suicide attempt.

- Bullying.

- Relationship problems with family or peers.

- Parental separation or divorce.

Research has found that adolescents are more likely to have engaged in nonsuicidal self-injury if they have close friends or peers who engage in similar behaviors (Kerr, Muehelekamp, & Turner, 2010).

What Are The Physical And Mental Health Risks Of Self-Injury?

Risk to well-being

People need positive ways of coping with problems. But one risk with self-injury is that it can become the person's central strategy for coping, making it very hard to use better ways of coping.

Over time, a person who self-injures may find that their fear of pain and injury is reduced; without this fear, they are at risk of suicidal thoughts, plans, and attempts.

It is possible that the same person is at times suicidal and at other times self-injuring without the intent to die by suicide.

For some people, self-injury can be a very difficult habit to break.

Risk to physical health

Injuries to the skin often go untreated. Wounds can take a long time to heal, and complications from infection can occur. Hitting body parts against hard surfaces may result in small fractures that may become complicated if untreated.

Trauma And Nonsuicidal Self-Injury

An individual who experiences trauma has a higher risk of developing mental illnesses or behaviors like nonsuicidal self-injury. In fact, according to the ACE Study detailed in Chapter 6: Trauma and Trauma-related and Stressor-related Disorders, that risk increases dramatically for each additional adverse childhood experience.

A person who has experienced trauma might show the symptoms of depression, bipolar disorder, anxiety disorder, or might engage in nonsuicidal self-injury. A recent study shows that children and adolescents who were physically abused had 49 percent higher odds of engaging in nonsuicidal self-injury. Children and adolescents who were sexually abused had 60 percent higher odds of engaging in nonsuicidal self-injury when compared to their non-abused counterparts (Baiden, 2017).

If trauma is addressed and appropriate treatment and supports are provided sooner than later, a person's chances of recovery are much more likely.

The impact of trauma shapes a person's behavior and impacts different individuals differently. Understanding the impact of trauma also goes a long way in reducing the shame and stigma that many people experience when they self-harm.

Stigma Around Nonsuicidal Self-Injury

There is stigma associated with behaviors such as nonsuicidal self-injury. People who engage in nonsuicidal self-injury may hide their scars, burns, and bruises because they feel embarrassed, rejected, or criticized about their physical appearance. They often do not seek treatment and support because of concerns about what others will think.

IMPORTANCE OF EARLY INTERVENTION

Many people who engage in nonsuicidal self-injury don't seek help. This may be because of shame or embarrassment. It may also be because the person finds the behaviors they are engaging in helpful (American Psychiatric Association, 2013). But the sooner someone gets help, the more likely they are to have a positive outcome.

Remember that nonsuicidal self-injury is usually a sign of deeper distress or another mental illness. Taking the time to explore how the person is feeling (rather than focusing on the behavior) can be helpful.

THE MHFA ACTION PLAN FOR NONSUICIDAL SELF-INJURY

See Chapter 2: Mental Health First Aid to read about how to use ALGEE. In this section, we discuss each step briefly and add information about treatments for nonsuicidal self-injury.

ALGEE is a useful way to remember the steps of the action plan you can use to help a person with signs and symptoms of mental disorders. Not every step must be done, and they don't have to be done in order.

Special Considerations for Nonsuicidal Self-Injury in People with Developmental Disabilities

If you know the person's family, caregiver, or legal guardian, you may wish to first engage with them to talk about your concerns and see if they have noticed similar concerns. However, recall that you must ask the person whether it is okay to speak with the family member. If the person does not have the capacity to make their own health care treatment decisions, find out who is permitted to give consent for these decisions for the person.

When navigating consent to care, it is important to consider the individual's capacity to make their own health care treatment decisions, known as decisional capacity. When adults with developmental disabilities have incomplete decisional capacity, consent is obtained from a surrogate (such as a family caregiver who serves as a legal guardian) and assent, uncoerced willingness to undergo treatment, from the individual.

If you are able to speak with the family, caregiver, or legal guardian, you might listen nonjudgmentally, provide reassurance and information, and then help them connect to professional help or other resources to get help for the person. The way that you engage with the person's family will depend on your role and relationship.

If you are the parent or relative, you might be talking directly to your adult relative using the relevant ALGEE action steps. If the person appears to be at risk of self-harm and says that they intend to die, call 911 and do not leave the person alone.

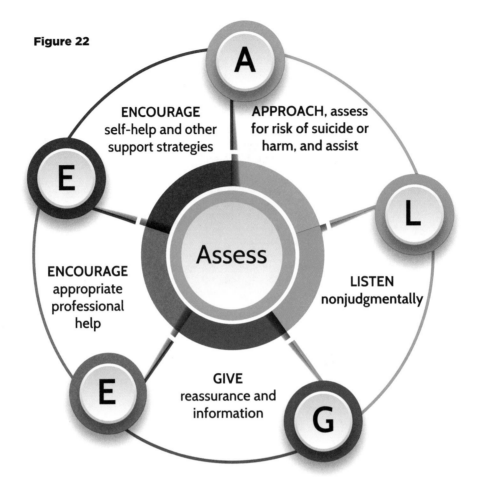

Figure 22

ACTION A: Assess for Risk of Suicide or Harm

Take all self-injuring behavior seriously, regardless of the severity of the injuries or the intent. Do not ignore suspicious injuries you have noticed on the person's body. Discuss your concerns with the person.

What should I do if I suspect someone is injuring themselves?

Before talking to the person, acknowledge and deal with your own feelings about self-injuring behaviors. If you feel you are unable to talk to the person who is self-injuring, try to find someone else who can talk to them.

If you find you are able, your first step is to choose a private place for the conversation.

Directly express your concerns that the person may be injuring themselves. Ask about self-injury in a way that makes it clear to the person that you understand a bit about self-injury, for example, "Sometimes, when people are in a lot of emotional pain, they injure themselves on purpose. Is that how your injury happened?"

Self-injury is a very private thing and is hard to talk about. Do not demand to talk about things the person is not ready to discuss.

You should avoid expressing a strong emotional response of anger, fear, revulsion, or frustration.

If the person is receiving psychiatric care, ask if their treating professional knows about the injuries.

What should I do if I find someone deliberately injuring themselves?

If you have interrupted someone who is in the act of self-injury and there is no crisis, intervene in a supportive and nonjudgmental way. Although it is natural to feel upset, helpless, and even angry upon finding out someone self-injures, try to remain calm and avoid expressions of shock or anger.

Tell the person that you are concerned about them and ask whether you can do anything to alleviate the distress. Ask if medical attention is needed.

When should I call 911?

Avoid over-reacting; medical attention is required only if the injury is severe.

Call 911:

- The person has harmed themselves by overdosing or by consuming poison, call 911, as the risk of death or permanent harm is high.

- Deliberate overdose is more frequently intended to result in death but is sometimes a form of self-injury. Regardless of a person's intentions, emergency help must be sought.

- The person is confused, disoriented, or unconscious.

- The person has bleeding that is rapid or pulsing. Take immediate steps to address the bleeding.

When should I get medical attention (but not call 911)?

Get medical attention for:

- Any serious wound or injury.

- Any cut that is gaping requires medical attention.

- Any burn that is three-quarters of an inch or larger in diameter.

- Any burn on the hands, feet, or face.

ACTION L: Listen Nonjudgmentally

Keep in mind that stopping self-injury should not be the focus of the conversation. Instead, look at what can be done to make the person's life more manageable or their environment less distressing.

Understand that self-injury cannot be stopped overnight, and people need time to recover and learn healthy coping mechanisms.

Avoid expressing anger or a desire to punish the person for self-injuring. Be comfortable with silence, allowing the person time to process what has been talked about. Be prepared for the expression of intense emotions.

Don't promise the person that you will keep their self-injury a secret. If you need to tell somebody about the person's self-injury to keep them safe, speak to them about this first. Avoid gossiping or talking to others about it without their permission.

Things to avoid when talking with someone about nonsuicidal self-injury include:

- Do not minimize the person's feelings or problems.

- Do not use statements that don't take the person's pain seriously, for example, "But you've got a great life" or "Things aren't that bad."

- Do not try to solve the person's problems for them.

- Do not touch (for example, hug or hold hands with) the person without their permission.
- Do not use terms such as "self-mutilator," "self-injurer," or "cutter" to refer to the person.
- Do not accuse the person of seeking attention.
- Do not make the person feel guilty about the effect their self-injuring is having on others.
- Do not set goals or pacts, such as "If you promise not to hurt yourself between now and next week, you're doing really well," unless the person asks you to do this.
- Do not try to make the person stop self-injuring, for example, by removing self-injury tools, or giving them ultimatums such as, "If you don't stop self-injuring, you have to move out."
- Do not offer drugs, prescription pills, or alcohol to the person.

What do I do if the person is not ready to talk?
Respect the person's right not to talk about their self-injuring. If the person doesn't want to talk right away, let them know that you want to listen when they are ready. Ask the person what would make them feel safe enough to be able to discuss their feelings. Do not force the issue unless the injury is severe. If the person still doesn't want to talk later, ask a health professional for advice on what to do.

ACTION G: Give Reassurance and Information

After you have listened attentively and sensitively to the person and given them a chance to fully express and explore their issue, you can begin to discuss possible courses of action. Spending time talking and listening means you are less likely to offer ill-considered or inappropriate advice or to minimize or dismiss the issue based on incomplete information.

It is important to do the following:

- Tell the person that you care and that you want to help.
- Express empathy.
- Find out if they have received treatment in the past.
- Clearly state that professional help is available and that a person can find other ways of managing distress, as this may instill a sense of hope.
- Remind the person that while the urge to harm oneself may be powerful, they do not have to act on these urges.

ACTION E: Encourage Professional Help

Self-injury is often a symptom of a mental health challenge that can be treated. Encourage the person to seek professional help. Let them remain in control over seeking help as much as possible. Suggest and discuss options for getting help rather than directing the person what to do. Help the person map out a plan of action for seeking help. Talk about how you can help them to seek treatment and who they can talk to, for example, a mental health service or a mental health professional.

Provide praise for any steps the person takes toward getting professional help. Follow up with the person to check whether they have found professional help that is suitable for them.

You should seek assistance on the person's behalf even without their permission if:

- The injury is severe or getting more severe, such as cuts getting deeper or bones being broken.
- The self-injurious behavior is interfering with daily life.
- The person has injured their eyes.
- The person has injured their genitals.
- The person has expressed a desire to die.

Discuss options for seeking professional help

Ask the person if they are interested in seeking professional help for managing the symptoms they have shared with you, including feelings of sadness, reduced ability to work or maintain social relationships, and increase in negative thinking. If they feel they need help, discuss the options they have to seek help and encourage them to reach out to a professional.

It is important to encourage the person to get appropriate professional help and effective treatment as early as possible. You might support the individual in finding a local mental health professional.

It may take some time to find a health care provider with whom the person is able to establish a good relationship. Encourage the person not to give up seeking appropriate professional help and offer to provide support during this time.

Professionals who can help

Information about professionals who can help is in Chapter 1: Mental Health in the United States. Professionals are skilled at assessing the extent of mental health and substance use issues. For example, a professional can identify an episode of depression that is so severe that the person is unable to care for themselves or where the person is a danger to themselves or others, and which may require that they may be admitted to a hospital.

Therapy with a mental health professional

Psychological therapies have shown to be effective to treat depressive symptoms associated with nonsuicidal self-injury. Here are some examples of these treatments:

- **Problem solving therapy,** a form of CBT, encourages positive and rational approaches to problem-solving. It also focuses on reducing avoidance of problem-solving. Research suggests this therapy works best in conjunction with other treatments (Washburn et al., 2012).
- **CBT** helps the person recognize unhelpful thoughts and change them to more realistic ones (Craske, 2010) and can include related components such as stress management, relaxation techniques, and sleep management.
- **DBT** teaches skills to help the person recognize patterns of thoughts, emotions, and behaviors, and learn techniques to regulate intense difficult emotions before they result in unhealthy or self-harm behaviors.

ACTION E: Encourage Self-Help

Other people who can help

You can suggest that the person surround themselves with supportive people. There are organizations that provide information and support for people who engage in nonsuicidal self-injury (see the Helpful Resources section).

Self-help strategies

Self-help books based on CBT or DBT can work for nonsuicidal self-injury. It is best to work through these books under the guidance of a therapist, but there is also benefit in using these books as self-help.

Encouraging alternatives to self-injury

Encourage the person to seek other ways to relieve their distress. You might offer the person informational materials like a website or fact sheet about alternatives to self-injury. Help the person identify coping strategies that do not involve self-injuring and help them to make a plan about what to do when they feel like self-injuring. Coping strategies may include:

- Sharing their feelings with other people, such as a close friend or family member, when they are feeling distressed or have the urge to self-injure.

- Having a hot bath, listening to music, or doing something kind for themselves.

Encouraging appropriate professional help and self-help strategies are ways to help a person to recovery and well-being. The Introduction of this manual presents more information about recovery and well-being.

CHAPTER 12: SUICIDE

WHAT IS SUICIDE?

Suicide is defined as death caused by self-directed injurious behavior with intent to die as a result of the behavior.

A suicide attempt is a non-fatal, self-directed, potentially injurious behavior with intent to die as a result of the behavior. A suicide attempt might not result in injury.

Suicidal ideation refers to thinking about, considering, or planning suicide.

Although some people think that asking about suicide can put the idea in a person's mind, research suggests this is not true. First Aiders should always ask a person about suicide if they are concerned.

When you work with someone who is not suicidal at that moment, use respectful terms as shown in the table.

RESPECTFUL TERM	DO NOT USE
☑ Lost to suicide	☒ Committed suicide
☑ Died by suicide	☒ Committed suicide
☑ Attempted suicide	☒ Had an unsuccessful suicide

An Important Note

Self-injury can indicate a number of different things.

Some people who are hurting themselves may be at risk of suicide, while others engage in self-injury over weeks, months, or years but are not suicidal.

If the person you are assisting is self-injuring but is not suicidal, see Chapter 11: Nonsuicidal Self-Injury for more information about this topic.

Mental Health First Aid USA has added this chapter to make the material relevant for the United States. This additional content has been added with input from mental health experts.

Prevalence Of Suicide And Of Suicidal Thoughts And Behaviors

Suicide is the 10th leading cause of death in the United States (CDC, 2016). See Figure 23 for rates of suicidal thoughts and behaviors.

SIGNS AND SYMPTOMS WHEN A PERSON IS THINKING ABOUT, CONSIDERING, OR PLANNING SUICIDE

The table shows how someone thinking about, considering, or planning suicide thinks, feels, behaves, and appears.

Figure 23

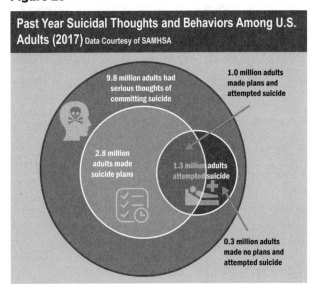

Past Year Suicidal Thoughts and Behaviors Among U.S. Adults (2017) Data Courtesy of SAMHSA

9.8 million adults had serious thoughts of committing suicide

1.0 million adults made plans and attempted suicide

2.8 million adults made suicide plans

1.3 million adults attempted suicide

0.3 million adults made no plans and attempted suicide

HOW SOMEONE THINKING ABOUT, CONSIDERING, OR PLANNING SUICIDE THINKS, FEELS, BEHAVES, AND APPEARS	
Thoughts	• Thoughts of revenge • Believes that there is no way out • No reason for living, no sense of purpose in life (Rudd et al., 2006)
Emotions	• Dramatic changes in mood, including sudden improvement in mood following an episode of depression • Hopelessness • Rage, anger • Anxiety, agitation
Behaviors	• Threatening to hurt or kill themselves • Looking for ways to kill themselves, seeking access to pills, weapons, or other means • Talking or writing about death, dying, or suicide • Withdrawing from friends, family, or society • Seeking revenge • Expressing hopelessness • Giving away possessions • Acting recklessly or engaging in risky activities, seemingly without thinking • Increasing alcohol or other drug use
Appearance and Well-being	• Experiencing anxiety or agitation • Being unable to sleep or sleeping all the time

CAUSES FOR SUICIDE AND SUICIDAL BEHAVIOR

The main reasons people give for attempting suicide are:

- A need to escape or relieve unmanageable emotions and thoughts.
  - The person wants relief from unbearable emotional pain, feels their situation is hopeless, feels worthless, and believes that other people would be better off without them.
- A desire to communicate with or influence another individual.
  - The person wants to communicate how they feel to other people, change how other people treat them, or get help (May & Klonsky, 2013).

Having major depression increases suicide risk compared to the rate of people without depression. Research shows that the risk of death by suicide is greater when depression is severe (U.S. Department of Health and Human Services, 2014).

Risk Factors For Suicide

While risk factors for suicide are possible to identify, keep in mind that the relevance of each risk factor can vary by age, race, gender, sexual orientation, where they live, and their socio-cultural and economic status.

People are at greater risk of suicide if they:

- Have a mental illness.
  - Having depression increases the risk of suicide. Many people with depressive disorders do not seek professional help. In the United States, only 57 percent of people who had major depressive disorder in the past year received professional mental health care or other services. Even when people do seek help, they can delay for many years (Wang et al., 2005). These delays affect long-term recovery. People with depressive disorders are more likely to seek help if someone close to them suggests it (Jorm, 2011).
  - Of the people who die by suicide, 43 percent had a mood disorder (Kelly et al., 2008). A person may feel so overwhelmed and helpless about life events that the future appears hopeless. The person may think suicide is the only way out. However, not every person who is depressed is at risk for suicide, nor is everyone who is at risk for suicide necessarily depressed. Encourage people to talk about their feelings, symptoms, and what is going on in their mind.
- Have poor physical health and disabilities.
- Have attempted suicide or harmed themselves in the past.
- Have had bad things happen recently, particularly with relationships or their health.
- Have been physically or sexually abused as a child.
- Have been recently exposed to suicide by someone else.
- Are a member of certain groups, including males, those who are LGBTQI+, Native American/Alaskan Native, the unemployed, and prisoners.
  - At all ages, men are significantly more likely than women to complete suicide.
  - Men die by suicide about 3.5 times more often than women, but there are three female attempts for each male attempt (American Foundation for Suicide Prevention, 2018).
  - Native American/Alaskan Native men have the highest rates of completed suicide, followed closely by White men (NIMH, May 2018).

- ○ Identifying as LGBQ alone does not put a person at higher risk for suicide, but not having family acceptance and being bullied and harassed are specific stressors for this population. Gay and bisexual men are four times as likely to attempt suicide as heterosexual men. Gay and bisexual men who were the victims of cruel or unjust treatment because of their sexual orientation were more likely to have a lifetime substance abuse problem, suicidal ideation, and suicide attempts than gay and bisexual men without victimization (Mereish, O'Cleirigh, & Bradford, 2014).

Stigma around mental illness is also a risk factor for suicide.

In 2016, the highest suicide rate (18.7 percent) was among adults between 45 and 54 years of age (Xu et al., 2018).

Trauma And Suicide

Trauma such as childhood sexual abuse is directly linked to an increased risk of suicide attempts (Lopez-Castroman et al., 2013). If trauma is addressed and appropriate treatment and supports are provided sooner than later, a person's chances of recovery are much more likely.

Stigma Around Suicide

The stigma around suicide is dangerous because it means suicide that might be prevented is not prevented. People tend to believe that suicide is due to personal weakness, irresponsibility, cowardice, and attention-seeking (Carpiniello & Pinna, 2017).

Self-stigma in someone having suicidal thoughts may keep the person from seeking appropriate professional help. And stigma against people with suicidal thoughts may prevent another person from offering a nonjudgmental listening ear to someone who needs it (Carpiniello & Pinna, 2017).

IMPORTANCE OF EARLY INTERVENTION FOR SUICIDE RISK

Strategies for prevention and early intervention focus on creating protective environments, promoting connectedness, teaching coping and problem-solving skills, identifying and supporting people at risk, and lessening harms and preventing future risk.

Early intervention is important to prevent suicide.

It is important to prevent a first suicide attempt, because people who have one suicide attempt are prone to more attempts (Goñi-Sarriés et al., 2018).

THE MHFA ACTION PLAN FOR SUICIDAL THOUGHTS AND BEHAVIORS

See Chapter 2: Mental Health First Aid to read about how to use ALGEE. In this section, we discuss each step briefly and add information about treatments for suicidal thoughts and behaviors.

ALGEE is a useful way to remember the steps of the action plan you can use to help a person with signs and symptoms of mental disorders. Not every step must be done, and they don't have to be done in order.

Special Considerations for Suicidal Thoughts and Behaviors in People with Developmental Disabilities

If you know the person's family, caregiver, or legal guardian, you may wish to first engage with them to talk about your concerns and see if they have noticed similar concerns. However, recall that you must ask the person whether it is okay to speak with the family member. If the person does not have the capacity to make their own health care treatment decisions, you will find out who is permitted to give consent for these decisions for the person.

When navigating consent to care, it is important to consider the individual's capacity to make their own health care treatment decisions, known as decisional capacity. When adults with developmental disabilities have incomplete decisional capacity, consent is obtained from a surrogate (such as a family caregiver who serves as a legal guardian) and assent, uncoerced willingness to undergo treatment, from the individual.

If you are able to speak with the family, caregiver, or legal guardian, you might listen nonjudgmentally, provide reassurance and information, and then help them connect to professional help or other resources to get help for the person. The way that you engage with the person's family will depend on your role and relationship.

If you are the parent or relative, you might be talking directly to your adult relative using the relevant ALGEE action steps. If the person appears to be at risk of self-harm and says that they intend to die, call 911 and do not leave the person alone.

Figure 24

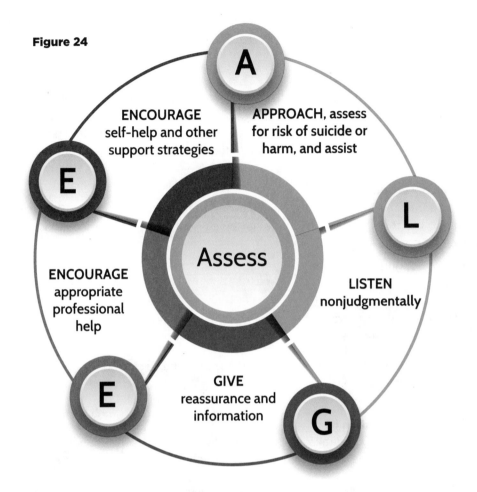

ACTION A: Assess for Risk of Suicide or Harm

How to assess

If a person tells you they are feeling suicidal, take them seriously.

Preparing yourself to approach the person

Be prepared to ask the person directly about suicide. Sometimes people do not ask directly about suicide because they think they will put the idea in the person's head or that they will increase the risk of the person attempting suicide. This is not true (Harris & Goh, 2017). Instead, asking the person about suicidal thoughts will allow them the chance to talk about their problems and show them that somebody cares.

Be aware of your own attitudes about suicide and the impact of these on your ability to provide assistance. It is very important to stay calm. If your attitudes about suicide will not allow you to stay calm, offer to help them find someone else to talk to. Even so, do not leave a suicidal person alone.

Understand that the person may not want to talk with you. In this instance, you should offer to help them find someone else to talk to.

If the person is from a different cultural or religious background than your own, keep in mind that they might have beliefs and attitudes about suicide that differ from yours. Yet the topic of suicide should be treated as all we treat other illnesses. Safety is paramount and this is not a time for moral or spiritual judgment.

Remain aware that it is more important to genuinely want to help than to be of the same age, gender, or cultural background as the person.

Making the approach

Act promptly if you think someone is considering suicide. Even if you have only a mild suspicion that the person is having suicidal thoughts, you should still approach them. Tell the person your concerns about them, describing behaviors that have caused you to be concerned about suicide. However, understand that the person may not want to talk with you. In this instance, you should offer to help them find someone else to talk to.

Asking about thoughts of suicide

Anyone could have thoughts of suicide. Unless someone tells you, the only way to know if they are thinking about suicide is to ask. If you think someone might be having suicidal thoughts, you should ask that person directly. For example, you could ask:

- "Are you having thoughts of suicide?"

- "Are you thinking about killing yourself?"

It is more important to ask the question directly than to be concerned about the exact wording. However, do not ask about suicide in leading or judgmental ways, such as, "You're not thinking of doing anything stupid, are you?"

Do your best to appear calm, confident, and empathic in the face of the suicide crisis, as this may have a reassuring effect for the suicidal person.

How can I tell how urgent the situation is?

Take all thoughts of suicide seriously and take action. Do not dismiss the person's thoughts as "attention seeking" or a "cry for help." Determine the urgency of taking action based on the warning signs of suicide.

Ask about issues that affect the person's immediate safety by asking them:

- Whether they have a plan for suicide.

- How they intend to die by suicide; ask them direct questions about how and where they intend to die by suicide.

- Whether they have decided when they will carry out their plan.

- Whether they have already taken steps to secure the means to end their life.

- Whether they have been using alcohol or other drugs. Intoxication can increase the risk of a person acting on suicidal thoughts.

- Whether they have ever attempted or planned suicide in the past.

If the suicidal person says they are hearing voices, ask what the voices are telling them.

This is important in case the voices are relevant to their current suicidal thoughts.

It is also useful to find out what supports are available to the person. Ask the person:

- Whether they have told anyone about how they are feeling.

- Whether there have been changes in their employment, social life, or family.

- Whether they have received treatment for mental health challenges or are taking any medication.

Be aware that those at the highest risk for acting on thoughts of suicide in the near future are those who have a specific suicide plan, the means to carry out the plan, a time set for doing it, and an intention to do it. Understand, however, that the lack of a plan for suicide does not mean the person is safe.

ACTION L: Listen Nonjudgmentally

In the table are actions that are supportive for suicidal thoughts and behaviors actions and actions that are not supportive.

WHAT IS SUPPORTIVE?	WHAT IS NOT SUPPORTIVE?
☑ Be patient and calm while the person is talking about their feelings.	☒ Do not argue or debate with the person about their thoughts of suicide.
☑ Listen to the person without expressing judgment, accepting what they are saying without agreeing or disagreeing with their behavior or point of view.	☒ Do not discuss with the person whether suicide is right or wrong.
☑ Ask open-ended questions, that is, questions that cannot be simply answered with "yes" or "no," to find out more about the suicidal thoughts and feelings and the problems behind them.	☒ Do not use guilt or threats to prevent suicide, for example, do not tell the person they will go to hell or ruin other people's lives if they die by suicide.
☑ Show you are listening by summarizing what the person is saying.	☒ Do not minimize the suicidal person's problems.
☑ Clarify important points with the person to make sure they are fully understood.	☒ Do not give glib reassurance such as, "Don't worry," "Cheer up," "You have everything going for you," or "Everything will be all right."
☑ Express empathy for the person.	☒ Do not interrupt with stories of your own.
	☒ Do not communicate a lack of interest or negative attitude through your body language.
	☒ Do not "call their bluff" (dare or tell the suicidal person to "Just do it").
	☒ Do not try to give the suicidal person a diagnosis of a mental illness.

ACTION G: Give Support and Information

It is more important to be genuinely caring than to say all the "right" things. Be supportive and understanding of the suicidal person and listen to them with undivided attention. Suicidal thoughts are often a plea for help and a desperate attempt to escape from problems and distressing feelings.

Ask the person who is suicidal what they are thinking and feeling. Keep in mind that it's okay to use the word "suicide." Reassure them that you want to hear whatever they have to say. Allow them to talk about these thoughts and feelings and their reasons for wanting to die and acknowledge these. Let the suicidal person know it is okay to talk about things that might be painful, even if it is hard. Allow them to express their feelings, allow them to cry, express anger, or scream. The person may feel relief at being able to do so.

Remember to thank the suicidal person for sharing their feelings with you and acknowledge the courage this takes.

How can I keep the person safe?
Once you have established that a suicide risk is present, you need to take action to keep the person safe. A person who is suicidal should not be left alone. If you suspect there is an immediate risk of the person acting on suicidal thoughts, act quickly, even if you are unsure.

Work collaboratively with the suicidal person to ensure their safety, rather than acting alone to prevent suicide. For example, you can ask if they could text "MHFA" to 741741 so a professional can be reached for immediate support.

Remind the suicidal person that suicidal thoughts need not be acted on. Reassure them that there are solutions to problems or ways of coping other than suicide.

Find out who or what has supported the person in the past and whether these supports are still available.

When talking to the suicidal person, focus on the things that will keep them safe for now, rather than the things that put them at risk. Examples include calling the suicide hotline or texting the crisis text line, talking about feelings and experiences, or making plans to get help in the future.

Although you can offer support, you are not responsible for the actions or behaviors of someone else and cannot control what they might decide to do.

ACTION E: Encourage Appropriate Professional Help

Encourage the person to get appropriate professional help as soon as possible.

If they don't want to talk to someone face-to-face, encourage them to contact a suicide helpline.

If the suicidal person is reluctant to seek help, keep encouraging them to see a mental health professional and contact a suicide prevention hotline for guidance on how to help them. If the suicidal person refuses professional help, call a mental health center or crisis telephone line and ask for advice on the situation.

For people at more urgent risk, additional action may be needed. If you believe the suicidal person will not stay safe, seek their permission to contact their regular doctor or mental health professional about your concerns. (It can be helpful if you are able to contact a professional who the suicidal person already knows and trusts.)

If the person has a specific plan for suicide, or if they have the means to carry out their suicide plan, call a mental health center or crisis telephone line and ask for advice on the situation.

If the suicidal person has a weapon, contact the police. When contacting the police, inform them that the person is suicidal.

Make sure you do not put yourself in any danger while offering support to the suicidal person.

Be prepared for the suicidal person to possibly express anger and feel betrayed by your attempt to prevent their suicide or help them get professional help. Try not to take personally any hurtful actions or words of the suicidal person.

What should I do if the person has acted on suicidal thoughts?
If the suicidal person has already harmed themselves, administer first aid and call 911, asking for an ambulance.

Keep in mind that despite our best efforts, we may not be successful in preventing suicide.

ACTION E: Encourage Self-Help and Other Support Strategies

People struggling with suicidal thoughts and feelings frequently use self-help strategies. The person's ability and desire to use self-help strategies will depend on their interests and the severity of their mental health or substance use issues. Therefore, do not be overly forceful when trying to encourage the person to use self-help strategies.

Some people with mental health issues gain support from peers with similar experiences. Similarly, if the person is dealing with substance use issues or has grown up with substance use in their family, 12-step programs such as AA, Al-Anon, or Adult Children of Alcoholics (ACOA) may be very helpful.

REMEMBER

The goals of Mental Health First Aid are to:

- Encourage adults to practice nonjudgmental listening
- Empower adults with the skills to promote help-seeking skills and behaviors
- Reduce stigma around mental health and substance use challenges

NOT to diagnose and/or treat themselves or others

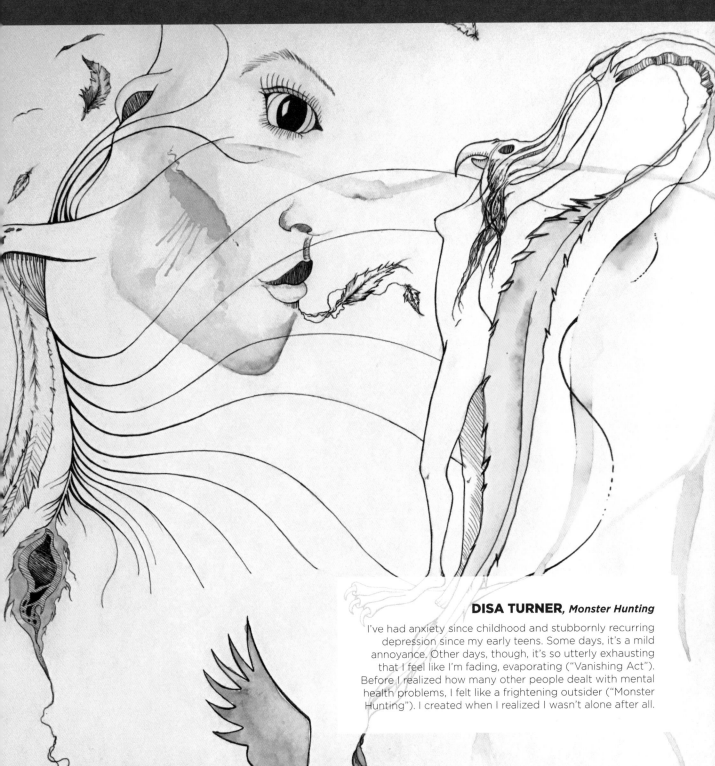

SECTION 3
FIRST AID FOR CRISES

This section provides First Aiders with information on what to do in a mental health or substance use-related crisis. It consists of one chapter addressing crises related to several behaviors and mental health disorders and the Helpful Resources section. For each crisis, you will learn when to call 911 or seek medical attention. You'll learn how to put someone in the recovery position, what to say to a person in a specific type of crisis, and much more.

Specific crises addressed are suicidal thoughts and behaviors, nonsuicidal self-injury, effects of a traumatic event, panic attacks, severe psychotic states, severe effects from alcohol use, severe effects from drug use, opioid over-dose, and aggressive behaviors.

DISA TURNER, *Monster Hunting*

I've had anxiety since childhood and stubbornly recurring depression since my early teens. Some days, it's a mild annoyance. Other days, though, it's so utterly exhausting that I feel like I'm fading, evaporating ("Vanishing Act"). Before I realized how many other people dealt with mental health problems, I felt like a frightening outsider ("Monster Hunting"). I created when I realized I wasn't alone after all.

PETE MORELEWICZ, *First Impression*

I often use the creative process as an avenue to explore and temper my anxiety disorder. In particularly rough times, I find it helpful to dive into an art project that is larger than myself. That is, to get outside of my own head and acknowledge and appreciate the anxiety that others feel, too. Making a connection to the larger world helps break the cycle of an inner-anxiety spiral.

CHAPTER 13: FIRST AID FOR MENTAL HEALTH CRISES

INTRODUCTION

This chapter recommends ways for you to assess and assist in mental health crisis situations.

The role of the First Aider is to assist the person until appropriate professional help is received or the crisis resolves.

Each individual is unique, so you will tailor your support to that person's needs. These recommendations may not be appropriate for every person who is in crisis. Crises vary in severity, and the Mental Health First Aid given also varies.

To read more about mental health crises in a person with developmental disabilities, refer to Chapter 2: Mental Health First Aid.

This chapter contains Mental Health First Aid recommendations for:

- Suicidal thoughts and behaviors.
- Nonsuicidal self-injury.
- A traumatic event.
- Panic attacks.
- Severe psychotic states.
- Severe effects from alcohol use.
- Severe effects from drug use.
- Opioid overdose.
- Aggressive behaviors.

MENTAL HEALTH FIRST AID FOR SUICIDAL THOUGHTS AND BEHAVIORS

When a person is suicidal, you should always call 911. If the person has a weapon or is behaving aggressively toward you, you must call 911 for your own safety.

If the suicidal person has harmed themselves, administer first aid and call 911, asking for an ambulance.

What Should I Do If I Think Someone Is Considering Suicide?

Act quickly. Even if you only have a mild suspicion that the person is having suicidal thoughts, you should still approach them.

- Tell the person your concerns about them.
- Describe behaviors that have caused you to be concerned about suicide.

Mental Health First Aid USA has added this chapter to make the material relevant for the United States. This additional content has been added with input from mental health experts.

Understand that the person may not want to talk with you. In this instance, you should offer to help them find someone else to talk to.

How Should I Talk With A Person Who Seems Suicidal?

Do your best to appear calm, confident, and empathetic in the face of the suicide crisis, as this may have a reassuring effect for the suicidal person.

It is important to:

- Tell the person that you are concerned and that you want to help.

- Express empathy for the person and what they are going through.

- Clearly state that thoughts of suicide are common, and that help is available to discuss these thoughts. This may instill the sense of hope that the person needs.

- Tell the person that thoughts of suicide do not have to be acted on.

- Encourage the person to do most of the talking, if they are able to. Allow them to cry, express anger, or scream. Suicidal thoughts are often a plea for help and a desperate attempt to escape from problems and distressing feelings. The person needs the opportunity to talk about their feelings and reasons for wanting to die and may feel great relief at being able to do this.

- Listen to the person and talk about some of the specific problems they are experiencing. Show you are listening by summarizing what the suicidal person is saying.

- Do not use guilt or threats. For example, do not tell the person they will ruin other people's lives if they complete suicide. Also, do not discuss whether suicide is right or wrong.

- Thank the suicidal person for sharing their feelings with you and acknowledge the courage this takes.

How Can I Tell How Serious Or Urgent The Situation Is?

As you talk with the person, you are assessing their risk of suicide. If you believe there is a risk, call 911 immediately.

Ask the person directly if they have a plan for suicide with these three questions:

- "Have you decided how you would kill yourself?"

- "Have you decided when you would do it?"

- "Have you taken any steps to secure the things you would need to carry out your plan?"

If they answer yes to any of these, they are at great risk. Call a mental health center or crisis helpline and ask for advice on the situation.

If the person mentions vague suicidal thoughts, such as, "What's the point of going on?" but does not answer yes to any of the questions above, they are still at risk. All thoughts of suicide must be taken seriously.

Next, you need to know about the following so you can inform the crisis team or the 911 operator:

- Has the person been using alcohol or other drugs? The use of alcohol or other drugs can make a person act on impulse.

- Has the person made a suicide attempt in the past? A previous suicide attempt makes a person more likely to make a future suicide attempt.

- Have there been changes in their employment, social life, or family?

- Have they told anyone about how they are feeling?

- Have they received treatment for mental disorders?

- Are they taking medication?

- Have they stopped any medication?

The Suicide Risk Assessment in Figure 25 guides you to take 4 main actions as detailed in this chapter: Assess, Ask the Question, Ask About Planning, and Get Help Immediately.

Figure 25

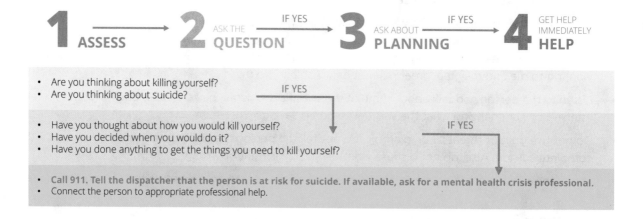

SUICIDE RISK ASSESSMENT

1 ASSESS → **2 ASK THE QUESTION** — IF YES → **3 ASK ABOUT PLANNING** — IF YES → **4 GET HELP IMMEDIATELY HELP**

- Are you thinking about killing yourself?
- Are you thinking about suicide?

IF YES

- Have you thought about how you would kill yourself?
- Have you decided when you would do it?
- Have you done anything to get the things you need to kill yourself?

IF YES

- **Call 911. Tell the dispatcher that the person is at risk for suicide. If available, ask for a mental health crisis professional.**
- Connect the person to appropriate professional help.

How Can I Keep The Suicidal Person Safe?

- Call 911 promptly.

- Do not leave a suicidal person on their own while waiting for the EMTs. If you cannot stay with them, arrange for someone else to do so.

- If the suicidal person refuses professional help, call a mental health center or crisis helpline and ask for advice on the situation.

- If you believe the suicidal person who refuses professional help will not stay safe, seek their permission to contact their regular doctor or mental health professional about your concerns.

- If the suicidal person wants a promise not to tell anyone else, do not agree. Never agree to keep a plan for suicide or risk of suicide a secret. In this case, explain why you are not agreeing. You might say, for example, "I care about you too much to keep a secret like this. You need help and I am here to help you get it." Treat the person with respect and involve them in decisions about who else knows about the suicidal crisis. If the person still refuses to give you permission to tell someone about their suicidal thoughts, you may call 911 or otherwise get help in order to ensure their safety. You do not need their permission. Tell the person who you will be notifying.

Keep in mind that it is much better to have the person angry at you for sharing their suicidal thoughts without their permission in order to get help than to lose the person to suicide.

What To Tell The 911 Operator

Tell the 911 operator clearly that the person needs mental health assistance.

Tell the 911 operator and EMTs if the person has:

- Access to a gun, medications, or other means of suicide.
- Stopped taking prescribed medicines.
- Stopped seeing a mental or behavioral health care professional or physician.
- Written a suicide note.
- Given possessions away.
- Been in or is currently in an abusive relationship.
- Recently suffered a loss or other traumatic event.
- An upcoming anniversary of a loss.
- Used alcohol or other drugs.
- Received treatment for any mental disorders.
- Recovered well from a previous suicidal crisis after getting a particular kind of help.

Your role as a First Aider ends when the EMTs or mental health professional arrives.

How Can I Keep The Person Safe If There Is No Risk Of Suicide, But The Person Is Having A Real Crisis?

Help the person get professional help as soon as possible. This may mean taking them to the emergency department of a hospital, a community mental health center, or a doctor's office.

If there is no risk of suicide and the person does not want help, keep encouraging them to see a mental health professional and contact a suicide prevention hotline for guidance on how to help them.

Give the person a suicide hotline number, a phone number for a friend or family member who has agreed to help, and contact information for a mental health professional.

Help the person think about people or things that have helped them in the past and find out whether these supports are still available. Perhaps a family member, friend, teacher, mental health professional, or an individual from a faith group, community organization, or recreational club might be helpful.

If the person you are trying to help has engaged in self-injury, but insists they are not suicidal, See Chapter 11: Nonsuicidal Self-injury to help you understand and assist.

After The Crisis Has Passed

Emergency care is short-term care only. After the suicide crisis has passed, help ensure that the person gets whatever psychological and medical help they need. The doctor who helped during the crisis can help refer the person to appropriate mental health care.

Accessing the appropriate services, supports, and treatment is not always easy and may take days or weeks, even when the situation is serious. If you have an ongoing role with the person, it may be helpful to assist them in developing a safety plan. However, keep in mind that a safety plan by itself is not enough to keep the suicidal person safe.

A safety plan is an agreement between the suicidal person and another person that outlines steps and actions to keep the person safe. The safety plan should:

- State what will be done, who will be doing it, and when it will be carried out.
  - For example, ask that the person agree to talk to a professional immediately to better understand their current feelings and what is going on.
- Be for a length of time that will be easy for the suicidal person to cope with, so that they can feel able to fulfill the agreement and have a sense of achievement.
- Include contact numbers that the person agrees to call if they are feeling suicidal, like the person's mental health professionals, a suicide helpline or 24-hour crisis line, or friends and family members who will help in an emergency.

As you talk with the person, focus on what they should do rather than what they shouldn't. For example, ask "Do you mind if I stay with you? I am concerned about you and want to make sure you are safe." This is a positive statement. Contrast this with "You can't be alone right now."

Do not make decisions for the person as you or they write the safety plan.

Recall that although you can offer support, you are not responsible for the actions or behaviors of someone else and cannot control what they might decide to do.

SELF-CARE

Be prepared for the suicidal person to express anger and feel betrayed by your attempt to prevent their suicide or get professional help. Try not to take personally any hurtful actions or words.

Recall that despite our best efforts, some people will still die by suicide. A suicide or attempted suicide of someone you have tried to help will have considerable impact on caregivers and First Aiders involved.

As a First Aider, it is important to pay attention to your own emotional state and physical needs and to make sure that you are asking for and accepting care from your social support network. Seek and accept support from trusted colleagues, friends, and family, and allow yourself time for reflection and healing.

Figure 26

 Remember you cannot assist others as a First Aider without taking care of yourself. Consider the following questions to guide your self-care plan.

Self-Care
1 Have I decided what I will do for self-care?
2 Who can I speak with now?
3 Who can I call if I feel upset or distressed later?

MENTAL HEALTH FIRST AID FOR NONSUICIDAL SELF-INJURY

An Important Note

This Mental Health First Aid advice applies only if the person is injuring themselves for reasons other than suicide. If the person you are assisting is injuring themselves and is suicidal, call 911 and refer to Chapter 12: Suicide.

How To Assess

Take all self-injuring behavior seriously, no matter the intent or how minor the injuries. Discuss your concerns with the person.

If you think someone you care about is deliberately injuring themselves, you need to discuss it with them. Do not ignore suspicious injuries you have noticed on the person's body.

The most common methods of self-injury are (Klonsky, 2011):

- Cutting.
- Scratching.
- Deliberately hitting body on hard surface.
- Punching, hitting, or slapping oneself.
- Biting.
- Burning.

How To Assist

What should I do if I suspect someone is injuring themselves?
If you feel you are unable to talk to the person who is self-injuring, try to find someone else who can talk to them.

Choose a private place for the conversation. Directly express your concerns that the person may be injuring themselves. Ask about self-injury in a way that makes it clear to the person that you understand self-injury, for example, "Sometimes, when people are in a lot of emotional pain, they injure themselves on purpose. Is that how your injury happened?"

Self-injury is a very private thing and is hard to talk about. Do not demand to talk about things the person is not ready to discuss. Do not express a strong emotional response of anger, fear, revulsion, or frustration.

If the person is receiving mental health treatment, ask if their mental health professional knows about the injuries.

What should I do if I find someone deliberately injuring themselves?
If you have interrupted someone who is in the act of self-injury, intervene in a supportive and nonjudgmental way. Although it is natural to feel upset, helpless, and even angry upon finding out someone self-injures, try to remain calm and avoid expressions of shock or anger. Tell the person that you are concerned about them and ask whether you can do anything to alleviate their distress. Ask if they need medical attention.

When is emergency medical attention necessary?
Medical attention is required only if the injury is severe. Do not overreact.

If a wound or injury is serious, get medical attention. For example:

- Any cut that is gaping and may need stitches.
- Any burn that is three-quarters of an inch or larger in diameter.
- Any burn on the hands, feet, or face.

If the person has harmed themselves by taking an overdose of medication or consuming poison, call 911 as the risk of death or permanent harm is high. Deliberate overdose is more frequently intended to result in death but is sometimes a form of self-injury. Regardless of a person's intentions, call 911.

How should I talk with someone who is deliberately injuring themselves?
Keep in mind that stopping self-injury should not be the focus of the conversation. Instead, look at what can be done to make the person's life more manageable or their environment less distressing. Understand that self-injury cannot be stopped overnight, and people need time to recover and learn healthy coping mechanisms.

Behave in a supportive and nonjudgmental way
Understand that self-injury makes the person's life easier and accept their reasons for doing it. Be supportive without being permissive of the behavior. Be aware of what your body language is communicating about your attitudes.

Use a calm voice when talking to the person
Avoid expressing anger or a desire to punish the person for self-injuring. Be comfortable with silence, allowing the person time to process what has been talked about. Be prepared for the expression of intense emotions.

Express concern and actively listen
When talking with the person, use "I" statements instead of "you" statements, like "I feel worried/angry/frustrated when you…" instead of "You make me feel worried/angry/frustrated…." Ask the person questions about their self-injury but avoid pressuring them to talk about it. Reflect what the person is saying by acknowledging their experience as they are describing it.

Give support and reassurance
Express empathy for how the person is feeling. Validate the person's emotions by explaining that these emotions are appropriate and valid.

Let them know they are not alone and that you are there to support them. Work collaboratively with the person in finding solutions by asking what they want to happen and discussing any possible actions with them.

Reassure the person that there are sources of help and support available. Tell the person that you want to help and let them know the ways in which you are willing to help them.

Don't promise the person that you will keep their self-injury a secret
If you need to tell somebody about the person's self-injury to keep them safe, speak to them about this first. Never talk to others about it without their permission.

When talking with someone about nonsuicidal self-injury:

- Do not minimize the person's feelings or problems.
- Do not use statements that don't take the person's pain seriously, like "But you've got a great life" or "Things aren't that bad."
- Do not try to solve the person's problems for them.
- Do not touch (for example, hug or hold hands with) the person without their permission.
- Do not accuse the person of seeking attention.
- Do not make the person feel guilty about the effect their self-injuring is having on others.
- Do not set goals or pacts, such as "If you promise not to hurt yourself between now and next week, you're doing really well," unless the person asks you to do this.
- Do not try to make the person stop self-injuring, for example, by removing self-injury tools, or giving them ultimatums, like "If you don't stop self-injuring, you have to move out."
- Do not offer drugs, prescription pills, or alcohol to the person.
- Do not use terms such as "self-mutilator," "self-injurer," or "cutter" to refer to the person.

What Do I Do If The Person Is Not Ready To Talk?

Respect the person's right not to talk about their self-injuring. If the person doesn't want to talk right away, let them know that you want to listen to them when they are ready. Ask the person what would make them feel safe enough to be able to discuss their feelings. If the person still doesn't want to talk, ask a health care professional for advice on what to do.

Seeking Professional Help

Self-injury is often a symptom of a mental disorder that can be treated. Encourage the person to seek professional help. Let them remain in control over seeking help as much as possible. Suggest and discuss options for getting help rather than directing the person as to what to do. Help the person map out a plan of action for seeking help. Talk about how you can help them to seek treatment and who they can talk to.

Praise the person for any steps they take toward getting professional help. Follow up with the person to check whether they have found professional help that is suitable for them.

You should seek mental health assistance on the person's behalf if:

- The person asks you to.
- The injury is severe or getting more severe, such as cuts getting deeper or bones being broken.
- The self-injurious behavior is interfering with daily life.
- The person has injured their eyes.
- The person has injured their genitals.
- The person has expressed a desire to die.

YOUR ROLE

Keep in mind that not all people who self-injure want to change their behavior. Even though you can offer support, you are not responsible for the actions or behavior of someone else and cannot control what they do.

Encouraging Alternatives To Self-Injury

Encourage the person to seek other ways to relieve their distress.

Help the person use their coping strategies that do not involve self-injuring and help them make a plan about what to do when they feel like self-injuring.

Suggest some coping strategies and discuss with the person what might be helpful for them. These may include:

- Encouraging the person to share their feelings with other people, such as a close friend or family member, when they are feeling distressed or have the urge to self-injure.

- Helping the person think of ways to reduce their distress, like having a hot bath, listening to loud music, or doing something kind for themselves.

MENTAL HEALTH FIRST AID FOLLOWING A TRAUMATIC EVENT

How To Assess

A person who has experienced a traumatic event may react strongly right away, showing you that they need immediate assistance. Others may have a delayed reaction. This means that if you are helping someone you know and see on a regular basis, you may be continually assessing them for signs of distress over the few weeks following their trauma.

How To Assist

What are the first priorities for helping someone after a traumatic event?

Ensure your own safety before offering help to anyone. Check for potential dangers, such as fire, weapons, debris, or other people who may become aggressive, before deciding to approach a person to offer your help.

If you are helping someone you do not know, introduce yourself and explain what your role is. Find out the person's name and use it when talking to them. Remain calm and do what you can to create a safe environment by taking the person to a safer location or removing any immediate dangers.

If the person is injured, offer first aid if you can and seek medical assistance.

If the person seems physically unhurt, you need to watch for signs that their physical or mental state is declining and be prepared to call 911. Be aware that a person may suddenly become disoriented, or an apparently uninjured person may have internal injuries that reveal themselves more slowly.

Try to determine what the person's immediate needs are for food, water, shelter, or clothing. However, if EMTs or other professionals are nearby and can better meet those needs, don't take over their role.

If the person has been a victim of assault, consider that evidence may need to be collected, like cheek swabs or evidence on clothing or skin. Work with the person to preserve that evidence when possible. For example, if they change their clothes and shower, it may destroy evidence, so put clothing in a bag for police to take as evidence and suggest to the person that they wait to shower until after a forensic exam. Recall that although collecting evidence is important, you should not force the person to do anything that they don't want to do.

Do not make any promises you may not be able to keep. For example, don't tell someone that you will get them home soon if this may not be the case.

What are the priorities if I am helping after a mass traumatic event?

Mass traumatic events affect large numbers of people. They include severe environmental events (such as fires and floods), acts of war and terrorism, and mass shootings. In addition to the general principles outlined above, there are a number of things you need to do.

If there are professional helpers at the scene, you should follow their directions. Call 911 if EMTs or other professional helpers are not at the scene or find out if the community has a local crisis team available.

Be aware of and responsive to the comfort and dignity of the person you are helping, for example, you might offer the person something to cover themselves with (such as a blanket) and ask bystanders or media to go away. Try not to appear rushed or impatient.

Give the person truthful information and if there is something you do not know, tell them you do not know. Tell the person about any information sessions, fact sheets, or phone numbers as they become available.

Do not try to give the person any information they do not want to hear, as this can be traumatic in itself.

How do I talk to someone who has just experienced a traumatic event?

When talking to a person who has experienced a traumatic event, it is more important to be genuinely caring than to say all the "right" things. Show the person that you understand and care and ask them how they would like to be helped.

Speak clearly and communicate with the person as an equal, rather than as a superior or expert.

If the person seems unable to understand what is said, you may need to repeat yourself several times.

The person may not be as distressed about what has happened as you might expect them to be, and that is fine. Don't tell the person how they should be feeling. Tell them that everyone deals with trauma at their own pace. Be aware that cultural differences may influence the way some people respond to a traumatic event; for example, in some cultures, expressing vulnerability or grief around strangers is not considered appropriate. The priorities do not change even if the person is not expressing themselves in a way that you expected.

How do I talk to someone who has experienced a traumatic event in the recent past?

Be aware that providing support doesn't have to be complicated; it can involve small things like spending time with the person, having a cup of tea or coffee, chatting about day-to-day life, or giving them a wanted hug.

Behavior such as withdrawal, irritability, and bad temper may be a response to the trauma, so try not to take such behavior personally. Try to be friendly, even if the person is being difficult.

Should we talk about what happened?

It is very important not to force the person to tell their story. Remember that you are not the person's therapist. Encourage the person to talk about their reactions only if they feel ready and want to.

If the person wants to talk, don't interrupt to share your own feelings, experiences, or opinions. Be aware that the person may need to talk about the trauma many times, so you may need to be willing to listen on more than one occasion.

Avoid saying anything that might trivialize the person's feelings, such as, "Don't cry" or "Calm down" or anything that might trivialize their experience, such as, "You should just be glad you're alive."

Be aware that the person may experience survivor's guilt, which is the feeling that it is unfair that others died or were injured while they were not. First Aiders can watch for signs and symptoms of mental health or substance use challenges.

How can I help the person cope over the next few weeks or months?

If you are helping someone you don't know, unless you are responsible for them in some professional capacity, it is not expected that you will have further contact with them.

If you are helping someone you know after a traumatic event, you can help them cope with their reactions over the next few weeks or months.

Encourage the person to tell others when they need or want something, rather than assume others will know what they want. Also encourage them to identify sources of support, including loved ones and friends, but remember that it is important to respect the person's need to be alone at times.

Encourage the person to take care of themselves; get plenty of rest if they feel tired; do things that feel good to them, like taking baths, reading, exercising, or watching television; and to think about any coping strategies they have successfully used in the past and use them again. Encourage them to spend time somewhere they feel safe and comfortable.

Be aware that the person may suddenly or unexpectedly remember details of the event and may or may not wish to discuss these details.

Discourage the person from using negative coping strategies such as working too hard, using alcohol or other drugs, or engaging in behavior that provides short-term relief or even pleasure, such as self-injury, binge eating, or suicide attempts.

When should the person seek professional help?

Not everyone will need professional help to recover from a traumatic event. However, if the person wants to seek help, you should support them.

Be aware of the kinds of professional help that are available locally, and if the person does not like the first professional they speak to, you should tell them that it is okay to try a different one.

If the person says they do not want professional help, keep track of time passing and note whether you see the person return to normal functioning after four weeks.

If, four weeks or more after the trauma, they are showing the following signs, encourage the person to seek professional help:

- They still feel very upset or fearful.
- They are unable to escape intense, ongoing distressing feelings.
- Their important relationships are suffering as a result of the trauma, for example, if they withdraw from their family or friends.
- They feel jumpy or have nightmares because of or about the trauma.
- They can't stop thinking about the trauma.
- They are unable to enjoy life at all as a result of the trauma.
- Their post-trauma symptoms are interfering with their usual activities (NIMH, Feb 2017).

If at any time the person becomes suicidal, call 911. And, if at any time the person uses alcohol or other drugs to deal with the trauma, you should encourage them to seek professional help.

MENTAL HEALTH FIRST AID FOR PANIC ATTACKS

How To Assess

Signs and symptoms of a panic attack

A panic attack is a distinct episode of high anxiety with fear or discomfort that develops abruptly and has its peak within 10 minutes. During the attack, several of the following symptoms are present.

- Palpitations, pounding heart, or rapid heart rate.
- Sweating, chills, or hot flashes.
- Trembling and shaking.
- Numbness or tingling.
- Sensations of being short of breath.
- Sensations of choking or smothering.
- Dizziness, light-headedness, feeling faint or unsteady.
- Chest pain or discomfort.
- Abdominal distress or nausea.
- Feelings of unreality or being detached from oneself.
- Fears of losing control or going crazy.
- Fear of dying (American Psychiatric Association, 2013).

If someone is experiencing any of these symptoms and you suspect that they are having a panic attack, ask them if they know what is happening and whether they have ever had a panic attack before.

How To Assist

If you are helping someone you do not know, introduce yourself. If the person says that they have had panic attacks before and believe that they are having one now, ask them if they need any kind of help and give it to them, when possible.

What if I am uncertain whether the person is really having a panic attack and not something more serious like a heart attack?

The symptoms of a panic attack sometimes resemble the symptoms of a heart attack or other medical problem. It is not possible to be totally sure that a person is having a panic attack. Only a medical professional can tell if it is something more serious.

If the person has not had a panic attack before and doesn't think they are having one now, you should follow physical first aid guidelines. The first step is to help the person into a supported sitting position (for example, against a wall).

Ask the person or check to see if they are wearing a medical alert bracelet or necklace. If they are, follow the instructions on the alert or seek medical assistance.

If the person loses consciousness, call 911. Use physical first aid until the EMTs arrive. Check for breathing and pulse.

What should I say and do if I know the person is having a panic attack?

Reassure the person that they are experiencing a panic attack. It is important that you remain calm and that you do not start to panic yourself. Speak to the person in a reassuring but firm manner and be patient. Speak clearly and slowly and use short sentences. Invite the person to sit down somewhere comfortable.

Rather than making assumptions about what the person needs, ask them directly what they think might help.

Do not downplay the person's experience. Acknowledge that the terror feels very real, but reassure them that a panic attack, while very frightening, is not life-threatening or dangerous. Reassure them that they are safe and that the symptoms will pass.

What should I say and do when the panic attack has ended?

After the panic attack has subsided, ask the person if they know where they can get information about panic attacks. If they don't know, offer some suggestions.

Tell the person that if the panic attacks recur and are causing them distress, they should speak to an appropriate health professional. Reassure the person that there are effective treatments available for panic attacks and panic disorder.

A Note On Breathing During A Panic Attack

It has been widely believed for many years that focusing on breathing during a panic attack can help, either by distracting the person or by bringing about a state of calm. But experts say that it is not a good idea to actively encourage a person to focus on their breathing, as this can become an emotional crutch, leading to difficulty with treatments later on (Salkovskis, Clark, & Gelder, 1996).

Because people have traditionally believed that focusing on breathing during a panic attack can help, you might find that the person wants to use breathing to help themselves. In this case, do not try to stop someone from focusing on their breathing.

If the person feels distressed, encourage them to seek professional help.

MENTAL HEALTH FIRST AID FOR SEVERE PSYCHOTIC STATES

Facts On Severe Psychotic States

If someone has a psychotic illness, they may at times experience severe psychotic states.

A severe psychotic state may develop gradually over a few days, or it may seem to come on very suddenly. For this reason, early signs of a psychotic state should be addressed as quickly as possible (Langlands et al., 2008).

How To Assess

A person in a severe psychotic state can have:

- Overwhelming delusions and hallucinations.
- Very disorganized thinking.
- Bizarre and disruptive behaviors.
- Severe distress.

When a person is in this state, they can be hurt because of their delusions or hallucinations. For example, the person might believe they have special powers to protect them from danger and may run through traffic to try to escape from terrifying hallucinations.

How To Assist

It is possible that the person might act upon a delusion or hallucination. It may help to invite the person to sit down. Make sure that you have access to an exit.

Your primary task is to de-escalate the situation, and you should not do anything to further agitate the person. Remain as calm as possible. Use short, simple sentences. Speak quietly in a nonthreatening tone of voice.

Talk to them about how they feel, not what they hear or believe. If the person asks you questions, answer them calmly. You should comply with requests unless they are unsafe or unreasonable. This gives the person the opportunity to feel somewhat in control.

Ask if there is an advance care directive or relapse prevention plan, and if there is, follow it. If there is not, then proceed with contacting a crisis team, calling 911, or calling a mental health crisis line.

Once you have gotten help for the person, try to find out if they have anyone they trust, like close friends or family, and try to enlist their help. If you believe it is not safe for the person to be alone, ensure that someone stays with them. If they say they have no one they trust, you may need to contact their parent or another caregiver against their wishes.

Be prepared to call 911 and tell them briefly what you have seen. When any EMTs or any other helpers arrive, explain to the person who they are and how they are going to help. If your concerns about the person are dismissed by the services you contact, you should persist in trying to seek support for them.

MENTAL HEALTH FIRST AID FOR SEVERE EFFECTS FROM ALCOHOL USE

The guidelines in this section were developed by an expert consensus study (Kingston et al., 2009).

Facts On Alcohol Intoxication, Poisoning, And Withdrawal

Alcohol intoxication substantially impairs the person's thinking and behavior. It can lead to risky activities, such as driving a car while under the influence. The person may also be at higher risk of attempting suicide. And, if someone is intoxicated enough to pass out, they are at risk of choking on their own vomit.

Alcohol poisoning is a toxic level of alcohol in the bloodstream, which can lead to the person's death. The amount of alcohol that causes alcohol poisoning is different for every person.

Alcohol withdrawal refers to the unpleasant symptoms a person experiences when they stop drinking or drink substantially less than usual. Unmedicated alcohol withdrawal may lead to seizures and delirium or confusion.

How To Assess

Alcohol intoxication

Common signs and symptoms of alcohol intoxication are:

- Loss of coordination.
- Slurred speech.
- Staggering or falling over.

- Loud, argumentative, or aggressive behavior.
- Vomiting.
- Drowsiness or sleepiness.

Alcohol intoxication and poisoning

When you see the signs and symptoms of alcohol intoxication and poisoning, call 911. These signs and symptoms are:

- Continuous vomiting.
- Cannot be awakened (is unconscious).
- Signs of a possible head injury, for example, they are vomiting and talking incoherently.
- Irregular, shallow, or slow breathing.
- Irregular, weak, or slow pulse rate.
- Cold, clammy, pale, or bluish colored skin.

Severe alcohol withdrawal

Signs and symptoms of severe alcohol withdrawal which may lead to a medical emergency:

- Delirium tremens — a state of confusion and visual hallucinations.
- Agitation.
- Fever.
- Seizures.
- Blackouts (when the person forgets what happened during the drinking episode).

How To Assist

If the person is intoxicated

Stay calm and communicate appropriately. Talk with the person in a respectful manner and use simple, clear language. Repeat simple requests and instructions because the person may find it difficult to comprehend what has been said. Do not laugh at, make fun of, or provoke the person.

Monitor for danger and assist. The person may engage in a wide range of activities that are risky to do while in a substance-affected state, such as driving, swimming, diving, or vandalizing property. Substance use can lead to a range of medical emergencies. Be aware that the person may be more affected than they realize. The following tips will help you keep them safe:

- Stay with the person or ensure they are not left alone.
- Move items that may cause them to trip.
- Encourage them to tell someone if they start to feel sick or uneasy and to call 911.
- Keep the person away from machines and dangerous objects.
- If they try to drive or to ride a bike, tell them about the risks to both self and others. If it is unsafe for you to prevent the person from driving, call 911 or the police. Tell the dispatcher that the person is intoxicated.

If they are a risk to self, drive them to the emergency room or see if someone else will drive them there. If they are not, organize a safe ride home for them after ensuring that they will not be left alone.

Call 911 if:

- The person is unconscious and cannot be woken.

- The person has irregular, shallow, or slow breathing.

- The person has an irregular, weak, or slow pulse rate.

- The person has cold, clammy, pale, or bluish colored skin.

- The person is continuously vomiting.

- The person shows signs of a possible head injury, for example, they are vomiting and talking incoherently.

- The person has a seizure.

- The person has delirium tremens.

- The person has blackouts and forgets what happened during the drinking episode.

- The person may have consumed a spiked drink (drink spiking is the illegal act of placing a substance into a drink with the intention of causing harm to the drinker; in recent years, media reports have shown drink spiking to be on the rise).

When to call 911

Do not be afraid to seek medical help for the person, even if there may be legal implications for them. Be aware that EMTs and hospital staff are there to help the person and not to enforce the law.

When you call 911

- Follow the 911 operator's instructions.

- When asked, describe the person's symptoms and explain that they have been drinking alcohol.

- Give the address of where you are.

- Stay with the person until the ambulance arrives.

- It is beneficial for a friend or family member to accompany the person to the hospital because they may be able to provide relevant information.

What to do while waiting for the ambulance

Ensure that:

- The person is not left alone.

- No food is given to the person, as they may choke on it if they are not fully conscious.

- The person's airway, breathing, and circulation are monitored.

- If the person is hard to wake, put them in the recovery position as in Figure 26.

- If the person is vomiting and conscious, keep the person sitting. Alternatively, put them in the recovery position. If necessary, clear the person's airway after they have vomited.

- An injury can go unnoticed when a person is intoxicated; you may need to check them for injury.

Can I help the person sober up?

No. Only time will reverse the effects of intoxication. The body metabolizes approximately one standard drink of alcohol an hour. Drinking black coffee, sleeping, walking, and taking cold showers will not speed this process up.

What do I do if the intoxicated person becomes aggressive?

Follow the advice in First Aid for Aggressive Behaviors later in this chapter.

Helping An Unconscious Person: The Recovery Position

Call 911 if someone is unconscious. The person needs immediate medical attention, and their airway must be kept open.

Putting the person in the recovery position will help to keep the airway open. If someone is left lying on their back, they could suffocate on vomit or the tongue could block the airway.

Before placing the person in the recovery position:

- Check the area for and remove any sharp objects such as broken glass or syringes.
- If the person has vomited and you need to clear their airway, you can use their fingers to clear vomit from the mouth.
- Keep the person warm without allowing them to overheat.

Figure 27

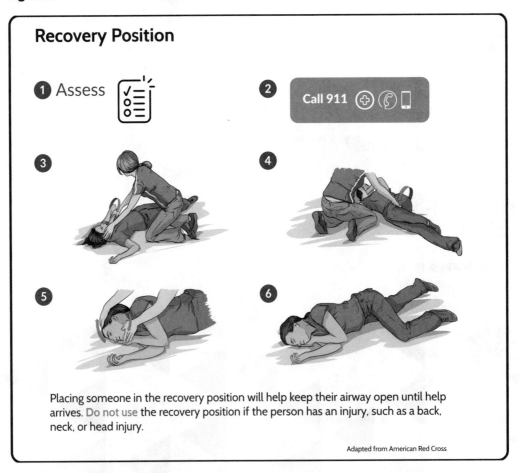

Recovery Position

① Assess

② Call 911

③ ④ ⑤ ⑥

Placing someone in the recovery position will help keep their airway open until help arrives. Do not use the recovery position if the person has an injury, such as a back, neck, or head injury.

Adapted from American Red Cross

Steps for putting someone in the recovery position

1. Assess the situation and find out what has happened to the person. Bump their foot gently with your foot and call their name. If you think a person may have a spinal injury, do not attempt to move them.

2. Call 911 right away.

3. Crouch by the unconscious person's side. Continue talking to the person so they know what you're doing. Bring the arm furthest away from you up so it is out of your way.

4. Bring the closest knee up and put the arm on the same side across the body.

5. With one hand on the shoulder closest and one hand on the raised knee, roll the person toward you. Move their arm and leg out so they are stable.

6. Adjust their head so it is resting on their high arm, making sure their mouth is pointed down so if they throw up, gravity helps them be safe.

Stay with the person until help arrives to ensure they do not roll forward and suffocate. If the person is on a couch or bed, remove pillows or other items that could cause them to suffocate. ·

Note

If you have physical first aid training, follow the protocol from your first aid course when responding to an emergency situation involving a physical injury.

MENTAL HEALTH FIRST AID FOR THE SEVERE EFFECTS FROM DRUG USE

The guidelines in this section were developed as part of an expert consensus study (Kingston et al., 2011).

Facts On Drug-Affected States

Drug-affected states are short-term changes in a person's state of mind or behavior as a result of drug use. These states distress the person or impair their ability to function.

The effects of drugs on behavior can vary from person to person depending on the sort of drug that has been used and the amount that is taken.

It is often difficult to make a distinction between the effects of different drugs.

Overdose

Overdose refers to use of an amount of a drug that could cause death, most typically opioid drugs. Overdose leads quickly to a loss of consciousness. If you think someone is overdosing, call 911 right away.

How To Assess

Some drugs make the person feel energetic and confident. Signs of more acute intoxication include:

- Becoming frustrated or angry.
- Having a racing heart.
- Overheating or dehydration.

Some drugs have hallucinogenic effects called "trips," including hallucinations and delusions and feelings of affection for others. Signs of more acute intoxication include:

- Having negative hallucinations and delusions.

- Becoming fearful or paranoid.

Some drugs have depressant effects, including fatigue, slurred speech, and slowed reflexes. Signs of more acute intoxication include:

- Feelings of having trouble moving.

- Vomiting.

- Loss of consciousness.

A medical emergency can result from overheating or dehydration from drug use. Symptoms of overheating or dehydration include:

- Feeling hot, exhausted, and weak.

- Persistent headache.

- Pale, cool, clammy skin.

- Rapid breathing and shortness of breath.

- Fatigue, thirst, and nausea.

- Giddiness and feeling faint.

Some drugs, such as ecstasy and cannabis, may have multiple effects. This is why it can be hard to tell what sort of drug has been used.

How To Assist

If the person is in a drug-affected state

- Stay calm and communicate appropriately. Talk with the person in a respectful manner and use simple, clear language. Repeat simple requests and instructions because the person may find it difficult to comprehend what has been said. Do not laugh at, make fun of, or provoke the person.

- Monitor for danger. The person may engage in a wide range of activities that are risky to do while in a substance-affected state, such as driving, swimming, diving, or vandalizing property. Substance use can lead to a range of medical emergencies. Be aware that the person may be more affected than they realize. The following tips will help you keep them safe:

  - Stay with the person or ensure they are not left alone.

  - Move items that may cause them to trip.

  - Encourage them to tell someone if they start to feel sick or uneasy and to call 911.

  - Keep the person away from machines and dangerous objects.

  - If they try to drive or to ride a bike, tell them about the risks to both self and others. If it is unsafe for you to prevent the person from driving, call 911 or the police. Tell the dispatcher that the person is intoxicated.

- If they are a risk to self, drive them to the emergency room or see if someone else will drive them there; otherwise, organize a safe ride home for the person after ensuring that they will not be left alone.

If the person seems to need 911

Call 911 in any of the following circumstances:

- You cannot get the person to wake up.

- Deteriorating or loss of consciousness.

- The person has irregular, shallow, or slow breathing.

- The person has an irregular, weak, or slow pulse rate.

- The person has cold, clammy, pale, or bluish colored skin.

- The person is continuously vomiting.

- The person shows signs of a possible head injury, for example, they are vomiting and talking incoherently.

- The person has a seizure.

- The person has delirium — a state of confusion and visual hallucinations.

- The person is overheated, dehydrated, or overhydrated.

When you call 911

- Follow the instructions of the 911 operator.

- When asked, describe the person's symptoms and explain that the person has been using drugs. Try to get detailed information about what drugs the person has taken by asking the person, their friends, or looking for clues.

- Give the 911 operator the address of where you are and stay with the person until the EMTs arrives.

- It is beneficial for a friend or family member to accompany the person to the hospital, as they may be able to provide relevant information.

> **Do not be afraid to** seek medical help for the person, even if there may be legal implications for them. Be aware that EMTs and hospital staff are there to help the person and not to enforce the law.

What to do while waiting for the EMTs

Ensure that:

- The person is not left alone.

- No food is given to the person, as they may choke on it if they are not fully conscious.

- The person's airway, breathing, and circulation are monitored.

- If the person is hard to wake, put them in the recovery position.

Helping a person who is overheating or dehydrated

If the person is showing symptoms of overheating or dehydration, you must keep the person calm and seek medical help immediately.

Encourage the person to rest somewhere quiet and cool. While waiting for help to arrive, reduce the person's body temperature gradually. Do this by loosening any restrictive clothing or removing any additional layers and encourage the person to sip nonalcoholic fluids like water and soft drinks.

Prevent the person from drinking too much water at once, as this may lead to over-hydration and even coma or death. Discourage the person from drinking alcohol as it may further dehydrate them.

What do I do if the intoxicated person becomes aggressive?
If this occurs, follow the advice in this chapter on aggressive behaviors.

MENTAL HEALTH FIRST AID FOR AN OPIOID OVERDOSE

Overdose happens when a toxic amount of a drug or combination of drugs overwhelms the body.

Opioid overdose is a very serious situation that requires immediate medical attention. If you think someone is overdosing, call 911 right away.

All drugs can cause an overdose, including prescription medication prescribed by a doctor.

See Chapter 10: Substance Use Disorders for more information.

How To Assess

It can be difficult to tell when a person is overdosing on opioids because the symptoms of being very intoxicated ("high") on opioids are similar to those of an overdose. The table shows the contrasting symptoms.

SYMPTOMS OF A PERSON BEING VERY HIGH ON OPIOIDS	SYMPTOMS OF A POTENTIAL OPIOID OVERDOSE
Slow movement and reactions	• Slow heartbeat/pulse • Pale clammy skin • Blue or purple-tinged fingernails or lips
Speech is slowed/slurred	• Deep snoring or gurgling (death rattle) • Very infrequent or no breathing
Sleepy looking but responds when you talk to the person, tap their shoulder, or rub your knuckles on the center of their ribcage	• Extreme sleepiness • Cannot be awakened verbally • Cannot be awakened when you rub your knuckles on the center of the person's ribcage
Nodding off or falling asleep	• Heavy nod • Not responsive to stimulation such as talking to the person, tapping their shoulder, or rubbing your knuckles over the person's ribcage

How To Assist

Naloxone is a medication that you can administer to save someone's life. Call 911 immediately for anyone who is given naloxone.

Naloxone is an opioid antagonist, which means it counters the effects of opioid overdose. Naloxone works to reverse the overdose by binding to the same receptors in the brain as opioid drugs and blocking them for approximately 30 minutes.

Naloxone is a temporary solution; it does not stop the overdose for good. It may provide time for medical professionals to arrive and give appropriate medical attention to the individual in need. Someone who is given naloxone may wake up immediately, but this does not mean they are in the clear. Everyone who gets naloxone needs immediate medical attention.

Figure 28

The SAMHSA Opioid Overdose Toolkit is for every First Aider who may encounter someone with opioid use disorder.

Naloxone is safe and can be given by anyone. It can be administered through an IV, into the muscle, underneath the skin, or in the nose as a spray.

First Aiders who know a person who uses opioids should carry naloxone and should tell the person that they wish to share information about naloxone with someone close to them.

Can I Be Arrested For Possession Of A Controlled Substance Or Paraphernalia If Emts Come In Because Someone Is Experiencing An Overdose?

Thirty-seven states and the District of Columbia have "Good Samaritan" statutes that prevent prosecution for possession of a controlled substance or paraphernalia if emergency assistance is sought for someone who is experiencing an overdose, including an opioid-induced overdose.

No matter what, when naloxone is given, 911 should be called.

How Do I Learn The Steps For Administering Naloxone?

Information about accessing naloxone and getting trained in how to administer naloxone is in the Helpful Resources section.

In particular, the SAMHSA Opioid Overdose Toolkit offers information that is indispensable for you as a First Aider. The toolkit is at https://store.samhsa.gov/system/files/sma18-4742.pdf. It will give you detailed information about opioid use, overdose, steps for administering naloxone, and ways to provide help.

How To Help When You Suspect An Opioid Overdose

If you suspect an opioid overdose and the person is extremely drowsy and unresponsive:

- Check for breathing and pulse.
- Administer naloxone if it is available.
- Call 911. State "Someone is unresponsive and not breathing" and give a specific address and/or description of the location.

- Sit with the person until medical help arrives.
- If the person is not breathing and has no pulse, start CPR.
- If the person does not respond to naloxone, or responds at first but then starts to drift off again, then give more naloxone.

Everyone who gets naloxone needs immediate medical attention.

MENTAL HEALTH FIRST AID FOR AGGRESSIVE BEHAVIORS

Aggressive, defiant, and hostile behaviors involve verbal or physical attacks.

Violent behavior can include explosive fits of rage, physical aggression, fighting, threats or attempts to hurt others (including thoughts of wanting to kill others), use of weapons, cruelty toward animals, fire setting, and intentional destruction of property (vandalism).

Important Note

Many communities have trained responders who handle mental health crises. If you call 911 because someone is showing aggressive behaviors, you can ask for responders trained in mental health crises. Some communities have a mobile crisis team available. (Of course, if the person poses a serious threat to the First Aider or others, the priority is to get the police or other first responders to the location.)

How To Assess

Aggressive behavior can be:

- Verbal (for example, insults or threats).
- Behavioral (for example, pounding, throwing things, or violating personal space).
- Emotional (for example, raised voice or looking angry).

If at any time during your assessment you are not comfortable approaching and performing Mental Health First Aid, you can always call a crisis team and/or a non-emergency line to get support for the person.

A person with an intellectual disability or some developmental disabilities may not be able to explain whether the aggressive behavior is related to a mental health challenge, disorder, or severe emotional distress.

Aggressive behaviors may be a response to fear. First Aiders can ask the person what has happened that has caused them to be upset. At times aggression can be the result of poor communication. What is seen as aggression can vary between individuals.

How To Assist

Your first steps are to:

- Ensure your own safety.
  - Always ensure you have access to an exit.
  - If you are frightened, remove yourself from the situation and call 911.
  - If the person's aggression escalates out of control at any time, you should remove yourself from the situation and call 911.

- ◦ Take any threats or warnings seriously. Remove yourself from the situation and call 911.
  - » When calling 911, tell the 911 operator if you believe that a mental health crisis team is needed.
- • If it is safe to stay with the person, remain as calm as possible and try to de-escalate the situation while you wait for help to arrive.

To de-escalate the situation:

- ◦ Speak to the person slowly and confidently with a gentle, caring tone of voice.
- ◦ Do not restrict the person's movement (for example, you can allow them to pace up and down the room if they want).
- ◦ Consider taking a break from the conversation to allow the person a chance to calm down.
- ◦ Consider inviting the person to sit down if they are standing.
- ◦ Ask "What happened?" rather than "What's wrong with you?"
- ◦ Use positive words (such as "Stay calm") instead of negative words (such as "Don't fight").
- ◦ Leave the room to call 911.

Important "do nots" include:

- ◦ Do not argue with the person.
- ◦ Do not threaten them.
- ◦ Do not sound hostile.
- ◦ Do not shuffle your feet, fidget, or make abrupt movements.

If you believe that the aggression is related to a mental health challenge, you may need to call the mental health crisis team. If you do so, describe the person's symptoms and behaviors. Recall that First Aiders do not diagnose. Be aware that the crisis team may not attend without a police presence.

Figure 29

Safety is your priority — Plan your exit.

If you are frightened

If the person's aggression gets out of control at any time

If the person issues a threat or warns you of something

Remove yourself from the situation and CALL 911.

We need a mental health crisis team.

HELPFUL RESOURCES

Numerous diverse resources can be found on the Mental Health First Aid website at
https://www.mentalhealthfirstaid.org/mental-health-resources/

National Suicide Prevention Lifeline
1–800–273–TALK (1-800-273-8255)

This is a crisis hotline that can help with many issues, not just suicide. For example, anyone who feels sad, hopeless, or suicidal; family and friends who are concerned about a loved one; or anyone interested in mental health treatment referrals can call the Lifeline. Callers are connected with a professional nearby who will talk with them about what they are feeling or their concerns for other family and friends. Call the toll-free lifeline, 24 hours/day, seven days/week.

Crisis Text Line
Text "MHFA" to 741741

Available 24/7, 365 days a year, this organization helps people with mental health challenges by connecting callers with trained crisis volunteers who will provide confidential advice, support, and referrals if needed.

Lifeline Crisis Chat
www.crisischat.org

Visit www.crisischat.org to chat online with crisis centers around the United States.

The Trevor Project
Call 866-488-7386 or Text "START" to 678678
https://www.thetrevorproject.org

Trained counselors available 24/7 to support people under 25 who are in crisis, feeling suicidal, or in need of a safe and judgment free place to talk. Specializing in supporting the LGBTQI+ community.

The National Council for Behavioral Health
https://www.TheNationalCouncil.org/providers/?region=

Search for organizations that are committed to providing mental health services to anyone in the community who needs it regardless of their ability to pay.

Substance Abuse and Mental Health Services Administration
https://www.samhsa.gov/find-help

SAMHSA provides information on mental health services and treatment centers through an online service locator. You can search by your location, whether or not they provide services for youth, payment options (private insurance, cash, or something else), languages spoken, etc.

Child Welfare Information Gateway's Mandatory Reporters of Child Abuse and Neglect: Summary of State Laws
www.childwelfare.gov/systemwide/laws_policies/state/index.cfm

This summary will also tell you whether you are required to report by law and specific statute information for a particular state.

See the Mental Health First Aid website for additional mental resources and answers to frequently asked questions at https://www.MentalHealthFirstAid.org/mental-health-resources/

GLOSSARY

Acute stress disorder
Feelings of distress that may occur following a traumatic event.

Addiction
A generic term for severe substance use disorders, generally referring to loss of control over use of substances leading to physical and psychological dependence.

Adult day treatment
A program that provides social skills, training, group and individual counseling, medication evaluations, and occupational or vocational therapy.

Advance care directive
A document describing how a person wants to be treated when they are unable to make their own decisions due to their present state of illness. This is an agreement made between the person, their family, and sometimes their primary health care provider.

Adverse childhood experience (ACE)
A traumatic experience that occurs before age 18. ACEs include physical, sexual, or emotional abuse; physical or emotional neglect; intimate partner violence; violence against a child's mother; substance misuse in the home; parental separation or divorce; and/or having an incarcerated household member.

Aggressive behavior
Behavior characterized by physical or verbal attack that may be appropriate or destructive to the self or others. Aggression that is not a response to a clear threat can sometimes be a sign of a mental health disorder (Liu, 2004).

Agoraphobia
Anxiety or extreme fear regarding situations perceived to be difficult to escape from or find help in. Situations such as using public transportation, standing in a grocery line, or being in a movie theater may cause extreme anxiety.

Alcohol
An intoxicating ingredient found in beer, wine, and liquor. It is socially acceptable to drink alcohol to socialize, celebrate, and relax. The effects of alcohol vary from person to person and depend on how much and how often a person drinks, their age, health status, tolerance, and genetics.

ALGEE
The 5-step MHFA Action Plan used to provide a person with a mental health or substance use issue or experiencing a mental health or substance use crisis. The five steps are:

1. Action A – Approach, assess for risk of suicide or harm, assist
2. Action L – Listen nonjudgmentally
3. Action G – Give reassurance and information
4. Action E – Encourage appropriate professional help
5. Action E – Encourage self-help and other support strategies

Alternative therapies
Treatments for mental health challenges other than the traditional mental health, hospitalization, and institutional care options (such as biofeedback, yoga, therapeutic massage, and light therapy).
Amphetamines
A group of drugs used to increase a person's alertness, attention, and energy. Amphetamines have legitimate medical uses, but are also commonly misused/abused.

Anorexia nervosa
An eating disorder characterized by extreme weight-loss strategies used in an attempt to control body weight that can include dieting, fasting, over-exercising, using diet pills, diuretics, laxatives, and vomiting.

Antidepressant medications
Drugs used to prevent or treat depression.

Antipsychotic medications
Drugs used to prevent or treat psychosis.

Anxiety
A feeling of worry caused by perceived threats in the environment. Although unpleasant, anxiety can be useful in helping a person avoid dangerous or risky situations. It can motivate the person to take action and address the immediate risk as well as everyday troubles.

Assertive community treatment (ACT)
ACT is an approach for people experiencing more severe, chronic, and persistent symptoms of psychotic disorders. The person's care is managed by a team of health professionals, such as a psychiatrist, nurse, psychologist, and social worker. Care is available 24 hours a day and is tailored to the person's individual needs. Support is provided to family members as well. ACT has been found to reduce relapse and the need for hospitalization.

Behavioral addiction
Similar to substance addiction, except the person is addicted to the feeling brought on by an action, such as gambling or viewing pornography, rather than a substance.

Behavioral health care
Assessment and treatment of both mental and substance use or abuse disorders.

Bereavement
Feelings of sadness and grief that occur with the death of a loved one.

The Big Five Personality Traits
A description of personality including:
- Extraversion — The level of sociability and enthusiasm.
- Agreeableness — The level of friendliness and kindness.
- Conscientiousness — The level of organization and work ethic.
- Emotional stability (also called neuroticism) — The level of calmness and tranquility.
- Intellect/imagination (also called openness) — The level of creativity and curiosity.

Binge eating disorder
An eating disorder characterized by recurring episodes of eating significantly more than most people would eat under similar circumstances. These binges occur at least once per week over three months or more.

Bipolar disorder
A mental disorder characterized by extreme swings in mood, with periods of depression, periods of mania, and long periods of a normal mood in between.

Bipolar disorder not otherwise specified
A diagnosis for a person whose symptoms do not fit under the other types of bipolar disorders but who has experienced episodes of significant mood swings.

Bipolar I disorder
A mental disorder characterized by manic episodes that last at least seven days and/or require hospitalization as well as depressive episodes that last approximately two weeks.

Bipolar II disorder
A mental disorder characterized by less severe manic episodes (hypomania) that last at least seven days and/or require hospitalization as well as depressive episodes that last approximately two weeks.

Brain stimulation therapies
Treatment approaches used to treat medicine-resistant depression. Some of these therapies include repetitive transcranial magnetic stimulation (rTMS) and vagus nerve stimulation (VNS).

Bulimia nervosa
An eating disorder characterized by recurrent episodes of uncontrolled eating or eating unusually large amounts of food and feeling a lack of control over the eating. This over-eating is followed by a type of behavior that compensates for the binge, such as purging, fasting, and/or excessive exercising (NIMH, Nov 2017).

Cannabis (marijuana)
The dried leaves, flowers, stems, and seeds from the hemp plant.

Certified peer support specialist
Specialists with training that enables them to use their own lived experiences to promote hope, personal responsibility, empowerment, education, and self-determination.

Clinical social workers
Social work specialists who focus on assessment, diagnosis, treatment, and prevention of mental, emotional, and behavioral health challenges or crises (National Association of Social Workers, 2019).

Cognitive behavioral therapy
A type of psychotherapy that challenges negative thought patterns about the self and the world in order to alter unwanted behavior patterns or treat mood disorders such as depression.

Comorbidity
When a person has more than one health condition at the same time.

Complementary treatments
Treatments like life coaching and lifestyle changes that involve using natural or alternative therapies and changing the way one lives.

Compulsive behaviors
Repetitive behaviors that the person feels driven to perform in response to an obsession in order to reduce anxiety.

Co-occurrence
When a person has more than one health condition at the same time.

Coordinated specialty care
This recovery-oriented treatment program connects individuals who have experienced first episode psychosis (FEP) with a team of specialists, who work with the patient to create a personal treatment plan toward recovery. The aim of this early intervention approach is to initiate support as early as possible following the first episode. A treatment plan can include some of the following: psychotherapy, medication management, family education and support, case management, and work or education support, depending on the individual's needs and preferences.

Counseling
A variety of treatment techniques that aim to help a person identify and change troubling emotions, thoughts, and behavior.

Culture
A combination of a person's values, norms, expectations, and identity that can affect one's perceptions, the actions they take, how they interact with others, and impacts how communities and families are organized.

Delusions
Delusions are fixed beliefs that do not change even when there is conflicting evidence. Some delusions are bizarre, other are not.

Depression
A sad or low mood that persists for at least two weeks.

Depression with a seasonal pattern
A depressive disorder with episodes that occur during a specific time of year, generally fall or winter, and lift during other times of year. Formerly seasonal affective disorder.

Dialectic behavioral therapy
A combination of cognitive and behavioral therapies designed to help a person transform negative thought patterns and destructive behaviors into positive outcomes.

Disability
A health condition that disrupts people's ability to work, care for themselves, attend school, and carry on relationships.

Discrimination
Negative behaviors against a person based on perceived belonging to a social group.

Disease burden
The combined effect of premature death and years lived with disability caused by illness (World Health Organization, 2018).

Drug
A chemical substance that can change how a person's body and mind work by affecting the brain in different ways.

Dual-diagnosis
When a person has more than one health condition at the same time.

Dysthymia
A persistent depressive disorder where a person experiences a depressed mood with at least two other symptoms of depression for at least two years.

Early intervention
Recognizing the warning signs of a mental health or substance use problem and taking action before a problem becomes worse.

Eating disorder
A serious illness tied to irregular eating habits, severe stress, or concerns about body image, characterized by too much or too little food intake.

Electroconvulsive therapy
A procedure done under general anesthesia, usually in a hospital setting, where controlled electric currents are passed through the brain. It is used to treat severe depression and sometimes severe bipolar disorder.

Emergency psychiatric services
Immediate assessment, crisis counseling, and referral for people at immediate risk of harm to self or others. Often this service precedes admission to inpatient hospitalization, but most people who seek emergency psychiatric services stabilize and can return to their community setting after the evaluation.

Enduring power of attorney
A legal agreement where a person appoints someone of their choice to manage their legal and financial affairs. This is developed when a person is of sound mind. As the agreement is "enduring," it will continue to apply if the person becomes unable to make their own decisions (legally described as being of "unsound mind").

Enduring power of guardianship
A legal agreement where a person appoints someone of their choice to manage, where necessary, medical and welfare decisions on their behalf. It only comes into effect when the person becomes unable to make their own decisions.

Exposure therapy
See cognitive behavior therapy.

Eye movement desensitization (EMDR) therapy
A therapeutic technique designed to alleviate the distress related to traumatic memories. Using eye movement to help the person focus on external stimuli allows for internal processing of traumatic memories.

First Aider
An individual certified to provide Mental Health First Aid to a person experiencing a mental health or substance use problem or crisis.

Gender identity
A person's self-identification as male, female, or a combination of both or neither. A person's gender identity can be the same as or different from their biological sex.

Generalized anxiety disorder
Long-term anxiety across a whole range of situations that interferes with a person's life.

Hallucinations
Seeing, hearing, feeling, or smelling things that others do not see, hear, feel, or smell.

Hallucinogens
Drugs that affect a person's perceptions of reality. Some hallucinogens also produce rapid, intense emotional changes.

Individual trauma
An event, series of events, or set of circumstances that is experienced by an individual as physically or emotionally harmful or life threatening and that has lasting adverse effects on the individual's functioning and mental, physical, social, emotional, or spiritual well-being (SAMHSA, May 2018).

Integrated care
A combination of primary health care with mental and behavioral health care in one setting.

Interpersonal psychotherapy (IPT)
An evidence-based approach that allows a person to focus on improving the quality of their interpersonal relationships, increasing social support and functioning to alleviate their stress.

LGBTQI+
Lesbian, gay, bisexual, transgender, queer/questioning, intersex, and other gender and sexual identities.

Major depressive disorder
A mental disorder characterized by persistently depressed mood or loss of interest in activities, causing significant impairment in daily life.

Mania
A state of excitement manifested by mental and physical hyperactivity, disorganization of behavior, and elevation of mood.

Mental disorder
See mental illness.

Mental health
A state of well-being in which the individual realizes his or her own abilities, can cope with the normal stresses of life, can work productively and fruitfully, and is able to make a contribution to their community (WHO, 2004).

Mental Health First Aid
The help offered to a person developing a mental health or substance use issue or experiencing a mental health or substance use crisis. The first aid is given until appropriate treatment and support are received or until the crisis resolves.

Mental health challenge
A broad term that includes both mental disorders and symptoms of mental disorders that may not be severe enough to warrant the diagnosis of a mental disorder.

Mental illness
A diagnosable illness that affects a person's thinking, emotional state, and behavior and disrupts the person's ability to work or carry out other daily activities and engage in satisfying personal relationships.

Mental wellness, mental well-being
A state that allows a person to perform well at work, in their studies, and in family and other social relationships.

Mindfulness
Being conscious and accepting of the present moment while acknowledging one's thoughts, feelings, and bodily sensations.

Mindfulness-based cognitive therapy
A strategy that utilizes concepts of mindfulness and accepting the "present moment" to encourage individuals with depression to pay attention to their experiences and disengage from triggering or stressful factors moment by moment (Lu, 2015).

Mood stabilizers
A general term for medications that are used to control extreme variations in a person's mood.

Negative symptoms
Associated with disruptions in an individual's regular emotions and behaviors. They are called negative symptoms because they are aspects of well-being that a person does not have.

Nonsuicidal self-injury (NSSI)
Deliberate, self-inflicted damage to the body without the intent to die by suicide (American Psychiatric Association, 2013).

Nutritional counselors
Experts who can provide education about nutritional needs, meal planning, and monitoring eating choices.

Obsessive-compulsive disorder
Obsessive thoughts and compulsive behaviors accompany feelings of anxiety. Obsessions are recurrent thoughts and images that are experienced as intrusive, unwanted, and inappropriate and cause marked anxiety.

Opioids
Opioids are a type of drug used to reduce pain. Opioids work by binding to specific brain receptors to minimize the body's perception of pain.

Panic attack
The sudden onset of intense worry, fear, or terror. These attacks begin suddenly and develop rapidly and briefly and involve an intense fear that is out of proportion to the circumstances in which it is occurring.

Panic disorder
Recurrent unexpected panic attacks that interfere with daily living activities at home, work, and in social situations.

Partial hospitalization
The comprehensive staffing and programming of inpatient hospitalization for people who are not at immediate risk of harm to self and others and who can go to a stable and supportive living environment at the end of the day.

Peer counseling
A practice of having people with lived experience of a mental disorder trained to work with others in a number of different settings in conjunction with other treatments.

Positive symptoms
Behaviors not generally seen in the person's typical healthy behavior. They are called positive symptoms because these symptoms are present.

Post-traumatic stress disorder
Feelings of distress that last longer than one month following a traumatic event.

Prejudice
Negative attitudes against a person based on perceived belonging to a social group.

Primary care physician
The medical doctor responsible for overseeing your medical care.

Problem solving therapy
A form of cognitive behavior therapy that encourages positive and rational approaches to problem-solving. It also focuses on reducing avoidance of problem-solving.

Protective factor
Something that decreases the chances of a person being adversely affected by a circumstance or disorder.

Psychiatric mental health nurses
Registered nurse specialists who work with patients, families, and communities to diagnose, treat, and promote mental health (American Psychiatric Nurses Association, 2018).

Psychiatrist
A medical doctor who specializes in the treatment of mental disorders with severe or long-lasting impact.

Psychoeducation
A type of psychological therapy that can help reduce psychotic symptoms by helping the person develop alternative explanations of schizophrenia symptoms, reducing the impact of the symptoms, and encouraging the person to take their medication.

Psychologist
A mental health professional with advanced training who can diagnose and treat mental health conditions. Psychologists are not medical doctors and cannot prescribe medication.

Psychosis
A general term used to describe a mental health condition in which a person has lost some contact with reality. Psychosis causes a person's thoughts and perceptions to be disrupted, and the person may not understand what is real and what is not. Psychosis is a syndrome, or collection of symptoms, not an illness.

Psychotic episodes
A period of psychotic thoughts and behaviors that can involve three different phases: the prodromal phase, the acute phase, and the recovery phase.

Recovery
The process of change through which individuals improve their health and well-being, live a self-directed life, and strive to reach their full potential and personal journey with the goals of hope, empowerment, and autonomy.

Recovery position
A body position where an unconscious-but-breathing person is placed on their left side with the left arm supporting the head and the right knee drawn towards the abdomen.

Remission
In the recovery process, remission refers to a reduction of key symptoms of substance use.

Resilience
A person's ability to "bounce back" or overcome challenging experiences.

Risk factor
Something that increases the chances of a person being adversely affected by a circumstance or disorder.

Schizoaffective disorder
A disorder where a person has had at least one separate episode each of psychosis and depressive/manic disorder but may not meet the criteria for bipolar disorder.

Schizophrenia
A chronic and severe mental disorder that involves a breakdown in the relationships between how a person thinks, feels, and behaves.

Self-care

The active practice of seeing to your own physical and mental health needs, particularly during or after a stressful event.

Self-directed violence

Behavior directed at oneself that deliberately results in injury or the potential for injury. Self-directed violence may be suicidal or nonsuicidal in nature.

Self-help

The practice of improving yourself or coping with your own problems using resources and strategies you access on your own.

Sexual orientation

An inherent or immutable enduring emotional, romantic or sexual attraction to other people (Human Rights Campaign, 2019).

Social anxiety disorder

A fear of situations in which a person may be observed and judged by others.

Social skills training

Training used to improve social and independent living skills.

Social support

Having a network of family and friends available to turn to in challenging times.

Specific phobia

Intense anxiety and fear about a specific situation or object.

Spectrum of interventions

The entire service array, including institutional and community mental health services, social support groups, public education programs, and volunteer services that can be customized to meet the individual's needs.

Stigma

Negative attitudes and behaviors carried by a group towards another group, person, or circumstance.

Stimulants

Substances that increase a person's alertness, attention, and energy and also increase blood pressure, heart rate, and respiration.

Substance- or medication-induced psychotic disorder

Delusions or hallucinations brought on by the use of or withdrawal from substances or medications.

Substance use disorder

A problematic pattern of using alcohol or another substance that results in impairment in daily life or noticeable distress (American Psychiatric Association, 2013).

Suicidal ideation

Thoughts or plans about suicide.

Suicide

A death caused by self-injurious behavior with the intent to die.

Suicide attempt

A non-fatal, self-directed, and potentially injurious behavior with an intent to die. A suicide attempt may or may not result in injury.

Supported employment and education (SEE)

An important part of coordinated specialty care; offers a way to help individuals return to work or school. A SEE specialist helps people develop the skills they need to achieve their personal school and work goals, further supporting their recovery.

Tolerance (substance use)

A person's ability to function while under the influence of a substance. Tolerance generally increases as a person continues to use a substance. The person needs to use increasing amounts to get the desired effect, or they get less effect with the same amount of the substance.

Trauma

An event, series of events, or set of circumstances that is experienced by an individual as physically or emotionally harmful or life threatening and that has lasting adverse effects on the individual's functioning and mental, physical, social, emotional, or spiritual well-being.

Traumatic disorders

Specific mental disorders with definable symptoms, causes, and treatments.

Vaping

The act of inhaling and exhaling the aerosol, known as vapor, that is produced by an e-cigarette or similar device.

Well-being, wellness

A state that allows a person to perform in good condition at work, in their studies, and in family and other social relationships.

REFERENCES

Abdullah, T., & Brown, T. (2011). Mental illness stigma and ethocultural beliefs, values, and norms: An integrative review. Clinical Psychology Review, 31, 934-948.

Abuse, S., US, M. H. S. A., & Office of the Surgeon General (US. (2016). Early Intervention, Treatment, and Management of Substance Use Disorders. In Facing Addiction in America: The Surgeon General's Report on Alcohol, Drugs, and Health. US Department of Health and Human Services.

Alsawy, S., Wood, L., Taylor, P., & Morrison, A. (2015). Psychotic experiences and PTSD: Exploring associations in a population survey. Psychological Medicine, 45(13), 2849-2859. doi:10.1017/S003329171500080X

American Board of Preventive Medicine. Overview. https://www.theabpm.org/become-certified/subspecialties/addiction-medicine/

American Foundation for Suicide Prevention. (2018). Suicide claims more lives than war, murder, and natural disasters combined. https://afsp.donordrive.com/index.cfm?fuseaction=cms.page&id=1226&eventID=5545

American Psychiatric Association. (2013). Diagnostic and Statistical Manual of Mental Disorders: Fifth Edition. Washington DC: American Psychiatric Publishing.

American Psychological Association. (2015). Definitions related to sexual orientation and gender diversity in APA documents. APA Dictionary of Psychology.

American Psychiatric Association. (2016, Jul). What is psychotherapy? (R. Parekh, Editor) https://www.psychiatry.org/patients-families/psychotherapy

American Psychiatric Nurses Association. (2018). Psychiatric-mental health nurses. APNA: https://www.apna.org/i4a/pages/index.cfm?pageid=3292

American Psychological Association. (2018). The road to resilience. http://www.apa.org/helpcenter/road-resilience.aspx

Anda, R., Felitti, V., Bremner, D. J., J., Walker, J., Whitfield, C., Perry, B., . . . Giles, W. (2006). The enduring effects of abuse and related adverse experiences in childhood: A convergence of evidence from neurobiology and epidemiology. European Archives of Psychiatry and Clinical Neuroscience, 256(3), 174-186. doi:10.1007/s00406-005-0624-4

Arcelus, J., Mitchell, A., Wales, J., & Nielsen, S. (2011, Jul). Mortality rates in patients with anorexia nervosa and other eating disorders: A meta-analysis of 36 studies. Archives of General Psychiatry, 68(7), 724-731. doi:10.1001/archgenpsychiatry.2011.74

Asnaani, A., Richey, A., Dimaite, R., Hinton, D., & Hofmann, S. (2010). A cross-ethnic comparison of lifetime prevalence rates of anxiety disorders. The Journal of Nervous and Mental Diseases, 198(8), 551-555. doi:10.1097/NMD.0b013e3181ea169f

Avalos, L. A., Flanagan, T., & Li, D. K. (2019). Preventing perinatal depression to improve maternal and child health—A health care imperative. JAMA Pediatrics, 173(4), 313-314.

Bagalman, E., & Napili, A. (2014). Prevalence of mentalillness in the United States: Data sources and estimates (CRS Report 7-5700). https://fas.org/sgp/crs/misc/R43047.pdf

Baiden, P. (2017). Non-suicidal self-injury and suicidal behaviours among children and adolescents: The role of adverse childhood experiences and bullying victimization. Doctoral thesis, University of Toronto, Factor-Inwentash Faculty of Social Work. https://tspace.library.utoronto.ca/bitstream/1807/80719/1/Baiden_Philip_201711_PhD_thesis.pdf

Bandelow, B., & Michaelis, S. (2015). Epidemiology of anxiety disorders in the 21st century. Dialogues in Clinical Neuroscience, 17(3), 327-325.

Banh, M., Chaikind, J., Robertson, H., Troxel, M., Achille, J., Egan, C., & Anthony, B. (2018). Evaluation of Mental Health First Aid USA using the Mental Health Beliefs and Literacy Scale. American Journal of Health Promotion. doi:10.1177/0890117118784234

Barnett, J. C., & Berchick, E. R. (2017). Health insurance coverage in the United States: 2016. Washington, D.C.: U.S. Government Printing Office.

Becker, A., Franko, D., Speck, A., & Herzog, D. (2003). Ethnicity and differential access to care for eating disorder symptoms. International Journal of Eating Disorders, 33(2), 205-212. doi:10.1002/eat.10129

Berke, J., & Gould, S. (2019). This Map Shows Every US State Where Pot Is Legal. Times Union.

Beyer, J., & Weisler, R. (2016). Suicide behaviors in bipolar disorder: A review and update for the clinician. The Psychiatric Clinics of North America, 39(1), 111-123. doi:10.1016/j.psc.2015.09.002

Bhughra, D., & Flick, G. (2005). Pathways to care for patients with bipolar disorder. Bipolar Disorders, 7(3), 236-45. doi:10.1111/j.1399-5618.2005.00202.x

Boelen, P. A., Reijntjes, A., & Smid, G. E. (2016). Concurrent and prospective associations of intolerance of uncertainty with symptoms of prolonged grief, posttraumatic stress, and depression after bereavement. Journal of Anxiety Disorders, 41, 65-72.

Bonanno, G. A., Westphal, M., & Mancini, A. D. (2011). Resilience to loss and potential trauma. Annual review of clinical psychology, 7, 511-535.

Bostwick, W. B., Boyd, C. J., Hughes, T. L., West, B. T., & McCabe, S. E. (2014). Discrimination and mental health among lesbian, gay, and bisexual adults in the United States. The American Journal of Orthopsychiatry, 84(1), 35–45. https://doi.org/10.1037/h0098851

Brisch, R., Saniotis, A., Wolf, R., Bielau, H., Bernstein, H., Steiner, J., . . . Gos, T. (2014, May). The role of dopamine in schizophrenia from a neurobiological and evolutionary perspective: Old fashioned, but still in vogue. Front Psychiatry, 5(110). doi:10.3389/fpsyt.2014.00047

Brody, D., Pratt, L., & Hughes, J. (2018). Prevalence of depression among adults aged 20 and over: United States, 2013-2016. https://www.cdc.gov/nchs/products/databriefs/db303.htm

Brown, B. (2015). Daring greatly: How the courage to be vulnerable transforms the way we live, love, parent, and lead. London: Penguin Books Ltd.

Bruce, M., & Hoff, R. (1994). Social and physical health risk factors for first-onset major depressive disorder in a community sample. Social Psychiatry and Psychiatric Epidemiology, 29(4), 165-171. doi:10.1007/BF00802013

Bystritsky, A., Kerwin, L., Niv, N., Natoli, J. L., Abrahami, N., Klap, R., Wells, K., & Young, A. S. (2010). Clinical and subthreshold panic disorder. Depression and Anxiety, 27(4), 381–389. https://doi.org/10.1002/da.20622

Campbell, L., Brown, T., & Grisham, J. (2003). The relevance of age of onset to the psychopathology of generalized anxiety disorder. Behavior Therapy, 34(1), 31-48. doi:10.1016/S0005-7894(03)80020-5

Cantor-Graae, E., & Selten, J. (2005, Jan). Schizophrenia and migration: A meta-analysis and review. American Journal of Psychiatry, 162(1), 12-24. doi:10.1176/appi.ajp.162.1.12

Carpiniello, B., & Pinna, F. (2017). The reciprocal relationship between suicidality and stigma. Frontiers in Psychiatry, 8(3). doi:10.3389/fpsyt.2017.00035

Center for Behavioral Health Statistics and Quality. (2017). 2016 National Survey on Drug Use and Health: Methodological summary and definitions. https://www.samhsa.gov/data/sites/default/files/NSDUH-MethodSummDefs-2016/NSDUH-MethodSummDefs-2016.htm

Centers for Disease Control and Prevention. (2012). Key findings: Trends in the prevalence of developmental disabilities in US children, 1997–2008. Atlanta: Department of Health and Human Services.

Centers for Disease Control and Prevention. (2013). Vital signs: Current cigarette smoking among adults aged ≥18 years with mental illness — United States, 2009–2011. Morbidity and Mortality Weekly Report, 62(05), 81-87. https://www.cdc.gov/mmwr/preview/mmwrhtml/mm6205a2.htm

Centers for Disease Control and Prevention. (2014). Surveillance for violent deaths - National Violent Death Reporting System, 16 states, 2010 surveillance summaries. Morbidity and Mortality Weekly Report, 63(SS01), 1-33. https://www.cdc.gov/mmwr/preview/mmwrhtml/ss6301a1.htm

Centers for Disease Control and Prevention. (2016, Apr 1). Adverse childhood experiences. https://www.cdc.gov/violenceprevention/acestudy/index.html

Centers for Disease Control and Prevention. About the CDC-Kaiser ACE Study. https://www.cdc.gov/violenceprevention/childabuseandneglect/acestudy/about.html

Centers for Disease Control and Prevention. (2016). WISQARS Fatal Injury Data. Washington DC. https://www.cdc.gov/injury/wisqars/fatal.html

Centers for Disease Control and Prevention. (2017, Jun 21). LGBT youth. https://www.cdc.gov/lgbthealth/youth.htm

Centers for Disease Control and Prevention. Synthetic cannabinoids: What are they? What are their effects? https://www.cdc.gov/nceh/hsb/chemicals/sc/default.html

Center for Substance Abuse Treatment. (2014). Understanding the impact of trauma. In Trauma-informed care in behavioral health services. Substance Abuse and Mental Health Services Administration.

Cicero, T., Ellis, M., & Surratt, H. (2014). The changing face of heroin use in the United States. JAMA Psychiatry, 71(7), 821-826. doi:10.1001/jamapsychiatry.2014.366

Cipriano, A., Cella, S., & Cotrufo, P. (2017). Nonsuicidal self-injury: A systematic review. Frontiers in Psychology, 8, 1946. doi:10.3389/fpsyg.2017.01946

Cohen Veterans Network and National Council for Behavioral Health. (2018). America's Mental Health 2018. https://www.cohenveteransnetwork.org/wp-content/uploads/2018/10/Research-Summary-10-10-2018.pdf

Coleman, E., Bockting, W., Botzer, M., Cohen-Kettenis, P., DeCuypere, G., Feldman, J., ... & Monstrey, S. (2012). Standards of care for the health of transsexual, transgender, and gender-nonconforming people, version 7. International Journal of Transgenderism, 13(4), 165-232.

Corrigan, P., & Shah, B. (2017). Understanding and addressing the stigma experienced by people with first episode psychosis. Alexandria, VA: National Association of State Mental Health Program Directors. https://www.nasmhpd.org/sites/default/files/DH-Stigma_research_brief_0.pdf

Corrigan, P., & Watson, A. (2002). Understanding the stigma on people with mental illness. World Psychiatry, 1(1), 16-20.

Coute, R. A., Nathanson, B., Kurz, M. C., Haas, N. L., McNally, B., & Mader, T. J. (2019). National Institutes of Health Research Investment for the Leading Causes of Disability-Adjusted Life Years in the United States. Circulation, 140(Suppl_2), A310-A310.

Craske, M. (2010). Theories of psychotherapy series: Cognitive-behavioral therapy (1 ed.). Washington DC: American Psychological Association.

Crow, S., Peterson, C., Swanson, S., Raymond, N., Specker, S., Eckert, E., & Mitchell, J. (2009). Increased mortality in bulimia nervosa and other eating disorders. American Journal of Psychiatry, 166(12), 1342-1346. doi:10.1176/appi.ajp.2009.09020247

Cuijpers, P., Sijbrandij, M., Koole, S., Andersson, G., Beekman, A., & Reynolds, C. (2014). Adding psychotherapy to antidepressant medication in depression and anxiety disorders: A meta-analysis. World Psychiatry, 13(1), 56-67. doi:10.1002/wps.20089

Danieli, Y., Norris, F., & Engdahl, B. (2016). Multigenerational legacies of trauma: Modeling the what and how of transmission. American Journal of Orthopsychiatry, 86(6), 639-651. doi:10.1037/ort0000145

Danzer, G., Rieger, S., Schubmehl, S., & Cort, D. (2016). White psychologists and African Americans' historical trauma: Implications for practice. Journal of Aggression, Maltreatment & Trauma, 25(4), 351-370. doi:10.1080/10926771.2016.1153550

Darvishi, N., Farhadi, M., Haghtalab, T., & Poorolajal, J. (2015). Alcohol-related risk of suicidal ideation, suicide attempt, and completed suicide: a meta-analysis. PlOs One, 10(5), e0126870.

DeAngelis, T. (2015-a). A new look at self-injury. American Psychological Association, 46(7), 58. http://www.apa.org/monitor/2015/07-08/self-injury.aspx

DeAngelis, T. (2015-b). Who self-injures? Monitor on Psychology, 46(7), 60. http://www.apa.org/monitor/2015/07-08/who-self-injures.aspx

Deegan, P. (1988). Recovery: The lived experience of rehabilitation. Psychosocial Rehabilitation Journal, 11(4), 11-19. https://www.nami.org/getattachment/Extranet/Education, Training-and-Outreach-Programs/Signature-Classes/NAMI-Homefront/HF-Additional-Resources/HF15AR6LivedExpRehab.pdf

Duehring, S. (2011, Mar 04). Why did the steps for CPR change from A-B-C to C-A-B? https://www.emccprtraining.com/blog/emc-news-and-updates/cpr-c-a-b/why-did-the-steps-for-cpr-change-from-a-b-c-to-c-a-b

Eagles, J., Carson, D., Begg, A., & Naji, S. (2003). Suicide prevention: A study of patients' views. The British Journal of Psychiatry, 182(3), 261-265. doi:10.1192/bjp.182.3.261

Edwards, J., & McGorry, P. (2002). Implementing Early Intervention in Psychosis: A Guide to Establishing Early Psychosis Services. London: Martin Dunitz.

Emerson, D., Sharma, R., & Chaudhry, J. (2009). Trauma-sensitive yoga: Principles, practice, and research. International Journal of Yoga Therapy, 19(1), 123-128. http://www.traumacenter.org/products/..%5Cproducts%5Cpdf_files%5Cijyt_article_2009.pdf

Esang, M. & Ahmed, S. A Closer Look at Substance Use and Suicide. (2018). American Journal of Psychiatry Resident Journal, 13(6). https://doi.org/10.1176/appi.ajp-rj.2018.130603

Fairburn, C., & Harrison, P. (2003). Eating disorders. The Lancet, 361(9355), 407-416. doi:10.1016/S0140-6736(03)12378-1

Farrell, M. (1994, Nov). Opiate withdrawal. Addiction, 89(11), 1471-1475.

Feigin, V. L., Nichols, E., Alam, T., Bannick, M. S., Beghi, E., Blake, N., ... & Fisher, J. L. (2019). Global, regional, and national burden of neurological disorders, 1990–2016: A systematic analysis for the Global Burden of Disease Study 2016. The Lancet Neurology, 18(5), 459-480.

Felitti, V., Anda, R., Nordenberg, D., Williamson, D., Spitz, A., Edwards, V., . . . Marks, J. (1998). Relationship of childhood abuse and household dysfunction to many of the leading causes of death in adults: The Adverse Childhood Experience (ACE) study. American Journal of Preventive Medicine, 14(4), 245-258. doi:10.1016/S0749-3797(98)00017-8

Figley, C. R., & Ludick, M. (2017). Secondary traumatization and compassion fatigue. In S. N. Gold (Ed.), APA handbooks in psychology®. APA handbook of trauma psychology: Foundations in knowledge (p. 573–593). American Psychological Association. https://doi.org/10.1037/0000019-029

Forty, L., Smith, D., Jones, L., Jones, I., Caesar, S., Cooper, C., . . . Craddock, N. (2008, May). Clinical differences between bipolar and unipolar depression. British Journal of Psychiatry, 192(5), 388-389. doi:10.1192/bjp.bp.107.045294

Fukutomi, A., Austin, A., McClelland, J., Brown, A., Glennon, D., Mountford, V., ... & Schmidt, U. (2020). First episode rapid early intervention for eating disorders: A two-year follow-up. Early Intervention in Psychiatry, 14(1), 137-141.

Gautam S., Jain, A., Gautam, M., Vahia, V., & Gautam, A. (2017). Clinical practice guidelines for the management of generalised anxiety disorder (GAD) and panic disorder (PD). Indian Journal of Psychiatry, 59(Suppl 1), Jan. doi:10.4103/0019-5545.196975

Galderisi, S., Heinz, A., Kastrup, M., Beezhold, J., & Sartorius, N. (2015). Toward a new definition of mental health. World Psychiatry : Official Journal of the World Psychiatric Association (WPA), 14(2), 231-233. https://doi.org/10.1002/wps.20231

Garnaat, S. L., Greenberg, B. D., Sibrava, N. J., Goodman, W. K., Mancebo, M. C., Eisen, J. L., & Rasmussen, S. A. (2014). Who qualifies for deep brain stimulation for OCD? Data from a naturalistic clinical sample. The Journal of neuropsychiatry and clinical neurosciences, 26(1), 81-86.

GBD 2016 Disease and Injury Incidence and Prevalence Collaborators. (2017). Global, regional, and national incidence, prevalence, and years lived with disability for 328 diseases and injuries for 195 countries, 1990-2016: A systematic analysis for the Global Burden of Disease Study 2016. Lancet, 390(10100), 1211-1259. doi:10.1016/S0140-6736(17)32154-2

Ghio, L., Gotelli, S., Marcenar, M., Amore, M., & Natta, W. (2014). Duration of untreated illness and outcomes in unipolar depression: A systematic review and meta-analysis. Journal of Affective Disorders, 152-154, 45-51. doi:10.1016/j.jad.2013.10.002

Goldstein, R., Smith, S., Chou, S., Saha, T., Jung, J., Zhang, H., . . . Grant, B. (2016). The epidemiology of DSM-5 posttraumatic stress disorder in the United States: Results from the National Epidemiological Survey on Alcohol and Related Conditions III. Social Psychiatry and Psychiatric Epidemiology, 51(8), 1137-1148.

Gone, J. P., Hartmann, W. E., Pomerville, A., Wendt, D. C., Klem, S. H., & Burrage, R. L. (2019). The impact of historical trauma on health outcomes for indigenous populations in the USA and Canada: A systematic review. American Psychologist, 74(1), 20.

Goñi-Sarriés, A., Blanco, M., Azcárate, L., Peinado, R., & López-Goñi. (2018). Are previous suicide attempts a risk factor for completed suicide? Psicothema, 30(1), 33-38. http://www.psicothema.com/pdf/4447.pdf

Gonzalez, J. M., Alegría, M., Prihoda, T. J., Copeland, L. A., & Zeber, J. E. (2011). How the relationship of attitudes toward mental health treatment and service use differs by age, gender, ethnicity/race and education. Social Psychiatry and Psychiatric Epidemiology, 46(1), 45-57.

Gopalkrishnan, N. (2018). Cultural diversity and mental health: Considerations for policy and practice. Frontiers in Public Health, 6, 179.

Grant, B., Stinson, F., Dawson, D., Chou, S., Dufour, M., Compton, W., . . . Kaplan, K. (2004). Prevalence and co-occurrence of substance use disorders and independent mood and anxiety disorders: Results from the National Epidemiologic Survey on Alcohol and Related Conditions. Archives of General Psychiatry, 61(8), 807-816. doi:10.1001/archpsyc.61.8.807

Grant, J., Potenza, M., Weinstein, A., & Gorelick, D. (2010). Introduction to behavioral addictions. The American Journal of Drug and Alcohol Abuse, 36(5), 233-241. doi:10.3109/00952990.2010.491884

Green, A., & Brown, E. (2006). Comorbid schizophrenia and substance abuse. Journal of Clinical Psychiatry, 67(9), e08.

Harris, K., & Goh, M. (2017). Is suicide assessment harmful to participants? Findings from a randomized controlled trial. International Journal of Mental Health Nursing, 26(2), 181-190. doi:10.1111/inm.12223

Harrison, I., Joyce, E., Mutsatsa, S., Hutton, S., Huddy, V., Kapasi, M., & Barnes, T. (2008). Naturalistic follow-up of co-morbid substance use in schizophrenia: The West London first-episode study. Psychological Medicine, 38(1), 79-88. doi:10.1017/S0033291707000797

Hartz, S. P., Medeiros, H., Cavazos-Rehg, P., Sobell, J., Knowles, J., Bierut, L., & Pato, M. (2014). Comorbidity of severe psychotic disorders with measures of substance use. JAMA Psychiatry, 71(3), 248-254. doi:10.1001/jamapsychiatry.2013.3726

Harvard Health Publishing. (2018, May 9). Yoga for anxiety and depression. https://www.health.harvard.edu/mind-and-mood/yoga-for-anxiety-and-depression

Harvard Medical School. (2007). Table 2. 12-month prevalence of DSM-IV/WMH-CIDI disorders by sex and cohort 1 (n=9282). https://www.hcp.med.harvard.edu/ncs/ftpdir/NCS-R_12-month_Prevalence_Estimates.pdf

Hedegaard, H., Warner, M., & Miniño, A. (2017). Drug overdose deaths in the United States, 1999-2016. National Center for Health Statistics Data Brief, no. 294. https://www.cdc.gov/nchs/data/databriefs/db294.pdf

Hequembourg, A., Livingston, J., & Parks, K. (2013). Sexual victimization and associated risks among lesbian and bisexual women. Research Institute on Addictions, 19(5), 634-657. doi:10.1177/1077801213490557

Herrán, A., Vázquez-Barquero, J., & Dunn, G. (1999). Recognition of depression and anxiety in primary care: Patients' attributional style is important factor. British Medical Journal, 318(7197), 1558. https://www.ncbi.nlm.nih.gov/pmc/articles/PMC1115924/

Hoertel, M., Blanco, C., Oquendo, M., Wall, M., Olfson, M., Falissard, B., . . . Limosin, F. (2017). A comprehensive model of predictors of persistence and recurrence in adults with major depression: Results from a national 3-year prospective study. Journal of Psychiatric Research, 95, 19-27. doi:10.1016/j.psychires.2017.07.022

Hudson, J., Hiripi, E., Pope Jr., H., & Kessler, R. (2007). The prevalence and correlates of eating disorders in the National Comorbidity Survey Replication. Biological Psychiatry, 61(3), 348-358. doi:10.1016/j.biopsych.2006.03.040

Human Rights Campaign. (2019). Sexual orientation and gender identity definitions. https://www.hrc.org/resources/sexual-orientation-and-gender-identity-terminology-and-definitions

Hundt, N., Robinson, A., Arney, J., Stanley, M., & Cully, J. (2015, Aug 1). Veterans' perspectives on benefits and drawbacks of peer support for posttraumatic stress disorder. Military Medicine, 180(8), 851-856. doi:10.7205/MILMED-D-14-00536

Jones, C. (2013). Heroin use and heroin use risk behaviors among nonmedical users of prescription opioid pain relievers - United States, 2002-2004 and 2008-2010. Drug and Alcohol Dependency, 132(1-2), 95-100. doi:10.1016/j.drugalcdep.2013.01.007

Jorm, A. F. (2011, Oct 31). Mental health literacy: Empowering the community to take action for better mental health. American Psychologist, 67(3), 231-243. doi:10.1037/a0025957

Jorm, A., Christensen, H., Griffiths, K., Parslow, R., Rodgers, B., & Blewitt, K. (2004). Effectiveness of complementary and self-help treatments for anxiety disorders. Medical Journal of Australia, 181(7 (Supplement)), S29-46.

Jorm, A., Griffiths, K., Christensen, H., Parslow, R., & Rogers, B. (2004). Actions taken to cope with depression at different levels of severity: A community survey. Psychological Medicine, 34(2), 293-299.

Jordan, G., Lutgens, D., Joober, R., Lepage, M., Iyer, S. N., & Malla, A. (2014). The relative contribution of cognition and symptomatic remission to functional outcome following treatment of a first episode of psychosis. The Journal of Clinical Psychiatry, 75(6), e566-72.

Keitner, G., Ryan, C., Miller, I., Kohn, R., Bishop, D., & Epstein, N. (1995). Role of the family in recovery and major depression. American Journal of Psychiatry, 152(7), 1002-1008. doi:10.1176/ajp.152.7.1002

Kelly, C., Jorm, A., & Kitchener, B. (2009). Development of mental health first aid guidelines for panic attacks: A Delphi study. BMC Psychiatry, 9(49). doi:10.1186/1471-244X-9-49

Kelly, C., Jorm, A., Kitchener, B., & Langlands, R. (2008, Jul). Development of mental health first aid guidelines for deliberate non-suicidal self-injury: A Delphi study. BMC Psychiatry, 8(62). doi:10.1186/1471-244X-8-62

Kelly, C., Jorm, A., Kitchener, B., & Langlands, R. (2008). Development of mental health first aid guidelines for suicidal ideation and behaviour: A Delphi study. BMC Psychiatry, 8, Article ID 17. doi:10.1186/1471-244X-8-17

Kelly, J., Saitz, R., & Wakeman, S. (2016). Language, substance use disorders, and policy: The need to reach consensus on an "addiction-ary". Alcoholism Treatment Quarterly, 34(1), 116-123. doi:10.1080/07347324.2016.1112103

Kerr, P., Muehelekamp, J., & Turner, J. (2010). Nonsuicidal self-injury: A review of current research for family medicine and primary care physicians. Journal of the American Board of Family Medicine, 240-259. doi:10.3122/jabfm.2010.02.090110

Kessler, R., Berglund, P., Demler, O., Jin, R., Merikangas, E., & Walters, E. (2005). Lifetime prevalence and age-of-onset distributions of DSM-IV disorders in the National Comorbidity Survey Replication (NCS-R). Archives of General Psychiatry, 62(7), 593-602. doi:10.1001/archpsyc.62.6.593

Kessler, R., Birnbaum, H., Demler, O., I.R., F., Gagnon, E., Guyer, M., . . . Wu, E. (2005). The prevalence and correlates of nonaffective psychosis in the National Comorbidity Survey Replication (NCS-R). Biological Psychiatry, 58(8), 668-76.

Kessler, R., Petukhova, M., Sampson, N., Zaslavsky, A., & Wittchen, H. (2012). Twelve month and lifetime prevalence and lifetime morbid risk of anxiety and mood disorders in the United States. International Journal of Methods in Psychiatric Research, 21(3), 169-184.

Khoury, L., Tang, Y., Bradley, B., Cubells, J., & Ressler, K. (2010, Dec). Substance use, childhood traumatic experience, and posttraumatic stress disorder in an urban civilian population. Depression and Anxiety, 27(12), 1077-1086. doi:10.1002/da.20751

Kingston, A., Jorm, A., Kitchener, B., Hides, L., Kelly, C., Morgan, A., & Lubman, D. (2009). Helping someone with problem drinking: Mental Health First Aid guidelines—A Delphi expert consensus study. BMC Psychiatry, 9. doi:10.1186/1471-244X-9-79

Kingston, A., Morgan, A., Jorm, A., Hall, K., Hart, L., Kelly, C., & Lubman, D. (2011, Jan). Helping someone with problem drug use: A Delphi consensus study of consumers, carers, and clinicians. BMC Psychiatry, 11. doi:10.1186/1471-244X-11-3

Klonsky, E. (2011). Non-suicidal self-injury in United States adults: Prevalence, sociodemographics, topography and functions.

Psychological Medicine, 41(9), 1981-1986. doi:10.1017/S0033291710002497

Klonsky, E., & Muehlenkamp, J. (2007). Self-injury: A research review for the practitioner. Journal of Clinical Psychology, 63(11), 1045-1056. doi:10.1002/jclp.20412

Lai, H. M. X., Cleary, M., Sitharthan, T., & Hunt, G. E. (2015). Prevalence of comorbid substance use, anxiety and mood disorders in epidemiological surveys, 1990–2014: A systematic review and meta-analysis. Drug and Alcohol Dependence, 154, 1-13.

Langlands, R., Jorm, A., Kelly, C., & Kitchener, B. (2008). First aid for depression: A Delphi consensus study with consumers, carers and clinicians. Journal of Affective Disorders, 105(1-3), 157-165. doi:10.1016/j.jad.2007.05.004

Langlands, R., Jorm, A., Kelly, C., & Kitchener, B. (2008, May). First aid recommendations for psychosis: Using the Delphi method to gain consensus between mental health consumers, carers, and clinicians. Schizophrenia Bulletin, 34(3), 435-443. doi:10.1093/schbul/sbm099

Lazowski, L., Koller, M., Stuart, H., & Milev, R. (2012). Stigma and discrimination in people suffering with a mood disorder: A cross-sectional study. Depression Research and Treatment, Article ID 724848. doi: http://dx.doi.org/10.1155/2012/724848

Lee, R. J. (2017). Mistrustful and misunderstood: a review of paranoid personality disorder. Current Behavioral Neuroscience Reports, 4(2), 151-165.

Leonard, S., Mexal, S., & Freedman, R. (2007). Smoking, genetics, and schizophrenia: Evidence for self medication. Journal of Dual Diagnosis, 3(3-4), 43-59. doi:10.1300/J374v03n03_05

Lijster, J., Dierckz, B., Utens, E., Verhults, F., Zieldorff, C., Dieleman, G., & Legerstee, J. (2017). The age of onset of anxiety disorders: A meta-analysis. Canadian Journal of Psychiatry, 62(4), 237-246. doi:10.1177/0706743716640757

Linardon, J., Wade, T. D., De la Piedad Garcia, X., & Brennan, L. (2017). The efficacy of cognitive-behavioral therapy for eating disorders: A systematic review and meta-analysis. Journal of Consulting and Clinical Psychology, 85(11), 1080.

Lipari, R., & Van Horn, S. (2017). Smoking and Mental Illness Among Adults in the United States.

Liu, J. (2004). Concept analysis: Aggression. Issues in Mental Health Nursing, 25(7), 693-714. doi:10.1080/01612840490486755

López, S., García, J., Ullman, J., Kopelowicz, A., Jenkins, J., Breitborde, N., & Placencia, P. (2009). Cultural variability in the manifestation of expressed emotion. Family Process, 48(2), 179-194. doi:10.1111/j.1545-5300.2009.01276.x

Lopez-Castroman, J., Melhem, N., Birmaher, B., Greenhill, L., Kolko, D., Stanley, B., . . . Oquendo, M. (2013). Early childhood sexual abuse increases suicidal intent. World Psychiatry: Official Journal of the World Psychiatric Association, 149-154. doi:10.1002/wps.20039

Lu, S. (2015). Mindfulness holds promise for treating depression. Monitor on Psychology, 46(3), 50. http://www.apa.org/monitor/2015/03/cover-mindfulness.aspx

Madowitz, J., Matheson, B., & Liang, J. (2015). The relationship between eating disorders and sexual trauma. Eating and Weight Disorders, 20(3), 281-293. doi:10.1007/s40519-015-0195-y

Marques, L., Alegria, M., Becker, A., Chen, C., Fang, A., Chosak, A., & Belo Diniz, J. (2011). Comparative prevalence, correlates of impairment, and service utilization for eating disorders across U.S. ethnic groups: Implications for reducing ethnic disparities in health care access for eating disorders. International Journal of Eating Diroders, 44(5), 412-420. doi:10.1002/eat.20787

Marshall, M., Lewis, S., Lockwood, A., Drake, R., Jones, P., & Croudace, T. (2005). Association between duration of untreated psychosis and outcome in cohorts of first-episode patients: A systematic review. Archives of General Psychiatry, 62, 975-983.

Marshall, M., Shannon, C., Meenagh, C., McCorry, N., & Mulholland, C. (2018, Mar). The association between childhood trauma, parental bonding and depressive symptoms and interpersonal functioning in depression and bipolar disorder. Irish Journal of Psychological Medicine, 35(1), 23-32. doi:10.1017/ipm.2016.43

Masten, A. S., & Wright, M. O. D. (2010). Resilience over the lifespan: Developmental perspectives on resistance, recovery, and transformation. In J. W. Reich, A. J. Zautra, & J. S. Hall (Eds.), Handbook of adult resilience (pp. 213-237). Guilford Press.

Mattar, S. (2010). Cultural considerations in trauma psychology education, research, and training. Traumatology, 16(4), 48-52. http://dx.doi.org.ezproxy.umuc.edu/10.1177/1534765610388305

May, A., & Klonsky, E. (2013). Assessing motivations for suicide attempts: Development and psychometric properties of the inventory of motivations for suicide attempts. Suicide and Life-Threatening Behavior, 43(5), 532-546. doi:10.1111/sltb.12037

Mayo, D., Corey, S., Kelly, L., Yohannes, S., Youngquist, A., Stuart, B., . . . Loewy, R. (2017). The role of trauma and stressful life events among individuals at clinical high risk for psychosis: A review. Frontiers in Psychiatry, 8(55). doi: https://doi.org/10.3389/fpsyt.2017.00055

Mays, V. M., Jones, A. L., Delany-Brumsey, A., Coles, C., & Cochran, S. D. (2017). Perceived Discrimination in Health Care and Mental Health/Substance Abuse Treatment Among Blacks, Latinos, and Whites. Medical Care, 55(2), 173–181. https://doi.org/10.1097/MLR.0000000000000638

McIntosh, D., Kutcher, S., Binder, C., Levitt, A., Fallu, A., & Rosenbluth, M. (2009). Adult ADHD and comorbid depression: A consensus-derived diagnostic algorithm for ADHD. Neuropsychiatric Disease and Treatment, 5, 137–150. https://doi.org/10.2147/ndt.s4720

McKenzie, K., Milton, M., Smith, G., & Ouellette-Kuntz, H. (2016). Systematic review of the prevalence and incidence of intellectual disabilities: current trends and issues. Current Developmental Disorders Reports, 3(2), 104-115.

McQueen, M., Blinkhorn, A., Broad, A., Jones, J., Naeem, F., & Ayub, M. (2018). Development of a cognitive behavioural therapy-based guided self-help intervention for adults with intellectual disability. Journal of Applied Research in Intellectual Disabilities, 31(5), 885-896.

Mental Health America. (2018). How to become a peer support specialist. http://www.mentalhealthamerica.net/how-become-peer-support-specialist

Mereish, E., O'Cleirigh, C., & Bradford, J. (2014). Interrelationships between LGBT-based victimization, suicide, and substance use problems in a diverse sample of sexual and gender minorities. Psychological Health Medicine, 19(1), 1-13. doi:10.1080/13548506.2013.780129

Merikangas, K., Jin, R., He, J., Kessler, R., Lee, S., Sampson, N., . . . Zarkov, Z. (2011, Mar). Prevalence and correlates of bipolar spectrum disorder in the world mental health survey initiative. Archives of General Psychiatry, 68(3), 241-251. doi:10.1001/archgenpsychiatry.2011.12

Merrick, M. T., Ports, K. A., Ford, D. C., Afifi, T. O., Gershoff, E. T., & Grogan-Kaylor, A. (2017). Unpacking the impact of adverse childhood experiences on adult mental health. Child abuse & neglect, 69, 10-19.

Mitchell, K., Mazzeo, S., Schlesinger, M., Brewerton, T., & Smith, B. (2012). Comorbidity of partial and subthreshold PTSD among men and women with eating disorders in the National Comorbidity Survey-Replication study. The International Journal of Eating Disorders, 45(3), 307-315. doi:10.1002/eat.20965

Mohit, V., Mahapatra, A., Krishnan, V., Gupta, R., & Sinha Deb, K. (2015). Violence and mental illness: What is the true story? Journal of Epidemiology & Community Health, 70(3). doi:10.1136/jech-2015-205546

Monroe, S., & Harkness, K. (2011). Recurrence in major depression: A conceptual analysis. Pyschological Review, 118(4), 655-74. doi:10.1037/a0025190

Moos, R. (2007). Theory-based processes that promote the remission of substance use disorders. Clinical Psychology Review, 27(5), 537-551. doi:10.1016/j.cpr.2006.12.006

Morgan, A., & Jorm, A. (2008). Self-help interventions for depressive disorders and depressive symptoms: A systematic review. Annals of General Psychiatry, 7(13). doi:10.1186/1744-859X-7-13

Morrison, A., Frame, L., & Larkin, W. (2003). Relationships between trauma and psychosis: A review and integration. British Journal of Clinical Psychology, 42(Pt 4), 331-353. doi:10.1348/014466503322528892

Naslund, J., Marsch, L., McHugo, G., & Bartels, S. (2015). Emerging mHealth and eHealth interventions for serious mental illness: A review of the literature. Journal of Mental Health, 24(5), 321-332.

National Academies of Sciences, Engineering, and Medicine. (2018). Public health consequences of e-cigarettes. Washington DC: National Academies Press. doi:10.17226/24952

National Alliance on Mental Illness. (2017, Aug). Bipolar disorder.

https://www.nami.org/learn-more/mental-health-conditions/bipolar-disorder

National Association of Social Workers. (2019). Clinical social work. https://www.socialworkers.org/Practice/Clinical-Social-Work

National Child Traumatic Stress Network. (2008). Making the connection: Trauma and substance abuse. https://www.nctsn.org/sites/default/files/resources//making_the_connection_trauma_substance_abuse.pdf

National Child Traumatic Stress Network. (n.d.). Complex trauma. https://www.nctsn.org/what-is-child-trauma/trauma-types/complex-trauma

National Council for Behavioral Health. (2018). Integrated health care & health homes. https://www.thenationalcouncil.org/areas-of-expertise/integrated-healthcare/

National Eating Disorder Association. (2018). What are eating disorders.

National Eating Disorders Association. (2018-a). Statistics & research on eating disorders. https://www.nationaleatingdisorders.org/statistics-research-eating-disorders

National Eating Disorders Association. (2018-b). Binge eating disorder. https://www.nationaleatingdisorders.org/learn/by-eating-disorder/bed

National Institute of Mental Health. (2015, Apr. 23). A new look at racial/ethnic differences in mental health service use among adults. https://www.nimh.nih.gov/news/science-news/2015/a-new-look-at-racial-ethnic-differences-in-mental-health-service-use-among-adults.shtml

National Institute of Mental Health. (2015, Aug). Fact sheet: First episode psychosis. https://www.nimh.nih.gov/health/topics/schizophrenia/raise/fact-sheet-first-episode-psychosis.shtml

National Institute of Mental Health. (2015). Schizophrenia. https://www.nimh.nih.gov/health/publications/schizophrenia/nih_15-3517_155600.pdf

National Institute of Mental Health. (2016, Mar). Seasonal affective disorder. https://www.nimh.nih.gov/health/topics/seasonal-affective-disorder/index.shtml

National Institute of Mental Health. (2016, April). Bipolar disorder. https://www.nimh.nih.gov/health/topics/bipolar-disorder/index.shtml

National Institute of Mental Health. (2016, Nov). Psychotherapies. https://www.nimh.nih.gov/health/topics/psychotherapies/index.shtml

National Institute of Mental Health. (2017, Feb). Coping with traumatic events. https://www.nimh.nih.gov/health/topics/coping-with-traumatic-events/index.shtml

National Institute of Mental Health. (2017, Feb). Integrated care. https://www.nimh.nih.gov/health/topics/integrated-care/index.shtml

National Institute of Mental Health. (2017, Nov). Eating disorders. https://www.nimh.nih.gov/health/statistics/eating-disorders.shtml

National Institute of Mental Health. (2017, Nov). Mental illness. https://www.nimh.nih.gov/health/statistics/mental-illness.shtml#part_154785

National Institute of Mental Health. (2018). Eating Disorders: About more than food. www.nimh.nih.gov/health/publications/eating-disorders/index.shtml.

National Institute of Mental Health. (2018, Feb). Depression. https://www.nimh.nih.gov/health/topics/depression/index.shtml

National Institute of Mental Health. (2018, May). Suicide. https://www.nimh.nih.gov/health/statistics/suicide.shtml

National Institute of Mental Health. (2018, Jul). Anxiety disorders. https://www.nimh.nih.gov/health/topics/anxiety-disorders/index.shtml

National Institute on Alcohol Abuse and Alcoholism. (2000). 10th Special report to the U.S. Congress on alcohol and health: Highlights from current research. National Institutes of Health. Bethesda, MD: U.S. Department of Health and Human Services. https://pubs.niaaa.nih.gov/publications/10report/intro.pdf

National Institute on Alcohol Abuse and Alcoholism. (2016). Rethinking drinking: Alcohol and your health. NIH Publication No. 15-3770. Bethesda, MD: National Institutes of Health.

National Institute on Alcohol Abuse and Alcoholism. (2016). What is a standard drink? https://www.niaaa.nih.gov/alcohol-health/overview-alcohol-consumption/what-standard-drink

National Institute on Drug Abuse. (2010). Comorbidity: Addiction and other mental illnesses. NIH Publication No. 10-5771. Bethesda, MD: National Institutes of Health.

National Institute on Drug Abuse. (2018, Mar). Opioid overdose crisis. https://www.drugabuse.gov/drugs-abuse/opioids/opioid-overdose-crisis#one

National Institute on Drug Abuse. (2018, Jan 17). Which classes of prescription drugs are commonly misused? https://www.drugabuse.gov/publications/research-reports/misuse-prescription-drugs

National Institutes of Health (US). (2007). Information about mental illness and the brain. Biological Sciences Curriculum Study. Bethesda, MD. https://www.ncbi.nlm.nih.gov/books/NBK20369/

Nelson, J., Bundoc-Baronia, R., Comiskey, G., & McGovern, T. (2017). Facing addiction in America: The Surgeon General's report on alcohol, drugs, and health: A commentary. Alcoholism Treatment Quarterly, 35(4), 445-454. doi:10.1080/07347324.2017.1361763

Nepon, J., Belik, S., Bolton, J., & Sareen, J. (2010, Aug). The relationship between anxiety disorders and suicide attempts: Findings from the National Epidemiologic Survey on Alcohol and Related Conditions. Depression and Anxiety, 27(9), 791-798. doi:10.1002/da.20674

New Freedom Commission on Mental Health. (2003). Achieving the promise: Transforming mental health care in America. DHHS Pub. No. SMA-03-3832. http://govinfo.library.unt.edu/mentalhealthcommission/reports/finalreport/downloads/finalreport.pdf

Nock, M., Joiner Jr., T., Gordon, K., Lloyd-Richardson, E., & Prinstein, M. (2006, Sep 30). Non-suicidal self-injury among adolescents: Diagnostic correlates and relation to suicide attempts. Journal of Psychiatric Research, 144(1), 65-72. doi: https://doi.org/10.1016/j.psychres.2006.05.010

O'Donnell, M. L., Alkemade, N., Creamer, M., McFarlane, A. C., Silove, D., Bryant, R. A., ... & Forbes, D. (2016). A longitudinal study of adjustment disorder after trauma exposure. American Journal of Psychiatry, 173(12), 1231-1238.

Olfson, M., Gerhard, T., Huang, C., Crystal, S., & Stroup, T. S. (2015). Premature mortality among adults with schizophrenia in the United States. JAMA Psychiatry, 72(12), 1172-1181.

Ouellet-Plamondon, C., Abdel-Baki, A., Salvat, É., & Potvin, S. (2017). Specific impact of stimulant, alcohol and cannabis use disorders on first-episode psychosis: 2-year functional and symptomatic outcomes. Psychological Medicine, 47(14), 2461.

Palmer, B., Pankratz, V., & Bostwick, J. (2005). The lifetime risk of suicide in schizophrenia: A reexamination. Archives of General Psychiatry, 62(3), 247-253. doi:10.1001/archpsyc.62.3.247

Parker, G., & Crawford, J. (2007). Judged effectiveness of differing antidepressant strategies by those with clinical depression. Australia & New Zealand Journal of Psychiatry, 41(1), 32-37. doi:10.1080/00048670601057726

Patton, G., Coffey, C., & Sawyer, S. (2003). The outcome of adolescent eating disorders: Findings from the Victorian Adolescent Health Cohort Study. European Child & Adolescent Psychiatry, 12 Suppl, I25-I29. doi:10.1007/s00787-003-1104-x

Peeters, F., Huibers, M., Roelofs, J., van Breukelen, G., Hollon, S., Markowitz, J., . . . Arntz, A. (2013, Mar 5). The clinical effectiveness of evidence-based interventions for depression: A pragmatic trial in routine practice. Journal of Affective Disorders, 145(3), 349-355. doi:10.1016/j.jad.2012.08.022

Perälä, J., Suvisaari, J., Saarni, S., Kuoppasalmi, K., Isometsä, E., Pirkola, S., . . . Lönnqvist, J. (2007). Lifetime prevalence of psychotic and bipolar I disorders in a general population. Archives of General Psychiatry, 64, 19-28. doi:10.1001/archpsyc.64.1.19

Pérez, C., & Ariadna, P. (2015). Culture or psychosis: Social behavior inducing psychopathology or psychopathology inducing social behavior? International Journal of Health, Wellness & Society, 5(2), 1-5.

Perkins, S., Murphy, R., Schmidt, U., & Williams, C. (2006, July 19). Self-help and guided self-help for eating disorders. Cochrane Database of Systematic Reviews. John Wiley & Sons, Ltd. doi:10.1002/14651858.CD004191.pub2

Perry, B. (2002). Childhood experience and the expression of genetic potential: What childhood neglect tells use about nature and nurture. Brain and Mind, 79-100. doi:10.1023/A:1016557824657

Peterson, J., Freedenthal, S., Sheldon, C., & Andersen, R. (2008). Nonsuicidal self injury in adolescents. Psychiatry (Edgmont), 5(11), 20-26. https://www.ncbi.nlm.nih.gov/pmc/articles/PMC2695720/

Pies, R. (2014). The bereavement exclusion and DSM-5: An update and commentary. Innovations in Clinical Neuroscience, 11(7-8), 19-22. https://www.ncbi.nlm.nih.gov/pmc/articles/PMC4204469/

Pistrang, N., Barker, C., & Humphreys, K. (2008). Mutual help groups for mental health problems: A review of effectiveness studies. American Journal of Community Psychology, 42(1-2), 110-121. doi:10.1007/s10464-008-9181-0

Pompili, M., Serafini, G., Innamorati, M., Dominici, G., Ferracuti, S., Kotzalidis, G. D., Serra, G., Girardi, P., Janiri, L., Tatarelli, R., Sher, L., & Lester, D. (2010). Suicidal behavior and alcohol abuse. International Journal of Environmental Research and Public Health, 7(4), 1392–1431. https://doi.org/10.3390/ijerph7041392

Poobalan, A., Aucott, L., Ross, L., Smith, W., Helms, P., & Williams, J. (2007, Nov). Effects of treating postnatal depression on mother-infant interaction and child development: Systematic review. British Journal of Psychiatry, 191, 378-386. doi:10.1192/bjp.bp.106.032789

Prat, G., Escandell, M. J., Garcia-Franco, M., Martín-Martínez, J. R., Tortades, I., Vilamala, S., ... & Casas-Anguera, E. (2018). Gender differences in social functioning in people with schizophrenia in psychosocial rehabilitation services using one-dimensional and multidimensional instruments. Comprehensive Psychiatry, 87, 120-122.

Pratt, L., & Brody, D. (2014). Depression in the U.S. household population. Centers for Disease Control and Prevention. Hyattsville, MD: National Center for Health Statistics. https://www.cdc.gov/nchs/products/databriefs/db172.htm

Prochaska, J., Velicer, W., Rossi, J., Goldstein, M., Marcus, B., Rakowski, W., . . . Rosenbloom, D. (1994). Stages of change and decisional balance for 12 problem behaviors. Health Psychology, 13(1), 39-46.

Rafferty, J., & Committee on Psychosocial Aspects of Child and Family Health. (2018). Ensuring comprehensive care and support for transgender and gender-diverse children and adolescents. Pediatrics, 142(4).

Robinson, D., Woerner, M., McMeniman, M., Mendelowitz, A., & Bilder, R. (2004). Symptomatic and functional recovery from a first episode of schizophrenia or schizoaffective disorder. American Journal of Psychiatry, 161(3), 473-479. doi:10.1176/appi.ajp.161.3.473

Rockett, I., Wang, S., Stack, S., De Leo, D., Frost, J., Ducataman, A., . . . Kapusta, N. (2010). Race/ethnicity and potential suicide misclassification: Window on a minority suicide paradox? BMC Psychiatry, 10, 35. doi:10.1186/1471-244X-10-35

Ronningstam, E. (2014). Beyond the diagnostic traits: A collaborative exploratory diagnostic process for dimensions and underpinnings of narcissistic personality disorder. Personality Disorders: Theory, Research, and Treatment, 5(4), 434.

Rudd, M., Berman, A., Joiner Jr, T., Nock, M., Silverman, M., Mandrusiak, M., . . . Witte, T. (2006). Warning signs for suicide: Theory, research, and clinical applications. Suicide and Life-Threatening Behaviors, 255-262. doi:10.1521/suli.2006.36.3.255

Rueve, M., & Welton, R. (2008). Violence and mental illness. Psychiatry (Edgmont), 5(5), 34-48. https://www.ncbi.nlm.nih.gov/pmc/articles/PMC2686644/

Ryder, A., Yang, J., Zhu, X., Yao, S., Yi, J., Heine, S., & Bagby, R. (2008). The cultural shaping of depression: Somatic symptoms in China, psychological symptoms in North America? Journal of Abnormal Psychology, 117(2), 300-313. doi:10.1037/0021-843X.117.2.300

Sala, M., Reyes-Rodríguez, M., Bulik, C., & Bardone-Cone, A. (2013). Race, ethnicity, and eating disorder recognition by peers. Eating Disorders, 21(5), 423-436. doi:10.1080/10640266.2013.827540

Salkovskis, P., Clark, D., & Gelder, M. (1996). Cognition-behaviour links in the persistence of panic. Behaviour Research and Therapy, 34(5-6), 453-458.

Schoenborn, C. A., & Gindi, R.M. (2014). Electronic cigarette use among adults: United States. Centers for Disease Control and Prevention: National Center for Health Statistics Data Brief No. 217, October 2015.

Schwartz, R., & Blankenship, D. (2014). Racial disparities in psychotic disorder diagnosis: A review of empirical literature. World Journal of Psychiatry, 4(4), 133-140. doi:10.5498/wjp.v4.i4.133

Shrivastava, A., Johnston, M., & Bureau, Y. (2012). Stigma of Mental Illness-1: Clinical reflections. Mens Sana Monographs, 10(1), 70-84. https://doi.org/10.4103/0973-1229.90181

Sit, D., Rothschild, A., & Wisner, K. (2006). A review of postpartum psychosis. Journal of Women's Health, 15(4), 352-368. doi:10.1089/jwh.2006.15.352

Skarl, S. (2015). Anxiety and depression Association of America. Journal of Consumer Health on the Internet, 19(2), 100-106.

Smink, F., van Hoeken, D., & Hoek, H. (2012). Epidemiology of eating disorders: Incidence, prevalence and mortality rates. Current Psychiatry Reports, 14(4), 406-414. doi:10.1007/s11920-012-0282-y

Smolak, L., Striegel-Moore, R. H., & Levine, M. P. (Eds.). (2013). The developmental psychopathology of eating disorders: Implications for research, prevention, and treatment. Routledge.

Smoller, J., & Finn, C. (2003). Family, twin, and adoption studies of bipolar disorder. American Journal of Medical Genetics Part C: Seminars in Medical Genetics, 123C(1), 48-58. doi:10.1002/ajmg.c.20013

Squeglia, B., Jacobus, J., & Tapert, S. (2009). The influence of substance use on adolescent brain development. Clinical EEG and Neuroscience, 40(1), 31-38. doi:10.1177/155005940904000110

Stein, G. L., & Kerwin, J. (2010). Disability perspectives on health care planning and decision-making. Journal of Palliative Medicine, 13(9), 1059-1064.

Stone, D., Holland, K., Bartholow, B., Crosby, A., Davis, S., & Wilkins, S. (2017). Preventing suicide: A technical package of policies, programs, and practice. Atlanta: CDC Stacks Public Health Publications. doi:10.15620/cdc.44275

Strakowski, S., Adler, C., Almeida, J., Altshuler, L., Blumber, H., Chang, K., . . . Townsend, J. (2012, Jun). The functional neuroanatomy of bipolar disorder: A consensus model. Bipolar Disorders, 14(4), 313-325. doi:10.1111/j.1399-5618.2012.01022.x

Stuart, H. (2016). Reducing the stigma of mental illness. Global Mental Health, 3, e17. doi:10.1017/gmh.2016.11

Substance Abuse and Mental Health Services Administration. (2012, Mar 13). SAMHSA's working definition of recovery updated. https://blog.samhsa.gov/2012/03/23/samhsas-working-definition-of-recovery-updated

Substance Abuse and Mental Health Services Administration. (2014). Results from the 2013 National Survey on Drug Use and Health: Summary of National Findings. NSDUH Series H-48, HHS Publication No. (SMA) 14-4863. Rockville, MD: Substance Abuse and Mental Health Services Administration, 2014.

Substance Abuse and Mental Health Services Administration. (2017). Results from the 2016 national survey on drug use and health: Detailed tables. https://www.samhsa.gov/data/sites/default/files/NSDUH-DetTabs-2016/NSDUH-DetTabs-2016.pdf

Substance Abuse and Mental Health Services Administration. (2017, Sep 20). Recovery and recovery support. https://www.samhsa.gov/recovery

Substance Abuse and Mental Health Services Administration. (2018, Jan 17). Age- and gender-based populations. https://www.samhsa.gov/specific-populations/age-gender-based

Substance Abuse and Mental Health Services Administration. (2018, May 05). Trauma and violence. https://www.samhsa.gov/trauma-violence

Substance Abuse and Mental Health Services Administration. (2018, Jul 9). Adverse childhood experiences. https://www.samhsa.gov/capt/practicing-effective-prevention/prevention-behavioral-health/adverse-childhood-experiences

Substance Abuse and Mental Health Services Administration. (2018). Key Substance Use and Mental Health Indicators in the United States: Results from the 2017 National Survey on Drug Use and Health. (HHS Publication No. SMA 18-5068, NSUDH Series H-53). Rockville, MD: Center for Behavioral Health Statistics and Quality, Substance Abuse and Mental Health Services Administration. https://www.samhsa.gov/data/sites/default/files/cbhsq-reports/NSDUHFFR2017/NSDUHFFR2017.pdf.

Substance Abuse and Mental Health Services Administration. (2019). Key substance use and mental health indicators in the United States: Results from the 2018 National Survey on Drug Use and Health (HHS Publication No. PEP19-5068, NSDUH Series H-54). https://www.samhsa.gov/data/

Substance Abuse and Mental Health Services Administration. (n.d.). What is integrated care? https://www.integration.samhsa.gov/about-us/what-is-integrated-care

Suokas, J. T., Suvisaari, J. M., Grainger, M., Raevuori, A., Gissler, M., & Haukka, J. (2014). Suicide attempts and mortality in eating disorders: A follow-up study of eating disorder patients. General Hospital Psychiatry, 36(3), 355-357.

Svensson, B., Hansson, L., & Stjernswärd, S. (2015). Experiences of a Mental Health First Aid training program in Sweden: A descriptive qualitative study. Community Mental Health Journal, 51(4), 497-503. doi:10.1007/s10597-015-9840-1

Swarbrick, M., & Yudof, J. (2006). Wellness in the 8 Dimensions. Collaborative Support Programs of NJ, Inc. doi:10.13140/RG.2.1.2650.2804

Tagay, S., Schlottbohm, E., Reyes-Rodriguez, M., Repic, N., & Senf, W. (2014). Eating disorders, trauma, PTSD and psychosocial resources. Eating Disorders, 22(1), 33-49. doi:10.1080/10640266.2014.857517

Taylor, P., Hutton, P., & Wood, L. (2015). Are people at risk of psychosis also at risk of suicide and self-harm? A systematic review and meta-analysis. Psychological Medicine, 45, 911-926. doi:10.1017/S0033291714002074

The Hamilton Project. (2016, Dec). Rates of drug use and sales, by race; rates of drug related criminal justice measures, by race. http://www.hamiltonproject.org/charts/rates_of_drug_use_and_sales_by_race_rates_of_drug_related_criminal_justice

Thoits, P. A. (2011). Mechanisms linking social ties and support to physical and mental health. Journal of Health and Social Behavior, 52(2), 145-161.

Toh, W. L., Thomas, N., & Rossell, S. L. (2015). Auditory verbal hallucinations in bipolar disorder (BD) and major depressive disorder (MDD): A systematic review. Journal of Affective Disorders, 184, 18-28.

Tomiyama, A. J. (2014). Weight stigma is stressful. A review of evidence for the Cyclic Obesity/Weight-Based Stigma model. Appetite, 82, 8-15.

Tsai, J., & Rosenheck, R. (2013). Psychiatric comorbidity among adults with schizophrenia: A latent class analysis. Psychiatry Research, 210(1), 16-20. doi:10.1016/j.psychres.2013.05.013

Tsuchiya, K., Byrne, M., & Mortensen, P. (2003). Risk factors in relation to an emergence of bipolar disorder: A systematic review. Bipolar Disorders, 5(4), 231-242.

Udo, T., & Grilo, C. (2018). Prevalence and correlates of DSM-5 defined eating disorders in a nationally representative sample of U.S. adults. Biological Psychiatry, 84(5), 345-354.

University of North Carolina at Charlotte. (2014). Posttraumatic growth research group: What is PTG? https://ptgi.uncc.edu/

University of North Carolina Department of Medicine. (2018). Perinatal mood and anxiety disorders. https://www.med.unc.edu/psych/wmd/mood-disorders/perinatal

United States Census Bureau. (2017, Jul 1). QuickFacts. https://www.census.gov/quickfacts/fact/table/us/pst045217

U.S. Burden of Disease Collaborators. (2013). The state of US health, 1990-2010: Burden of diseases, injuries, and risk factors. JAMA, 310(6), 591-606.

U.S. Department of Health and Human Services. (2014, Sep 16). Does depression increase the risk for suicide?

https://www.hhs.gov/answers/mental-health-and-substance-abuse/does-depression-increase-risk-of-suicide/index.html

U.S. Department of Health and Human Services. (2017, Aug 29). Mental health myths and facts. https://www.mentalhealth.gov/basics/mental-health-myths-facts

U.S. Department of Health and Human Services and U.S. Department of Agriculture. (2015). 2015-2020 Dietary guidelines for Americans (8th Edition). https://health.gov/dietaryguidelines/2015/resources/2015-2020_Dietary_Guidelines.pdf

U.S. Department of Veterans Affairs. (2016, Oct 3). How common is PTSD? https://www.ptsd.va.gov/public/ptsd-overview/basics/how-common-is-ptsd.asp

U.S. Food & Drug Administration. (2018, Jun 25). FDA and marijuana. https://www.fda.gov/newsevents/publichealthfocus/ucm421163.htm

van Baal, P. H., Hoeymans, N., Hoogenveen, R., de Wit, G., & Westert, G. (2006, Apr 10). Disability weights for comorbidity and their influence on Health-adjusted Life Expectancy. Population Health Metrics, 4(1). doi:10.1186/1478-7954-4-1

Varshney, M., Mahaptara, A., Krishnan, V., Gupta, R., & Deb, S. (2016). Violence and mental illness: What is the true story? Journal of Epidemiology and Community Health, 70, 223-225. doi:10.1136/jech-2015-205546

Vasilenko, S., & Evans-Polce, R. (2017, Nov). Age trends in rates of substance use disorders across ages 18-90: Differences by gender and race/ethnicity. Drug & Alcohol Dependency, 180, 260-264. doi:10.1016/j.drugalcdep.2017.08.027

Vega, W., Rodriguez, M., & Ang, A. (2010). Addressing stigma of depression in Latino primary care patients. General Hospital Psychiatry, 32(2), 182-191. doi:10.1016/j.genhosppsych.2009.10.008

Victor, S., Muehlenkamp, J., Hayes, N., Lengel, G., Styer, D., & Washburn, J. J. (2018). Characterizing gender differences in nonsuicidal self-injury: Evidence from a large clinical sample of adolescents and adults. Comprehensive Psychiatry, 82, 53-60. doi:10.1016/j.comppsych.2018.01.009

Vigo, D., Thronicroft, G., & Atun, R. (2016). Estimating the true global burden of mental illness. Lancet Psychiatry, 3(1), 171-178. doi: https://doi.org/10.1016/S2215-0366(15)00505-2

Vogel, D., Wade, B., Wester, S., Larson, L., & Hackler, A. (2007). Seeking help from a mental health professional: The influence of one's social network. Journal of Clinical Psychology, 63(3), 233-245. doi:10.1002/jclp.20345

Volpe, U., Tortorella, A., Manchia, M., & Monteleone, P. (2016, Apr 30). Eating disorders: What age at onset? Psychiatry Research, 238, 225-227. doi:10.1016/j.psychres.2016.02.048

Wade, T., Keski-Rahkonen, A., & Hudson, J. (2011). Epidemiology of eating disorders. In M. Tsuang, M. Tohen, & P. Jones (Eds.), Textbook in Psychiatric Epidemiology (pp. 343-360). New York: Wiley.

Wang, P., Angermeyer, M., Borges, G., Bruffaerts, R., Chiu, W., de Girolamo, G., . . . Bedirhan Üstün, T. (2007). Delay and failure in treatment seeking after first onset of mental disorders in the World Health Organization's World Mental Health Survey Initiative. World Psychiatry, 6(3), 177-185.

Wang, P., Berglund, P., Olfson, M., Pincus, H., Wells, K., & R.C., K. (2005). Failure and delay in initial treatment contact after first onset of mental health disorders in the National Comorbidity Survey Replication. Archives of General Psychiatry, 62, 603-613.

Washburn, J., Richardt, S., Styer, D., Gebhardt, M., Juzwin, K., Yourek, A., & Aldridge, D. (2012). Psychotherapeutic approaches to non-suicidal self-injury in adolescents. Child and Adolescent Psychiatry and Mental Health, 6(14). doi:10.1186/1753-2000-6-14

Watson, N. N., & Hunter, C. D. (2015). Anxiety and depression among African American women: The costs of strength and negative attitudes toward psychological help-seeking. Cultural Diversity and Ethnic Minority Psychology, 21(4), 604.

Westerhof, G., & Keyes, C. (2010, Jun). Mental illness and mental health: The two continua model across the lifespan. Journal of Adult Development, 17(2), 110-119. doi:10.1007/s10804-009-9082-y

White, A., Kavanagh, D., Stallman, H., Klein, B., Kay-Lambkin, F., Proudfoot, J., . . . Young, R. (2010). Online alcohol interventions: A systematic review. Journal of Medical Internet Research, 12(5), e62. doi:10.2196/jmir.1479

Whiteford, H., Degenhardt, L., Rehm, J., Baxter, A., Ferrari, A., & Erskine, H. (2013). Global burden of disease attributable to mental and substance use disorders: Findings from the Global Burden of Disease Study 2010. The Lancet, 382(9904), 1575-1586. doi:10.1016/S0140-6736(13)61611-6

Whitesell, M., Bachand, A., Peel, J., & Brown, M. (2013). Familial, social, and individual factors contributing to risk for adolescent substance use. Journal of Addiction, 2013.

Wiener, A., Wessely, S., & Lewis, G. (1999). "You don't give me flowers anymore": An analysis of gift-giving to medical and psychiatric inpatients. Social Psychiatry and Psychiatric Epidemiology, 34(3), 136-140.

Willenbring, M., Massey, S., & Gardner, M. (2009). Helping patients who drink too much: An evidence-based guide for primary care clinicians. American Family Physician, 80(1), 44-50. https://www.aafp.org/afp/2009/0701/p44.html

Wisner, K., Sit, D., McShea, M., Rizzo, D., Zoretich, R., Hughes, C., . . . Hanusa, B. (2013). Onset timing, thoughts of self-harm, and diagnoses in postpartum women with screen-positive depression findings. JAMA Psychiatry, 70(5), 490-498. doi: 10.1001/jamapsychiatry.2013.87

Won Jeon, S., Amidfar, M., & Kim, Y. (2017). Bio-psycho-social risk factors for depression. In Y.-K. Kim (Ed.), Major depressive disorder: Risk factors, characteristics, and treatment options. Gojan-Dong, Danwon-Gu, Kyunggido, Republic of Korea: Nova Science Publishers, Inc. https://www.researchgate.net/profile/Yong-Ku_Kim/publication/318792471_Bio-Psycho-Social_Risk_Factors_for_Depression/links/599434c2aca272ec9087e736/Bio-Psycho-Social-Risk-Factors-for-Depression.pdf?origin=publication_list

Wong, C. (2015, Oct 23). Can culture affect the risk of suicide? https://www.nami.org/Blogs/NAMI-Blog/October-2015/Can-Culture-Affect-the-Risk-of-Suicide

Woody, C., Ferrari, A., Siskind, D., Whiteford, H., & Harris, M. (2017, Sep). A systematic review and meta-regression of the prevalence and incidence of perinatal depression. Journal of Affective Disorders, 219, 86-92. doi:10.1016/j.jad.2017.05.003

World Health Organization. (2004). Prevention of mental disorders: Effective interventions and policy options. Geneva: World Health Organization. https://www.who.int/mental_health/evidence/en/prevention_of_mental_disorders_sr.pdf

World Health Organization. (2018). About the Global Burden of Disease (GBD) Project. http://www.who.int/healthinfo/global_burden_disease/about/en/

World Health Organization. (2018, Mar 30). Mental health: Strengthening our response. http://www.who.int/en/news-room/fact-sheets/detail/mental-health-strengthening-our-response

Worrall, H., Schweizer, R., Marks, E., Yuan, L., Lloyd, C., & Ramjan, R. (2018). The effectiveness of support groups: Mental Health and Social Inclusion, 22(2), pp. 85-93.

Xu, J., Murphy, S., Kochanek, K., Bastian, B., & Arias, E. (2018, July 26). Deaths: Final data for 2016. National Vital Statistics and Reports, 67(5), 1-76. https://www.cdc.gov/nchs/data/nvsr/nvsr67/nvsr67_05.pdf

Yale School of Medicine. (2014, Feb 18). Phases of psychosis. https://medicine.yale.edu/psychiatry/step/psychosis/phasis.aspx

Yang, P., Tao, R., He, C., Liu, S., Wang, Y., & Zhang, X. (2018). The Risk Factors of the Alcohol Use Disorders-Through Review of Its Comorbidities. Frontiers in Neuroscience, 12, 303. https://doi.org/10.3389/fnins.2018.00303

Zbozinek, T. D., Rose, R. D., Wolitzky, T. K. B., Sherbourne, C., Sullivan, G., Stein, M. B., ... Craske, M. G. (2012). Diagnostic overlap of generalized anxiety disorder and major depressive disorder in a primary care sample. Depression and Anxiety (1091-4269), 29(12), 1065–1071. https://doi.org/10.1002/da.22026

NOTES